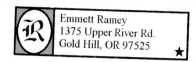
Emmett Ramey
1375 Upper River Rd.
Gold Hill, OR 97525

DMITRI ★ TRENIN

post-IMPERIUM

A EURASIAN STORY

D0973438

CARNEGIE ENDOWMENT

FOR INTERNATIONAL PEACE

WASHINGTON DC ▪ MOSCOW ▪ BEIJING ▪ BEIRUT ▪ BRUSSELS

© 2011 Carnegie Endowment for International Peace

All rights reserved. No part of this publication may be
reproduced or transmitted in any form or by any means without
permission in writing from the Carnegie Endowment.

Carnegie Endowment for International Peace
1779 Massachusetts Avenue, N.W., Washington, D.C. 20036
202-483-7600   www.ceip.org

The Carnegie Endowment does not take institutional positions on public
policy issues; the views represented here are the author's own and do not
necessarily reflect the views of the Endowment, its staff, or its trustees.

To order, contact Carnegie's distributor:
Hopkins Fulfillment Service
PO Box 50370, Baltimore, MD 21211-4370
1-800-537-5487 or 1-410-516-6956
Fax: 1-410-516-6998

Library of Congress Cataloging-in-Publication Data
Trenin, Dmitri.
Post-imperium : a Eurasian story / Dmitri Trenin.
p.   cm.
ISBN 978-0-87003-248-6 (pbk.)
ISBN 978-0-87003-249-3 (cloth)
1. Russia (Federation)–History–1991-
2. Russia (Federation)–Politics and government–1991-
3. Russia (Federation)–Social conditions–1991-
4. Russia (Federation)–Economic conditions–1991-
5. Russia (Federation)–Foreign relations.
6. Russia (Federation)–Foreign economic relations.
I. Title.
DK510.76.T73 2011
947.086–dc22

2011013975

Cover design by Zeena Feldman and Jocelyn Soly
Composition by Zeena Feldman
Maps by Robert Cronan, Lucidity Information Design
Printed by United Book Press

MIX
Paper from
responsible sources
FSC® C010236

To Petr Trenin-Strausov, 30,
of Russia's first free generation

CONTENTS

MAPS

TABLES

FOREWORD

Twenty-first century Russia is strikingly different from the Russia of old. The collapse of communism ushered in an era free of ideology and values. Forced collectivism gave way to rampant individualism. In today's Russia, the private trumps the public, for better and worse. With its five hundred-year-old empire a piece of history and its superpower ambitions put to rest, Russia is now looking inward, rather than outward.

In place of a historical empire and politico-military superpower status, Russia seeks to establish itself as a great power. In the eyes of Russia's leaders, this means Moscow's strategic independence from the principal centers of power in the new century: America and China. Shaping a new role after an imperial decline and fall is not easy, as several European nations discovered in the twentieth century. Performing the same feat without pooling sovereignty with others is virtually unprecedented.

Dmitri Trenin's *Post-Imperium: A Eurasian Story* details Russia's effort. This is not a story about the old empire—tsarist or Soviet—but about the new stage in Russia's development. Moscow's domestic and external actions during this period are critical—they will affect Russia and its neighbors for years to come and have a palpable impact on the global balance of power.

Trenin has been both an analyst of and a participant in Russia's struggle to transform itself. There are few, if any, more astute observers of this critical period, and certainly none with as clear and powerful a pen. In this new volume he takes up the challenge to illuminate Russia's path forward. In a world no longer defined by Cold War bipolarity or the immediate post–Cold War hegemony of the United States, Russia operates today in a post-imperial world where power is shifting from the West toward Asia and other non-Western actors, influence is defined by economics, knowledge, and information, and military power is increasingly exercised asymmetrically. To understand this new world, Trenin examines domestic conditions in Russia and its neighbors, detailing how the end of the empire has affected their political systems and institutions, economy, social structures, and values.

Trenin also examines the geopolitical and security relationships of Russia and its neighbors, looking at post-Soviet associations—from the Commonwealth of Independent States to the Shanghai Cooperation Organization—and the challenges posed by NATO and EU enlargement. He reflects on the roles other powers play in the various post-Soviet regions.

The post-imperial period has led to significant changes in how Russia conducts its economic relations with other nations. The country made immature attempts at integration into and with the West, first attempting to assert itself as an independent great power only to discover its glaring deficiencies. Energy figures prominently in Russia's sometimes contentious relationships with its trading partners, as demonstrated by the gas war with Ukraine and pipeline and transit politics. As a result, Russia's reputation in Europe and the rest of the world has suffered and it is clear that how Moscow handles its relationships with its neighbors will have far-reaching effects.

Russia's potentially disastrous demographic problems will also impact its prospects for post-imperial success. Since the collapse of communism, the country has faced diminishing life expectancy, higher mortality, declining standards of health care, greater incidences of substance and alcohol abuse, lower birth rates, and increased numbers of suicides. Government policies have done little to improve conditions. In addition, Russia's approach to immigration and labor migration—as well as the emergence of national identities, the renewed role of religion in society, language policies, and the debates over historical memory—will affect whether or not it succeeds.

An empire no more, Russia today faces a daunting list of challenges. The country must modernize to become competitive in the global economy and move away from the Cold War and zero-sum-game mentality that still underlies many of its actions. But, Trenin argues, there is reason to be hopeful. While no longer an empire or a superpower, Russia remains relevant—economically, culturally, and geopolitically. If it can adapt to twenty-first century realities and learn to cooperate with—not antagonize—its neighbors, Russia can emerge as a major and responsible player in the new world order.

—Jessica T. Mathews
President, Carnegie Endowment for International Peace

A NOTE FROM THE AUTHOR

Let me begin the book with a personal anecdote. In 1999 or 2000, I was flying from Shanghai to Moscow. At that time, many Russian citizens were still using passports with the old Soviet insignia, featuring the hammer and sickle emblazoned on the globe, with the star above it. After 1991, there were two basic reasons for the Russian government to continue to use the passport forms of a recently defunct state. One was sheer economy: The remaining stock of Soviet passports was just too large and too precious to be simply disposed of. The other one was the legal situation: The double-headed eagle was not officially approved by the State Duma as Russia's national emblem until 2000. There was a third reason, too. As a senior Duma member told me in the mid-1990s, there was no guarantee that the post-Soviet separation would last. He was by no means alone in holding that view.

Well, back to Pudong International Airport. At the check-in counter, I handed my Soviet-era passport, which inside clearly described me as a citizen of the Russian Federation, to a young Chinese airline assistant. She looked through my papers once, then leafed through them backward, then, without addressing me, went to see her superior. She did not speak English and could not tell me what the problem was with my passport. It took a while before a more senior person appeared, smiled, and said: "Sorry, the lady is too young to remember the Soviet Union." Indeed, a decade is a long time for youngsters.

The Soviet empire is long gone, but traces of it remain across a vast territory, from Minsk to Batumi to Bishkek. So do the traces, some physical, left by its immediate predecessor, the Russian empire. When I was taking off from Mariehamn Airport in the Aland Islands, a sprinkling of small pieces of wooded land at the entrance to the Gulf of Bothnia, much closer to Stockholm than to Helsinki or even Turku, Finland's ancient capital, I saw a huge white building below. A fellow passenger explained it was a telegraph station built in the nineteenth century to connect the Russian empire with the rest of Europe. The night before, as I had dined at Mariehamn's government house, I took note of the twin portraits in the hallway, depicting the Russian emperor and his empress—in their capacity, of course, as the grand duke and grand duchess of Finland.

On one of our many trips to China, my wife and I stayed at a hotel in downtown Harbin, built at the turn of the twentieth century in the very center of what was, then, a medium-sized Russian city in the middle of what was known at the time as Manchuria. When we later went for a walk, a nearby building caught my eye, and I immediately took a picture. When I showed the picture a week later to my colleagues at the Carnegie Moscow Center's office in Pushkin Square, right in the heart of the Russian capital, most of them were perplexed. Why, they said, would you be showing us a picture of the building where we presently are? That's how similar—identical—the basic designs of the two structures were. And that's why Harbin in the 1920s and 1930s, with its two hundred thousand Russian residents, was known as "little Moscow."

The book you are holding is a product of some research and reflection, and also of personal testimony. I was born in the historical center of Moscow, in the bulky shadow of the Soviet Foreign Ministry. The Stalinist skyscraper was completed just a year before the dictator's death, and three years before I was born. At the age of seven, I made my first major trip outside the Soviet capital, which, to me, was then—as now—simply my hometown. My grandmother took me to Riga, which, despite having been incorporated into the USSR two decades earlier, struck me as a thoroughly foreign city, with its Latin script and high medieval church spires. It looked definitely Germanic. When the older residents of Riga whom I met on that trip to Latvia wanted to refer to what we in Moscow used to call "the prewar days"—the 1920s and the 1930s—they said, "It happened in Latvia's time." When I now visit Riga and they ask me when I first came there, I answer: "In Soviet times."

A dozen years after my first trip to Riga, now as an officer cadet at Moscow's Defense Language Institute, I went on my first mission abroad. It took me to Iraq, which, in the Cold War setup, was chalked up as Moscow-leaning. My classmates went to similarly designated destinations: Algeria, Cuba, Syria, Uganda. At that time, a couple dozen countries in what was referred to, not without a note of contempt, as the third world, "hosted" Soviet military advisers and technical specialists. Some countries, such as Mozambique, even made the Kalashnikov rifle an element of their national emblem. When Egyptian President Anwar Sadat decided, in 1972, to send the Soviet advisers—but not the specialists—home, twenty thousand people had to pack up. Mid-1970s Iraq, by comparison, was not particularly crowded with Soviet military personnel: Only a few thousand were there.

When I graduated from the institute in 1977, I got my first assignment as a commissioned officer in East Germany, the centerpiece of the Soviet Union's Eastern European empire. From my house in Rembrandtstrasse in Potsdam's Berliner Vorstadt, it was a few hundred meters to the famous Glienicke Bridge where they used to swap spies, such as Rudolf Abel, and dissidents, such as Natan Sharansky. The white line across the bridge that marked the Cold War divide was barely ten inches wide. Slightly over a decade later, as a staff member of the Soviet delegation to the U.S.-USSR Nuclear and Space Talks in Geneva, I watched live pictures of the opening of the Berlin Wall. I had seen the wall countless times from both sides of divided Berlin but never thought I would see it gone. Walking through the Brandenburg Gate a few years later has remained, to this day, one of the most moving experiences of my life.

Because I was an English and German speaker, the army did not require me to serve in Afghanistan. However, many students at the Defense Language Institute where I taught after my return from Germany also studied Pashtu or Dari. They were young but already experienced veterans of what the Soviets, like the British before them and the Americans after them, called the Afghan war. In 2010, one of my former students, by then retired, went back to Afghanistan to work for the United Nations. There, he met his classmate from the institute days who was now working, also as a civilian, but a naturalized American, for the U.S. military. A little later my own friends got embroiled in wars closer to home, first in Tajikistan, and then in Chechnya.

This is not a book about the empire, tsarist or Soviet, but about the next stage, when the empire is gone. I took the demise of communism as liberation and Mikhail Gorbachev's efforts to reconfigure the USSR as a chance to build a genuine union, even if only on a loose confederal basis. This was not to be. The Soviet Union was not just a bunch of ethnic republics; nor was it simply a materialized, and later ossified, embodiment of communist ideology. Rather, it was another name for the Russian empire. It was in a fit of self-renewal, which also included an element of self-denial, that Russia in 1990–1991 simply shook off its empire—a move with few parallels in history. Now, twenty years hence, I am convinced that mankind was incredibly lucky that the demise of the Soviet Union, a communist state and a nuclear superpower, took the form of a soft landing rather than a hard one. The difference was made possible essentially by one factor: the aversion of Gorbachev, and even his *putschist* detractors, to the massive use of force.

When in December 1991 the Soviet Union was replaced by the Commonwealth of Independent States, I saw this as burden sharing in the wake of a political earthquake, with each republic-turned-independent state caring for its own population and taking up the hard issues of governance, while cooperating among themselves as equals. As to the new Russian Federation, I saw its future in a wider Europe. While I still stick to this basic concept, my opinions of how this noble vision can become a reality have certainly evolved.

I know the view from the borderlands is very different from where I sit in Moscow's Pushkin Square. One thing is clear, however. Exiting from an empire and building nation-states is not an event; it is a process for all parties concerned. The *post-imperium* is, of course, a transient phenomenon, like everything else in human history, but it is a crucible where new entities are shaped, consolidated, and socialized in broader frameworks. Having lived the process for the past two decades, I will now try to make sense of what I have been privileged to observe.

I address this book above all to post–Cold War generations around the world, like the young lady in the Shanghai airport, the students of Stanford University who came to my class in Moscow, and the student audiences at the London School of Economics and Sciences Po in Paris, where I spoke. To them, the Soviet Union is ancient history. They may hear stories that it fell apart as a result of the confrontation with the West, led by President Ronald Reagan and Pope John Paul II, with important assistance from the forces behind the iron curtain, symbolized by the Polish workers' leader Lech Walesa, who went on to become president of Poland. They may hear about Russia's undying imperialist urge, which leaves its smaller neighbors in perennial danger and in need of outside protection. They may pick up a copy of the *Economist* and wonder, as I sometimes do, why its cartoons depict other nations as human beings, and only Russia, by tradition, if not by some unwritten law, is represented by an animal. In this book, I will seek to show that there is a portrait behind the cartoon and a story behind the headline. I dedicate this book to my son Petr Trenin-Strausov, who, now thirty, was ten when the Soviet Union ceased to exist and who belongs, with his younger brother, Andrei, happily, to Russia's first free generation.

June 2011

ACKNOWLEDGMENTS

I would like to express my deep appreciation for the help, advice, and assistance that I received from a number of people. Carnegie Endowment Vice Presidents of Studies Thomas Carothers and George Perkovich, and Ambassador James F. Collins, director of the Carnegie Russia-Eurasia Program in Washington, D.C., read the manuscript and provided honest critiques and very useful comments, as did Natalia Bubnova, deputy director for communications at the Carnegie Moscow Center. Senior Publications Manager Ilonka Oszvald probably spent the most time on the book, overseeing its production process and patiently guiding the author through it. Marcia Kramer edited the text and Carlotta Ribar proofread the book. My research assistant Kristina Kudlaenko provided assistance with fact checking and other details. Zeena Feldman designed the book's cover and interior; Robert Cronan created the maps; and Jocelyn Soly was responsible for marketing. From the start, Carnegie Endowment President Jessica T. Mathews took a keen interest in the book project, and encouraged me throughout my work. Of course, the book would never have been written without the unfailing support of my wife Vera, who bravely put up with me spending inordinate amounts of time on weekends and holidays behind the computer. I thank them all, they did enormous good. The book's flaws and failings, however, are entirely mine.

INTRODUCTION

LIFE AFTER DEATH?

Like its predecessor, the Russian empire, the Soviet Union collapsed swiftly and, to both its inhabitants and outside observers, unexpectedly. A crude analogy with the Titanic would not be out of place. Winston Churchill famously wrote that the Russian ship of state sank, having withstood the most serious storms of the Great War, even as it was entering a safe harbor.[1] The Soviet Union went down as it was trying, under Mikhail Gorbachev's leadership, for the first time to put a human face on its system of government. On both occasions, it appeared that the giant construct that had taken centuries to build unraveled immediately, once its supreme authority, the autocratic tsar in 1917 and the reformist president in 1991, lost control of fast-moving events. The outcomes differ, however: At the beginning of the twentieth century, the empire was soon reconstituted, in a modified form; three-quarters of a century later, the imperial collapse was final.

A CHRONICLE OF THE SINKING EMPIRE[2]

It all happened incredibly fast. On February 15, 1989, the last Soviet commander in Afghanistan, General Boris Gromov, crossed the bridge across the river Panj to a small railhead town of Termez, in what was then the Soviet republic of Uzbekistan. Contrary to the popular notion, he was not the last Soviet soldier to leave Afghanistan. A small group of senior military officers, led by General Makhmut Gareyev, remained in Kabul to advise the government of President Muhammad Najibullah. They were not called back until 1991, a year before Kabul fell to the *mujahideen*. But the main news of the day was absolutely correct: After nearly ten years of fighting, and, officially, 14,354 soldiers dead, the Soviet intervention in Afghanistan was finally over.

Five weeks later, the Soviet Union held its first partially free election to a new-style legislative body, the Congress of People's Deputies. Astonishingly, the Communist Party candidates were soundly defeated in the major metropolitan centers—Moscow, Leningrad,* and Sverdlovsk.** When the new assembly met in May and June, its proceedings, aired live for two weeks, held the entire country virtually spellbound next to their radios and TV sets. Instead of giving a normal lecture in area studies to my officer cadets, I joined them in listening to the Congress broadcasts. At that moment, Andrei Sakharov—the nuclear physicist and a great human rights defender, only recently brought back from internal exile in Gorky***—was strongly condemning the Soviet invasion of Afghanistan. Gorbachev, presiding at the session, objected from the chair but did not silence him again. Glasnost was giving birth to a freedom of expression. Sakharov's denunciation of Moscow's Afghanistan policies, nuanced by his stated respect for the Soviet officers and men who had been sent to fight there, provoked a heated debate in the classroom.

That same summer, the Soviet empire in Eastern Europe developed serious cracks. In June, in an attempt at national reconciliation after the lifting of martial law, Poland swore in its first non-communist prime minister since the end of World War II, Tadeusz Mazowiecki. Moscow quietly acquiesced. At the Council of Europe in Strasbourg, Gorbachev himself called for a common European home built on shared, essentially Western, values—something Sakharov had been preaching for years, and for which he had been banished from Moscow under Leonid Brezhnev.

The Soviet Union's own home, however, started dividing against itself. In addition to Georgia—still reeling after military force had been used in April to dispel a peaceful rally, resulting in sixteen deaths—thousands across the three Baltic republics physically joined hands in a powerful gesture of defiance to denounce the Molotov-Ribbentrop Pact on its fiftieth anniversary that August. Several days later, Moldova, also an object of the 1939 Soviet-Nazi deal, passed a law establishing the primacy of the Romanian language over Russian. In Moscow, previous blanket denial of the

---

* Now St. Petersburg.

** Now Yekaterinburg.

*** Now Nizhny Novgorod.

very existence of the pact stopped; a commission to uncover the truth was formed, with the indomitable Alexander Yakovlev**** at the head of it.

All of these breathtaking events, however, were only a hint of what was to follow. The culmination came in the fall. In late summer, the German Democratic Republic, the bulwark of the Soviet politico-military posture in Europe, experienced the greatest hemorrhage since the building of the Berlin Wall in 1961. Thousands of East German holiday makers converged on Hungary, which suddenly and unexpectedly made an opening in the iron curtain to allow them to flee to the West via neighboring Austria. Thousands more occupied the West German Embassy in Prague and, under a hasty deal, were allowed to proceed to the West—but only on the condition that they take an absurd train journey across East Germany in order to be legally "expelled" from the GDR. The Soviet Union did not interfere.

The conservative communist rulers in East Berlin, preparing to celebrate the fortieth anniversary of the "first workers' and peasants' state on German soil," were shaken and shocked. Their regime started to unravel in earnest when Gorbachev, who came to the celebration in early October, made it plain that he no longer supported them. Absent the threat of a Soviet military crackdown—ever-present since the suppression of a workers' revolt in 1953—mass demonstrations filled the streets of Leipzig, Dresden, and other cities. The East German communists, left to their own devices, purged their conservative leaders and, bowing to the rising pressure, opened the gates of the Berlin Wall. Within six weeks, the mere change of an article in the demonstrators' slogans—from *Wir sind das Volk* to *Wir sind ein Volk*****— changed the course of Europe's history. Chancellor Helmut Kohl's plan to construct a German confederacy within ten years, which seemed incredible when it was unveiled in late November, was hopelessly overtaken by events on the ground. Germany was headed, unstoppably, toward full and instant unity. The 400,000 Soviet troops stayed in their barracks.

The German demonstrators were neither alone nor unaided. The fall of the wall reverberated across Eastern Europe. Revolutions in velvet toppled pro-Soviet regimes in Czechoslovakia, Hungary, and Bulgaria. In Poland, the anti-Communist trend, set by *Solidarnosc* a decade earlier, consolidated. Only Romania experienced serious street violence, and the execution of

---

**** Yakovlev (1923–2005), one of the principal ideologues of Gorbachev's perestroika, was pushing for opening the archives in order to counter Soviet-era myths with hard facts. He continued that work until his death.

***** i.e., from "We are the people" to "We are one people."

its dictator, Nicolae Ceauşescu, and his wife, Elena. Everywhere else the change was peaceful, acquiesced in by the Soviet Union, which immediately recognized the new regimes. At the same time, with the exception of Romania, the Soviet Union kept substantial military forces in every one of the still formally allied countries: 85,000 in Czechoslovakia, 58,000 in Poland, and 65,000 in Hungary.[3]

Finally, at their meeting off Malta in late November and early December 1989, Gorbachev and U.S. President George H. W. Bush publicly announced the end of the Cold War. With regard to the former satellite countries of Eastern Europe, Gorbachev's spokesman, Gennady Gerasimov, declared a replacement of the 1945 Yalta settlement—shorthand for the postwar division of Europe—with what he called a Sinatra Doctrine: *Do it your way.* Off Malta, Yalta was given a burial at sea.

The following year, the Soviet Union agreed to Germany's unity within the North Atlantic Treaty Organization (NATO)—that is, the GDR's absorption by the Federal Republic—and pledged to withdraw its forces from its eastern *Laender* within four years and from the other Warsaw Pact countries even earlier. It signed the Treaty on Conventional Armed Forces in Europe (CFE), which dramatically reduced troop levels across Europe and eliminated the potential for a major surprise attack anywhere on the continent. Under the CFE, Soviet troop reductions were particularly deep, constraints on troop movements strict, and redeployments sweeping. The ensuing hasty withdrawal from Central and Eastern Europe led to resentment among the uniformed military. This was not so much for its strategic implications as for the lack of minimal respect for the dignity of soldiers and airmen who, upon returning to the Soviet Union, where living quarters were in short supply, often were told to live in tents.[4] The new non-adversarial relationship among the countries of the Euro-Atlantic area was codified in a declaration signed in November 1990 and dubbed the Charter of Paris for a New Europe.

It was not just in Eastern Europe where the Soviet empire was being dismantled. To follow up on a reconciliation of relations with China achieved during Gorbachev's visit to Beijing in May 1989, Moscow agreed to withdraw its 75,000 troops from Mongolia and basically let that country follow its own path. Moscow leaned on Hanoi to start withdrawing Vietnamese forces from Cambodia, where they had been stationed since 1979. This withdrawal was part of a deal between the Soviet Union and the United States. The Vietnamese duly left, but at the same time they also left the Soviet orbit.

In similar ways, the termination of Cold War–era conflicts in Mozambique and Angola, Nicaragua and Namibia, resulted in the dramatic
reorientation of former Soviet clients, now suddenly left in the lurch by
Moscow. Cuba and Laos were simply and unceremoniously loaded off the
Soviet budget. A decade later, in 2000, President Vladimir Putin symbolically completed the withdrawal, by striking off the last vestiges of Soviet presence—the Cam Ranh naval facility in Vietnam and the Lourdes
intelligence-gathering station in Cuba. Like the previous concessions by
Moscow, this most recent one was taken for granted by the United States:
officials (privately) and analysts (overtly) believed that Moscow simply had
to face the music.

The equivalent of the fall of the Berlin Wall for the Soviet empire in
the third world was the Persian Gulf War. Not only did Moscow promptly
condemn, in a joint statement with Washington in August 1990, the bla-
tant aggression by its quasi-ally Baghdad against Kuwait, but it also progressively bought into the U.S. strategy, so that by the start of Operation
Desert Storm in January 1991 Moscow had essentially become a bystander.
This was a stunning end to the Soviet pretensions to offer a non-Western
alternative and provide protection, guidance, and support to dozens of clients in Asia, Africa, and Latin America.[5]

The Soviet Union was gone within a year of Saddam Hussein's defeat. Sovereignty declarations by its republics were touched off by Lithuania in March 1990 and were given a powerful boost by the decision of the
Russian republic's newly elected Supreme Soviet in June of that year. The
Russian move, led by Boris Yeltsin, seriously undermined the authority of
the Union. The central pillar of the Soviet state, the Communist Party's
"guiding role," embedded in the USSR Constitution, had been dismantled
by Gorbachev, who instead became the Soviet Union's first president in
March. Gorbachev, however, chose not to be popularly elected—a weakness that soon proved fatal for his political career.

It did not help that in March 1991 almost three-quarters of the USSR
population voted, in a referendum, to preserve a reformed Union. The Baltic states, Georgia, Armenia, and Moldova refused to participate. More
importantly, the referendum in Russia created the position of a republic's
president. In June, Yeltsin was elected to that post, and duality of power
in Moscow became official: a recipe for an imminent showdown. Conservatives feared that the new Union treaty, which Gorbachev negotiated
with leaders of the republics, would turn the Soviet Union into a loose
confederacy.

The last-ditch conservative putsch in August 1991 converted sovereignty claims into bids for independence. Three days after the putsch was defeated in Moscow on August 21, Ukraine declared independence; Belarus followed on August 25; Uzbekistan, on August 31. On September 6, the Baltic Three—Estonia, Latvia, and Lithuania—were released from the Soviet Union, with no strings attached. On December 1, 1991, the Ukrainian referendum overwhelmingly declared the largest Soviet republic, after Russia, a fully independent state. A week later, at Belovezhskaya Puscha, a *nomenklatura* hunting lodge on the Belarusian-Polish border, three of four original republics that in 1922 had formed the Soviet Union* declared it dissolved. On December 25, 1991, the Soviet flag was lowered from the Kremlin, and the Russian tricolor went up. In terms of history, the Soviet ship of state sank almost as fast as the Titanic. From the completion of the Soviet withdrawal from Afghanistan, the dismantlement of both the Soviet and classical Russian empires took a mere 34 months.

The Aftermath

The most stunning thing was that this imperial collapse, given the scale of the issue and the nature of the departing regime, was both orderly and relatively peaceful. The USSR, of course, was not replaced by a "more perfect union" that Gorbachev had been painfully negotiating with republic chiefs at his country residence of Novo-Ogaryovo, near Moscow. However, to many, the Commonwealth of Independent States (CIS), announced by the leaders of Russia, Ukraine, and Belarus on December 8, 1991, was not so different from a Union of Sovereign States that had been under discussion at Novo-Ogaryovo for months. The inter-republican borders became state borders but remained open; the armed forces were put under a nominally joint command; the Soviet ruble continued as legal tender. The classical Russian empire, after all, was not located overseas; nor were there clear borders between the "metropolitan area" and the "colonies." In any event, economically, the core Russian lands during the imperial period were not better off, and were often worse off, than many of the borderlands.

True, the Azeri-Armenian conflict over Nagorno-Karabakh, which broke out in 1988, claimed 100,000 lives and created 2 million refugees;

---

* The fourth original member of the Soviet Union, the Transcaucasian Federation, ceased to exist in 1936, when Armenia, Azerbaijan, and Georgia joined the USSR in their own right.

the war in Chechnya, between 1991 and 2001, cost 28,000 lives,[6] with many more wounded; the civil war in Tajikistan, which lasted from 1992 to 1997, left another 100,000 dead. The Georgian-Abkhazian and Georgian-Ossetian conflicts, the fighting on the Dniester in Moldova, and the Ingush-Ossetian violence added a few thousand more victims to those grim statistics. Moscow itself did not escape fully unscathed. While the 1991 putsch led to the deaths of three young people in the country's capital, the "mini-civil war" there two years later resulted in the official toll of 140 dead, while unofficial claims put the figure several times higher. Still, these figures pale in comparison to the victims of the partition of India in 1947; or the wars in Algeria in 1954–1962 and Indochina in 1946–1954, to name but a few. By comparison, the dissolution of the Soviet empire was surprisingly peaceful.

Except for the Karabakh conflict and the Russo-Georgian war of 2008, there were no major wars among the Soviet successor states. Strikingly, the first-ever collapse of a nuclear superpower did not lead to nuclear proliferation. Soviet strategic nuclear weapons remained under centralized control throughout and, by 1994, those deployed in Ukraine, Kazakhstan, and Belarus had been withdrawn to Russia, and the three new countries joined the Non-Proliferation Treaty as non-nuclear weapon states. Tactical nuclear weapons had been redeployed to the Russian Federation even before the breakup of the USSR. Over the past two decades, there have been no major breaches of the nonproliferation regime attributable to the collapse of the Soviet Union.

The astounding smoothness of the process was largely due to the fact that Russia, the imperial metropolis, led the process of imperial dismantlement. Even when the Soviet Union still existed, the Russian republic's authorities proceeded to conclude treaties with other republics, respecting their sovereignty. Once the USSR was no more, the Russian leadership immediately recognized the country's new, much-shrunken borders, and, while it fought separatism in Chechnya, it was wise enough to resist an impulse of irredentism in Crimea, northern Kazakhstan, and elsewhere. Compared with other empires in their final, usually not finest, hour—including the British, the French, and the Portuguese—Russia's did unbelievably well.

It is striking how virtually everyone took the incredible news for granted. That the ten-year presence in Afghanistan, the forty-year hold on Eastern Europe, and the three-hundred-year state unity with Ukraine would *all* evaporate within less than three years had been, of course, beyond anyone's wildest imagination. Right up until the late 1980s, the Soviet political system had been widely regarded as most stable. Dissident writer Andrei Amalrik's prophecy that the Soviet Union would not last until 1984[7] was seen as bizarre at the time of its publication in a 1969 book. In actual fact, he had undershot by only seven years. Even the author did not intend the title as anything other than an intellectual provocation: He simply played with the title of George Orwell's famous book.[8] Now that this impossible outcome was suddenly a reality, it was immediately accepted as a given, and as a starting point for a new status quo. This was a position fraught with serious consequences.

The dissolution of the historical Russian empire had not been an issue in the Cold War. Except for the three Baltic states, whose incorporation into the Soviet Union was seen as illegal by the United States and a few other (but by no means all) Western countries, the Soviet Union's territorial integrity was recognized. Moreover, centralized control over Soviet nuclear weapons and a vast territory in Eurasia with a diverse population was regarded in the West as one of the pillars of the global order. President George H. W. Bush was addressing more than just a Ukrainian audience when, in Kiev on August 1, 1991, he publicly rebuked those who sought independence from the Soviet Union.*

When the independence of Ukraine and other republics became a reality less than five months later, their separation was applauded in the United States and Europe. Now, it was Russia's *reimperialization*, to use Henry Kissinger's phrase,[9] that was identified as a new potential threat, but little thought was given to the impact of the loss of empire *on Russia*. After all, Russia had not been defeated, occupied, or controlled by outside powers. It was its own elites who had initiated the dissolution of the Soviet empire and the unbundling of the Soviet Union itself. The central thesis in the West was, of course, that by throwing off the imperial burden, Russia liberated itself as much as its former possessions and protectorates, and that it was thus making itself ready for democracy and integration into the community of free, democratic, and market-driven nations. The skeptics believed none of that and feared what they called a Weimar Russia.[10]

So much for how it all happened. What caused it to happen is a more interesting question.

---

* This later became known, rather unfairly, as Bush's "chicken Kiev speech." It is easy, of course, to be wise ex post facto; the forty-first president of the United States, it should be restated, was dealing with a tottering nuclear superpower.

WHY DID IT HAPPEN?

To many people now, the Soviet and classical Russian empires looked doomed almost from the beginning. Yet this was not the consensus view just a decade or so before the demise occurred. In 1979, as the Iranian revolution toppled the shah and terminated U.S. presence in that country, and the Soviet Union invaded Afghanistan, the USSR appeared to be on the offensive, and the United States, described by some Americans at the time as a "pitiful, helpless giant," was on the post-Vietnam retreat. Using Cuba as a stronghold, the Soviet Union was challenging U.S. power in Nicaragua and El Salvador, Grenada and Guyana. Its allies appeared triumphant in Angola and Yemen. When Gorbachev took power several years later, the Soviet Union, admittedly, experienced serious problems in a number of areas, yet none of them looked terminal.

Gorbachev's logic was clear, although his strategies evolved over time and his tactics were ever-changing. His prime motive for revamping Soviet foreign policy was to slow down the arms race, which was driving the Soviet economy into the ground.[11] In order to do so, he had to reach out for disarmament deals with the Reagan administration. Surprisingly, the very conservative U.S. president turned out to be a nuclear reduction advocate. The winding down of the Cold War, however, had the unintended effect of eroding the rationale for the legitimacy of the Soviet regime and the need to maintain a vast empire. If the Soviet Union was not threatened by the West, it had no reason to keep the eastern half of Europe under its control or to subsidize far-flung outposts of the empire such as Cuba, and it had no pressing business in Africa, Asia, or the Middle East. Most important, the mammoth Soviet military-industrial complex, its mission aborted, had to be converted to produce the consumer goods Soviet citizens had been denied in the name of fighting the Cold War. In 1961, Soviet Premier Nikita Khrushchev famously claimed (incorrectly: he was seeking, by means of colorful threats, to deter the United States) that the USSR was "producing missiles like sausages." Three decades later, the Soviet public wanted to reverse this process: The public could not eat missiles, which, by the time of Brezhnev, were being produced not so much like sausages, but instead of them. The problem was that reversing the process was impossible without changing the system.

Gorbachev, moreover, did not think much of the international communist movement, had the traditional Soviet disdain for the satellite states, and was barely interested in the developing world.[12] Like virtually everyone else in the Politburo, including longtime Foreign Minister Andrei Gromyko and his successor, Eduard Shevardnadze, he was squarely focused on the West, particularly the United States. It was that obsession that had led, in previous decades, to the dangerous overextension of the Soviet Union. It was out of the question for the Soviet leadership to engage in unilateral restraint and refuse to be drawn by the technologically and economically superior United States into an ever-more-intensive arms competition. Parity in nuclear armaments and superiority in conventional forces was the name of the game. It was the Soviet Union's to lose.

Gorbachev's later ambition was to replace the U.S.-Soviet rivalry with their global—and friendly—condominium. However, as economic difficulties mounted, spurred by a dramatic drop in oil prices starting in 1986, he made the fateful step of appealing to the West for financial assistance.[13] True, the Soviet Union had the unfortunate experience of its Eastern European satellites before its eyes: Poland, Romania, and East Germany had all borrowed, and all suffered for that. Yet Gorbachev was not deterred. At the Soviet Union's stage of development in the mid-1980s, it could not do what the Chinese did with great success at about the same time—allow the peasants to produce as much as they could and sell it on the market. Stalin had crushed the peasantry, thereby bequeathing his successors a perennial food problem. Nor could Stalin's heirs open up the country to foreign investors; both ideological constraints and the realities of the Cold War militated against that. Unlike Deng Xiaoping, Gorbachev had to plead for credits for a moribund economy. Western credits created dependence on the West, but more important, the penury led to the reordering of priorities. Gorbachev, who started as a bold leader of renewal, turned into one who mostly had to respond to events, always short of both time and money.

Historically in Russia, attempts at modernization, whether under Alexander II* or Mikhail Gorbachev, led simultaneously to growth in core Russian nationalism and ethnic nationalism in the borderlands. The empire was able to restore itself under the Bolsheviks, in some part *because* the Reds, unlike their White foes, ostensibly did not aim for that.[14] But the Soviet Union was living on borrowed time. In a quid pro quo, the Bolsheviks had to give their nationalist allies a vision of homelands. The borderlands became states, albeit within the Soviet state. They were encouraged to use local languages. Ethnic elites sprang up. This flowering of national cultures within the state ruled single-handedly by the Communist Party could only

---

* Reigned from 1855–1881; assassinated by revolutionaries.

be an uneasy compromise. It could be sustained only as long as the Communist Party was united and able to exert total control over the USSR.

Ironically, the Soviet totalitarian unitary state, which pretended to be a federation, laid the groundwork for its own orderly and legalistic disintegration. The right to secede was written into all three of the Soviet Union's constitutions: 1924, 1936, and 1977. In 1944, in a bid to gain more votes in the soon-to-be established United Nations organization, Joseph Stalin allowed the republics to have their own foreign ministries. Stalin, who believed himself to be the expert in ethnic relations, used the ethnic homelands to practice divide-and-rule policies, but the very idea of territorial homelands led to the establishment of embryos of new polities within the body of a seemingly monolithic Soviet state.

Just like the Russian empire before it, the USSR was undermined from within by the two opposing forces of reform and national awakening. The Russian republic declared its sovereignty ahead of all others, except the Baltics. Somewhat slower and more cautious, the borderlands followed with gusto. From the outset, the post-Soviet Commonwealth of Independent States was *not* Russia's third empire.[15] Just the opposite: It was an exit, not a continuation. It was the beginning of new states rather than a posthumous existence of an empire. Ukraine, for example, identifies itself as part of Europe, not of some "Eurasia." Russia allowed this to proceed primarily because, after 450 years, its imperial *élan* was gone. It, too, wanted to be "just" a Russia. But what was it, exactly—a Russia minus its empire?

AFTER THE EMPIRE

The turn of the twenty-first century has provoked a major surge of interest in the fate of empires—their rise, decline, and fall. Much of the writing done on the subject was to serve as reassurance, or, alternatively, warning to the premier power of today, the United States. This is understandable. Substantially less attention is paid to what happens after the decline and fall are complete, and the empire is no more. "What remains of a doughnut when it's eaten?" a character in Nikita Mikhalkov's film, *The Barber of Siberia*, asks. And answers, laughingly, "A hole. A hole remains." Well, not exactly.

All empires rise and fall. When they fall, they sometimes join with the mightier powers, whether their ex-adversaries or allies. The German Third Reich and the Japanese empire went down in flames in World War II, first defeated on the battlefield and occupied, then reformed and reeducated by the victorious powers. Great Britain and France, though among the victors in World War II, lost most of their overseas possessions within a few decades as a result of postwar decolonization. The smaller European colonial powers, such as Portugal and The Netherlands, waged bitter colonial wars, saw they could not prevail, and finally had to sail back to the "old country." Whatever the case, all of these countries managed relatively soon to reconstitute themselves as highly successful nation-states. It needs to be remembered, however, that in all those cases there had always been a nation behind the empire. Britain itself, for example, was only a united English-Scottish kingdom; its great empire lay overseas.

Unlike in the wake of the First World War (Austria-Hungary, Ottoman Turkey, tsarist Russia), the transition in post–World War II Europe from empire to nation-state—where this applied—was relatively smooth. It was helped, at a critical juncture, by an alliance with the United States. On the one hand, America reassured and protected the Europeans politically and militarily. On the other, it nudged them to shed their antiquated colonies. Even more important, the post-imperial transition was supported by the process of European economic integration, begun soon after the end of the war. The Common Market prevailed over old-time imperial preferences.

Once the physical separation had occurred and trade flows had been diversified or diverted, imperial nostalgia gradually subsided. What remained was cultural influence. The British empire has spawned several societies, which now form the English-speaking segment of the Western world alongside the United Kingdom: Australia, Canada, New Zealand, and the United States. But even non-Western countries as diverse as India and South Africa have borrowed from their former colonial power its language, legal system, and basic principles of government. The British empire is no more; its legacy, however, lives on.

Contiguous empires were more difficult to break up, but when it did happen, separation was much more complete. Usually this occurred as a result of major wars and massive geopolitical realignments. True, the cultural memories lingered, too. The Ottoman empire, which disintegrated as a result of World War I, has left an indelible Muslim mark on the Balkans, and the German-dominated *Mitteleuropa*, which partially survived the First World War to finally perish in the Second, could still evoke memories of a European vocation among the peoples of Soviet-controlled Eastern Europe. Yet Turkey for many decades after 1923 played a very limited international role, above all in its former imperial possessions. Likewise, West Germany after 1945 played a limited international role.[16] Similarly, maritime power Spain, having lost its American colonies in the nineteenth century, had to continue in relative obscurity, virtually up to the moment it became integrated with the rest of Europe, through membership in NATO (1982) and the European Economic Community/EU (1986).

Decades after the downfall of their empires, some of these countries rose to become regional powers, like Turkey; or emerged as the leader of united Europe, like Germany; or established an informal "guiding role" for itself in the Balkans and along the Danube, as Austria did. Imperial mentality of the respective elites, once demolished, came back later in a sublimated form of leadership, responsibility, and arbitration. In all these cases, however, the gap between empire and post-empire was lengthy, and during that time nation-states arose and matured.

Russia, which by 1980 had built a huge formal and informal empire— and lost much of it a decade later—is a rare case of a former imperial polity having neither disappeared nor reinvented itself as a nation-state, but seeking to reconstitute itself as a great power, with a regional base and global interests. This is not the kind of revanchism that, in the 1920s and 1930s, doomed post-Versailles, post-Weimar Germany. While no longer a pretender to world hegemony and staying within its new, shrunken borders, Russia has been trying hard to establish itself in the top league of the world's major players *and* as the dominant power in its neighborhood. Even more strikingly, as it promoted its bid on the world stage, it has been striving, simultaneously, to keep itself in one piece. This is a dual adventure almost unparalleled in modern history. Whether the adventure succeeds is a big question, and an important one.

DEFINING THE POST-IMPERIUM

I chose the notion of a *post-imperium* not for want of a better description of where Russia is today.* To me, the concept suggests a fairly prolonged exit from the imperial condition. The country is no longer an empire, and it is not going to be one again. However, the many features that

---

* Vadim Tsymbursky talked about two variants of imperial demise: one in which the empire is eliminated, and a new geopolitical setup emerges, as with the end of the Roman, Mongol, and Austro-Hungarian empires; and the other one in which the core of the imperial state keeps its state identity, and the state in question passes into its post-imperial stage. See Vadim Tsymbursky, "Ostrov Rossiya" (Russia the Island), *Polis*, issue 5, 1993.

were established in the imperial period are still felt to this day. Russia is not merely "lost in transition" but also in translation: The real name of the game is historical transformation, which takes much longer—generations rather than years or even decades—and has no immediately identifiable end station. The fact that unlike all the other members of the Soviet bloc or former republics of the Soviet Union, Russia has also had to deal with the imperial legacy, weighed heavily in Russia's failure to embrace integration into, or even with, the West.

The 2000s resulted in Russian society's acquiring a new quality, particularly through the rise of consumerism and the middle classes. However, the public space, including politics, has suffered a setback in comparison to the previous period. Elements of the empire are still visible—at home and abroad. Domestically, today's Russian Federation is a neo-tsarist, mildly authoritarian polity. Its current operation formula can be termed authoritarianism with the consent of the governed. As an international actor, Russia is at a point where it recognizes all former borderland republics as separate countries, even if it does not yet see all of them as foreign states.

A number of scholars and observers claim that Russia is an empire that has failed to dissolve completely. The idea is, of course, that the disintegration of the Soviet Union will have to be followed by a new round of disintegration, even partial, of the Russian Federation. According to this view, the process was only temporarily stopped at the turn of the twenty-first century; it will continue, engulfing the North Caucasus and possibly other regions of the Russian Federation.

There is no question that the contemporary North Caucasus is an area of high turbulence, with many uncertainties, to be discussed at length in this book. Yet many empires have failed to dissolve completely. Britain still holds on to Gibraltar, the Falklands, the Bermudas, Diego Garcia, and other small possessions; France has a sprawling DOM-TOM* community: Guyana, Guadeloupe, and Tahiti, to name but a few; even The Netherlands keeps a few islands off the coast of Venezuela. The common feature of all these former European colonial outposts, of course, is that their populations want to stay associated with the former overlord, as does Puerto Rico with the United States. Sovereignty per se is less important than economic prosperity and the degree of social development. Whether Russia will be able to offer something similar will be crucial, in the final count.

---

* Departements d'outre-mer–Territoires d'outre-mer.

Thus, post-imperial Russia is not a unique case. Postwar Britain offers a few interesting insights into the stages of post-imperialism and the psychological compensation for geopolitical losses, and so does Charles de Gaulle's France. It took Britain about a quarter-century to put its economic relations with the Continent of Europe above those with its far-flung colonies and dominions; to drop its pretensions to a politico-military presence east of Suez; and to reconcile itself with a much-diminished international power and role. Its "special relationship" with the United States was a major factor, both political and psychological.

France, by contrast, toned up the talk of its *grandeur* even as it toned down the discussion of its failings—all in order to compensate for the trauma of defeat and wartime collaboration with the Nazis. Whereas the British, in order to protect their distinct identity, sought to keep some distance from the Continent, the French aspired to lead Europe and turn the Continent into an instrument for reconstituting France's soft dominance. While post-imperial Britain sought greater closeness with America, post-imperial France raised a *fronde* against Washington's hegemonic ambitions.

One can argue that, in a way, neither Britain nor France is completely out of its post-imperial phase. Both countries' elites espouse a global approach to world affairs; both possess small nuclear arsenals; their conventional militaries, while much reduced, are highly capable and lethal, as the Serbs, Iraqis, and the Afghan Taliban can attest. As late as 1982, the United Kingdom projected power over thousands of miles to defend its sovereignty over the Falkland Islands, and France routinely sent paratroopers to intervene in Central Africa. Yet these are a few surviving vestiges of the past. The present, and the likely future, of both the United Kingdom and France are closely tied to NATO and the European Union. Neither of these clubs has much time for empires, or even great powers—except, of course, in NATO's case, the United States.

By comparison, Russia's post-imperial condition is complicated by a number of factors: lack of integration with the rest of Europe at the strategic and economic levels; continued cohabitation with the former borderlands-turned-independent states; and the mammoth task of comprehensive modernization to combat backwardness, to name but a few salient ones. This condition will persist, making Russia wonder about its place and role in the world, its policy priorities and methods of securing them. How Russia will be able to sort out these issues will be immensely important to itself and its neighbors, and for the big players to the east and the west, China and the European Union. It will also be very important to the United States.

While some American authors and commentators saw the United States as the dominant power in Eurasia since the demise of the Soviet empire, Washington's prevailing policy preoccupation was to prevent the restoration of the USSR, however fanciful that might have seemed, including to some senior American diplomats. Otherwise, the United States was interested in being a player there, having access and preventing Russia from denying it that access, even though dominance as such was not sought.*

What is at stake now in this continuing post-imperial story is the geopolitical setup of Eurasia in the mid–twenty-first century. Even though I dismissed the notion of Eurasia in an earlier book,** it is back—but with a different meaning. Rather than being another name for the Russian empire, which, as I argued, is *passé*, Eurasia now covers the entire Old World. For this new Eurasia to emerge, however, the old one had to go. Besides the Russian Federation, it is Central Asia, the Caspian, and the Caucasus that are now linking Eurasia's east and its west. It is Kazakhstan and Turkey that are acting as quintessential Eurasian countries, reaching to both Asia and Europe. The northern supply route to the NATO forces in Afghanistan includes a rail link from Riga to Termez and multiple air corridors that traverse Russia, Central Asia, and the Caucasus. Going in the opposite direction, from Afghanistan to Russia and Europe, are heroin, opium, and other drugs. More cheerfully, tourists from Siberia board charter flights to Hainan Island in the South China Sea, while Muscovites go to Goa to hang out, and quite a few of the rich from the Caucasus and Central Asia have made a second home in Dubai.

Enormous in size, and incredibly diverse, Eurasia is becoming ever closer-knit—economically, as well as politically and strategically. Regular ASEM summits—Asia-Europe meetings—are emblematic of the tightening ties. The eastward enlargement of the European Union (EU) and the rise of China, India, South Korea; the demographic and political dynamics of Turkey and Iran; the hazards and risks connected to Pakistan and Afghanistan; the new transportation links, from the revived Silk Road to the pipelines east and west of the Caspian—all put Russia into a situation where, beyond the still amorphous area of the CIS countries, it is surrounded by countries and their alliances and unions that are more affluent,

---

* I am indebted to James F. Collins, former U.S. ambassador to Russia (1997–2001), for his insights on that issue.

** Dmitri Trenin, *The End of Eurasia: Russia on the Border Between Geopolitics and Globalization* (Washington, D.C.: Carnegie Endowment for International Peace, 2002).

dynamic, powerful, or populous than Russia itself. It can no longer be the "last in Europe and the first in Asia."[17] Thus, it risks becoming a dual periphery in both half-continents.

The limits of China's continental reach; the modalities of Europe's future; the channeling of Muslim activism will depend, to a not insignificant extent, on how Russia deals with its post-imperial dilemmas. Will it become a (multiethnic) nation-state? Will it assert itself as a federation in more than just name? Will it be able to construct equitable relations with the new states that it used to own? Will it find a way to integrate its vast territory and, in particular, its eastern portion with the Pacific seaboard? What is the future of Russia's relations with the West: the EU, NATO, and the United States? Will Russia be able to strike a sustainable balance in its relations with China? Will it be able to integrate its Muslim populations and stabilize its immediate southern periphery? Will the Arctic be an area of peaceful collaboration or a new front in a truly cold war? This, in a nutshell, is Russia's post-imperial agenda.

Russia, however, is not the only post-imperial state in the former Soviet Union. In an ironic way, all the new states that have emerged from the USSR are also afflicted with elements of a post-imperial or, in some cases, post-colonial, syndrome. This can be described as seeking to distance themselves from the former hegemon, attempting to create new national myths and write new suitable histories of their nations, and yet exhibiting many of the features usually associated with the Soviet Union, among them doublespeak, lack of serious debate, and intolerance.

Now that notions such as the former Soviet Union and the post-Soviet space have a minimal utility in thinking about the future of Eurasia, where exactly the individual countries go will mean a lot. Obviously, Ukraine, the largest country wholly in Europe; Uzbekistan, with the biggest population in Central Asia; or neighboring Kazakhstan, with its mineral wealth, are likely to be important subregional players and trendsetters. But even the smaller countries such as Georgia, Moldova, or Kyrgyzstan can present challenges that reach beyond their immediate neighborhoods. Territorial integrity and minority rights; nation building and international orientation; pipeline politics and immigration issues are prominent on the new states' post-imperial, post-colonial agendas. However, to be able to understand and deal effectively with both agendas, one needs to revisit the recent and more distant past.

THE IMPERIAL RISE

Russia was born in geographical Europe, but on its periphery. It is essentially a borderland. A German would call it *Mark*, "a march"; a Slav, a *kraina, okraina, ukrayna*, "Ukraine." Physically isolated, due to the Mongol yoke, in its all-important formative period, from the thirteenth to the fifteenth centuries; economically and culturally backward, but resilient and sturdy, it always desired—and sometimes managed—to overcome its obvious drawbacks by a single powerful push. To survive and eventually prevail, Russia developed a high degree of political centralization, in the form of an autocratic government; in the interests of economic mobilization, it turned its peasants into serfs, who sustained the nobles-turned-servants; to defend against more advanced rivals and expand outward, it cultivated patriotism, militarism, and messianism.[18] It built a succession of empires, which, in some ways, lack a direct analogue.

What I will call, collectively, the historical Russian empire, has had several incarnations. The traditional empire, which is known as the Tsardom of Muscovy, was built from the mid-sixteenth century. The grand duchy of Moscow, its immediate predecessor, had been a largely ethnic Russian state, with the descendants of the Varanger at the top and some admixture of assimilated Finnish tribes at the other end. Grand Duke Ivan's assumption in 1547 of the title of a tsar, derived from "caesar," soon sent the country on a path to territorial expansion. The imperial story began with Ivan—soon to be named *Grozny* ("Awesome" rather than "Terrible" would be the correct translation), conquering two Tatar khanates: Kazan (1552) and Astrakhan (1556)—and his son Fyodor Sibir (1598). It went on to colonizing Siberia all the way from the Urals to the Pacific (1584–1689). The tsars established a protectorate in present-day eastern Ukraine, including Kiev, and then essentially annexed it (1654–1686). Finally, in a combination of Cossack colonization and Moscow's offers of protection to the indigenous rulers, the empire spread southward to the foothills of the Caucasus.

The traditional empire featured the triumph of the Russian state over its former overlord and oppressor, the Mongol Golden Horde or, rather, its successor khanates. This triumph endowed Russia with a sizable Turkic and Muslim element, firmly embedded ever since within the body of the Russian state. This inspired Russia's early twentieth-century Eurasianists[19] to refer to Russia's nature as Slavo-Turkic. Long held down, the Muslim/Turkic element in Russia has recently been growing and asserting itself.

Traditional Russian Empire, 1550 – 1650

However, there has also been a high degree of assimilation. The Tatars and Bashkirs have adopted ways rather similar to those of ethnic Russians. The Kazan khanate evokes only vague and distant memories; in Astrakhan and Tyumen, the seat of the former Sibir khanate, there is virtually none, the more so now that the majority of inhabitants are Russian.

Most of the territory added to the first empire was colonized rather than conquered. Cossacks led the drive across Siberia, reaching the Bering Strait in 1649, and peasants followed. Those peasants who had fled from their masters to become Cossacks populated the steppes of the Don, the Kuban, the Ural, and the Terek.

The traditional Moscow-Orthodox empire largely survived the collapse of the state in both 1917 and 1991. Rather than being "artificial," as some contemporary Russian authors claim, the borders of the Russian Federation today are strikingly close to those of the Tsardom of Muscovy circa 1650, before the absorption of Ukraine under Tsar Alexei Mikhailovich and Peter the Great's conquests.

The classical Russian empire was started by Peter the Great and centered in St. Petersburg, which he founded in 1703. Peter's was an outwardly

The Classical Russian Empire, 1650–1914

European-style imperial construct. Peter accepted the title of the Emperor of All Russias in 1721 as a result of a victorious war against Sweden that gave Russia wide access to the Baltic Sea. Peter's successors, actively engaging in European power politics, pushed Russia's borders westward to annex Finland (1809), Lithuania (1795), Belarus (1772–1795), Poland (1772–1815), and central Ukraine (1772–1795). In the southwest, they cut into the ailing Ottoman empire to take over Crimea (1783) and the northern coast of the Black Sea (1774–1791), including Bessarabia (1812).

Further along, they wrested the Transcaucasus from the Ottomans and the Persians (1801–1829; 1878). In a truly European-style colonial expansion, they then conquered the North Caucasus in a long series of bloody campaigns dubbed the Caucasus War (1817–1864), added Central Asia through a combination of the force of arms and diplomacy (1839–1895), and the Far Eastern provinces between Lake Baikal and Sakhalin Island, in a dual diplomatic coup vis-à-vis China (1858–1860). For more than a century, St. Petersburg's reach extended even to Alaska, which was sold to the United States in 1867. Beyond its formal borders, Russia built zones of influence in northern Persia (1907); Mongolia (1911); Tuva (1914); and Manchuria (1898–1905, 1917).

Unlike the traditional empire, most of the acquisitions from this classical imperial period were of territories that had formed their statehood before the Russian takeover, or of populations that put up fights to thwart the Russian advance. Some, like the Poles, had a very strong sense of national identity. Most of these territories seceded in 1917—some, like Poland and Finland, for good; others, such as the Baltic states and Bessarabia, for two decades; the rest only briefly, for the duration of the Civil War of 1918–1921. These formed the Soviet Union, only to secede definitely in 1991.

In Russia and then the Soviet Union, to paraphrase Sergei Witte, the prime minister in 1905–1906, there was nothing but the empire: no metropolitan area. Ordinary ethnic Russians did not enjoy a privileged status within the empire, while some non-Russians occasionally did: The Poles had a constitution from 1815 to 1830, and the Finns from 1809 to 1917; Central Asians were exempt from compulsory military service. The imperial elite included a large number of non-Russians: Tartars, Germans, Ukrainians, Georgians, and Armenians, and, much later, Jews.* This was greatly enhanced in the Soviet period.

---

* One could observe that while visiting Moscow's Cathedral of Christ the Savior, built to commemorate the victory against Napoleon in the Patriotic War of 1812. Roughly one-third of the names of hero officers on its walls are Slavic; another third, Muslim; the rest are Germanic and other West European.

The Soviet Russian Empire, 1922–1991

The Soviet Russian empire began by regaining control over the traditional and, partially, classical empires. This was achieved by a combination of revolutionary activity and military power during the Civil War; territorial annexation as a result partitioning the "lands between" Russia and Germany: western Ukraine, western Belarus, the three Baltic states, Bessarabia; and Eastern Karelia and Petsamo (later named Pechanga), resulting from a war with Finland (1939–1940); peaceful annexation of Tuva (1944); conquest of East Prussia, and of southern Sakhalin and the South Kuril Islands (1945); territorial handover from Czechoslovakia: Transcarpathia; and border adjustment with Poland (1945). After that, the Soviet Union was satisfied and forswore any more additions to its territory, whether of Finland or Poland, which had belonged to the Russian empire, or Mongolia or Bulgaria, which had not.

The Soviet Union claimed to be the very antithesis of an empire. It branded its enemies "imperialists," which, in the Leninist tradition, denoted the highest—and supposedly final—stage of capitalism. But "American imperialism," to Soviet propagandists, was also a policy of territorially expanding power and influence. Of course, the Soviet Union in practice sought to match America's international reach. It publicly rejected the title of a superpower but enjoyed it in private—and in practice.

Moreover, the Soviet Union itself was built as an empire, albeit a peculiar one. Formally a federation, it was ruled from an imperial center. The salient feature of all Russian empires was that they did not have a clearly identifiable metropolitan area, except for the capital, as noted by a Russian expert.[20] The regime at the center was as harsh as, or even harsher than, in the borderlands. By comparison, within the British empire, Britain itself was not the empire, as Robert Cooper observed:[21] India was. And, of course, Britain was a parliamentary democracy, even if the subjects of its empire did not enjoy many political rights. In the Russian case, the regime on the periphery might well be lighter than at the "center."

From 1945, the Soviet empire per se took the form of zones of control, often policed by Soviet forces. East Germany, including East Berlin (1945), Poland (1945), and Czechoslovakia, Hungary, Romania, and Bulgaria (1948) formed the hard core of that zone. Yugoslavia (1945–1948) and Albania (1945–1960) were also temporarily "in" but managed to sneak out. Outside of Eastern Europe, Mongolia joined this zone in the 1930s, while Tuva was simply incorporated into the USSR in 1944. The Warsaw Pact (1955–1991) and the Council for Mutual Economic Assistance, or COMECON, in Western parlance (1949–1991), were the main institutions of the Soviet empire.

Beyond the zone of control lay the Soviet zones of influence, where Moscow's domination was less direct and not backed by substantial military presence. North Korea (1945), Vietnam (1955), Cuba (1960), and Laos (1975) were closest to Moscow and heavily dependent on it, but they all retained a degree of autonomy. From the mid-1950s, Soviet influence spread to the Middle East, where Egypt (1955–1972), Syria (1958–1991), South Yemen (1971–1988), and the PLO (during the 1970s and 1980s) were at various times Moscow's regional strongpoints. Afghanistan joined this group in 1978, but it soon became a war zone, drawing the Soviet Union in.

In North Africa, Moscow maintained close political contacts with Algeria and Libya. In tropical Africa, it started in the early 1960s with Ghana, Guinea, and Mali. It saw its friends toppled in the former Belgian Congo but kept links to Congo-Brazzaville. It placed high hopes on Ethiopia (after 1974), Angola, Mozambique, Guinea-Bissau, and Cape Verde (after the breakup of the Portuguese empire in 1975), where Soviet-style political parties were formed as the backbone of the ruling regimes.

Soviet Zones of Influence

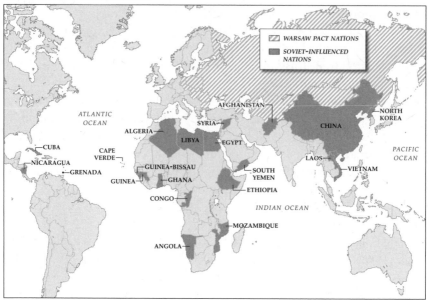

In Latin America beyond Cuba, Soviet gains were minimal. Nicaragua, which under the Sandinista government was leaning toward Cuba and the Soviet Union (1979–1991), was an exception. When tiny Grenada looked dangerously close to heading down that path, the United States intervened (1983).

The Soviet empire was ideological in concept. It adopted a political system dominated by a Soviet-style party. Its economic system was based on state control, and often bankrolled by the USSR. Most important, the Soviet empire was designed to change the "correlation of forces" in the world in favor of Soviet communism and the Soviet Union. It had a very strong military component, supplied by the Soviet Union, but rarely—outside of Eastern Europe and Mongolia—taking the form of direct Soviet military presence.

The Soviet "overseas" empire in Asia, Africa, and Latin America, which lasted at most four decades and in many cases half that time, was abandoned by Moscow without much thought or regret. These uncertain, expensive, but also expendable acquisitions were treated as ideological prizes, strategic positions, or bargaining chips. True, the Soviets did not separate themselves from the locals as overtly as their Western European predecessors had. Arab or African students often came back with Russian or

Soviet Zones of Control

Ukrainian wives. However, the Soviet impact on those countries was not particularly deep outside of the pattern of the governing structures from China to Cuba, all modeled on the Soviet Communist Party. When Vladimir Putin travels to Vietnam, or his aide and Deputy Premier Igor Sechin goes to Cuba, they meet with aging nostalgics. China's leader Jiang Zemin* also liked singing Russian songs he learned as a factory worker in Moscow in the 1950s. For today's youth in China, Vietnam, and Cuba alike, Russia is a very distant country. For most Russians themselves, going out that far was clearly an aberration.

The "near" empire, or the zone of control in Eastern Europe, was abandoned on condition that what had led to its acquisition in the first place—Moscow's security concerns—would not be revised as a result of its dissolution. Hence the Kremlin protests of NATO's enlargement and U.S. military deployments. Many countries in the region have long-standing ties to Russia, but those are checkered relationships. At different stages, Russian forces liberated, occupied, or divided up the same countries, which in

---

* Jiang Zemin was general secretary of the Communist Party of China from 1989 to 2002 and China's president from 1993 to 2003.

turn aligned with Russia or against it. To many East Europeans, the Russian state usually appeared oppressive; "high" Russian culture, from Tolstoy to Tarkovsky, by contrast, was appealing. Only one thing was constant: In modern times, Russia was always big, and the neighbors always small. All this changed after 1989. This *Zwischeneuropa*, the "lands between" Germany and Russia, joined the European Union. Russia remains geographically close, but politically, economically, and culturally, it has grown very distant.

The lands that had made up the historical "inner" empire form a different group. All had close economic, human, and political ties to Russia. Not a single one among them has joined the European Union (EU) or NATO. From Moscow's perspective, they constituted, collectively, Russia's historical patrimony. Two of them, Ukraine and Belarus, which used to form, with Russia, the core of the historical Russian state, are the inner sanctum in that group. Most Russians, in 1991, found it difficult or even perverse to treat them as foreign countries. They thought of separation as an aberration. They were wrong.

Twenty Years Later

Almost two decades later, just before the global economic crisis struck in 2008, a number of Western commentators dubbed Russia resurgent. Awash with oil money, it had gone off the Western orbit,[22] repaid its government-owed debts, amassed huge currency reserves, and was publicly discussing the ruble as a reserve currency in Eurasia. It stood up to the United States, applied the divide-and-rule tactic to the European Union, aspired to lead a virtual international counterculture group called BRIC,* and proclaimed the former Soviet republics a sphere of its privileged interests. Seeing its own soldiers attacked and its protégés in danger, it also fought a war against one such republic, Georgia, and as a result dropped its previous support for the principle of territorial status quo. For a brief moment, it appeared that Russia and the United States were back on a (cold) war path: in late summer and early fall of 2008, their relations plunged to the depths last visited in 1983–1984, just before Gorbachev came to power.

---

* Stands for Brazil, Russia, India, and China and denotes the world's major emerging economies; the phrase first appeared in a Goldman Sachs 2001 report, "Building Better Global Economic BRICs."

Much had been made in the Western media of President Putin's remark, in his 2005 annual address to the Russian parliament, that the collapse of the Soviet Union had been the greatest geopolitical catastrophe of the twentieth century. Putin's words were interpreted as evidence of an active Kremlin nostalgia for the recently lost empire, and even as a sign of his intention to bring back the USSR. This was a misinterpretation. An empire's collapse is, more often than not, a political earthquake, claiming lives. Suffice it to recall the immediate aftermath of the end of the British rule in India or in Palestine. Parts of southeastern Europe are still feeling the distant tremors that can be traced to the simultaneous end of the Ottoman and Habsburg empires.

Moreover, Putin had been on record as saying that "one who does not regret the passing of the Soviet Union has no heart; one who wants to bring it back has no brains." He also called the CIS a vehicle for civilized divorce.[23] Most Russians agreed with these words of wisdom. Most had not realized, however, that on both instances the sentiments were not originally their president's. Putin was quoting—without attribution—leading Ukrainian politicians: Rada Speaker Oleksandr Moroz and Ukraine's first president, Leonid Kravchuk, respectively. Putin himself, however, argued in 1999 in his so-called Millennium article that the Soviet Union had been a nonviable system,[24] and that what happened to it had resulted from a systemic failure. At a rally in Moscow eight years later, he again blamed the non-performing communist system for losing the Soviet Union.[25]

Contrary to most interpretations, Putin's catastrophe remark was not a precursor to a neo-imperialist, revanchist policy. Similarly, his much-noted remarks at the Munich security conference in February 2007,[26] when he lashed out at U.S. foreign policy, were not a declaration of a new Cold War on Washington. In reality, Putin was essentially trying to make the West accept new rules of engagement with Russia. Those could be summarized as "Accept us as we are; treat us as equals; and let's do business where our interests meet."[27] Two years later, these terms were tacitly accepted by the Obama administration. Speaking in Munich in February 2009, Vice President Joseph Biden announced a "reset" of U.S. policy toward Russia. This has ushered in a period of constructive and productive relations between the two countries, symbolized by the entry into force in February 2011 of the New START Treaty.

But in 2007, a real clash between Russia and America was looming as Ukraine edged toward NATO and the conflicts in Georgia became unfrozen. To many observers, it appeared that the former Soviet republics, in particular Ukraine, were about to become what Eastern Europe was in 1945–1947: the object and the prize of a new Cold War. In addition, the George W. Bush administration's plans to deploy ballistic missile defenses in Poland and the Czech Republic, ostensibly to counter Iranian missiles, created a sense in the Kremlin of a military threat. Some clearly authorized Russian voices started talking of Moscow's giving an "asymmetrical answer" in Cuba and Venezuela, in the form of bases for Russia's long-range bombers. The Russian navy started to hint about establishing naval facilities in the Mediterranean and the Gulf of Aden. Quite a few senior Russians publicly expressed something very similar to *Schadenfreude* at the sight of U.S./NATO difficulties in Afghanistan.

Events started to move at quickstep after the Ukrainian leadership—President Viktor Yushchenko, Rada Speaker Arseny Yatsenyuk, and Prime Minister Yuliya Tymoshenko—signed a letter early in January 2008 asking NATO to extend its Membership Action Plan to Ukraine. Coming so suddenly—the 2004 Orange Revolution with its radiant expectations had faded long before that—so late in the game, with the NATO Bucharest summit a mere ten weeks away, and first announced by none other than U.S. Senator Richard Lugar, the news was bound to look like a conspiracy to the Kremlin. Putin himself rushed to the summit, the first and only time he has done that, and tried to talk NATO out of embracing Ukraine. In dinner remarks attributed to him, Putin said that Ukraine was "not even a state." He probably wanted to say that the unity of the Ukrainian state was too brittle, not to be taken for granted, or tested. It sounded, however, as if he were denying Ukrainian statehood and advancing Russia's claim to its territory as its buffer zone vis-à-vis the West.

The NATO Bucharest summit decision, in fact, combined the worst of both worlds. In a compromise between the Franco-German and U.S. positions, it refused to award a membership action plan to either Ukraine or Georgia, thus giving Russia a sense of victory, but promised both that they will certainly become members one day, thus supposedly encouraging the Ukrainians and the Georgians.[28] That placated no one, and it angered Kiev, Tbilisi, and Moscow. Between Bucharest and the attack on Tskhinvali, the main town in South Ossetia, cold war–style tensions were constantly mounting. Both Moscow and Tbilisi saw the Bucharest decision as a shaky truce, unlikely to last a long time. In the ensuing war of nerves, Georgia jumped the gun.

The August 2008 five-day war in Georgia was a product of wrong assumptions, outright mistakes, and policy failures.[29] The actions by Georgian

President Mikheil Saakashvili were clearly adventurous, reckless, and brutal. He miscalculated his own strengths and his enemy's weaknesses. Saakashvili's plan was to retake South Ossetia in a lightning strike and present the habitually slow-moving Russia with a fait accompli. The administration of George W. Bush had aided and abetted Saakashvili, whose regime was hardly a democracy; worse, it failed to control him. Georgia was left to State Department senior officials. The Kremlin, for its part, had long relied on the frozen conflicts in the Caucasus as a means of preventing NATO accession by Georgia. Moscow's Georgia policy was essentially controlled by the military and later by the security services. The endless game of provocations and counter-provocations that was designed from the Russian perspective to make Georgia look unfit for any club—above all, NATO—and, from the Georgian angle, to raise alarm over Russia's growing assertiveness, had spun out of control.

In Russian government circles, Saakashvili's sudden attack on Tskhinvali confirmed the worst thinking about the United States. Both Putin (now the prime minister) and Dmitri Medvedev, the newly inaugurated president, were taken by surprise: They expected "provocations," but what they got instead was an outright attack. In the heady days that followed, even as people in Europe were wondering where Russia would strike next, the Russian leadership saw Saakashvili's action as a proxy war waged by Tbilisi on behalf of the United States. It was impossible for them to imagine that anything of this scale would not have been planned, or at least authorized, by the United States. After all, Secretary of State Condoleezza Rice had visited Tbilisi in mid-July 2008.

Moscow was now ready to believe Washington had known what it was doing as it was arming Georgia and virtually adopting "Misha" Saakashvili. The Georgian president's action suggested to Moscow that the "rogue elements" in the U.S. administration—Putin later named Vice President Dick Cheney—were trying to involve Russia in conflicts with neighbors (the war over Crimea being the next one), even as they were attempting to use these conflicts to bolster the chances of Senator John McCain to win the 2008 presidential race. The Kremlin logic was that as Russia was rising and turning resurgent—a popular phrase in the West during 2007 and early 2008—the United States would seek to hold it down. The method to achieve that goal was to involve Russia in a string of conflicts along Russia's periphery. Not only would these conflicts drain Russian resources, but they would also help restore the unity of the West on an anti-Russian platform.

An additional concern related to the reconfiguration of the Russian leadership itself was that Medvedev imagined himself in the position of a Cold War leader tested by the other side, a latter-day John F. Kennedy or Jimmy Carter. When he entered office in May 2008, Medvedev vowed to focus his presidency on building institutions, promoting innovation, developing infrastructure, and making smart investments. Instead, he was thrust into the thick of real battle, for which the trained lawyer had to rely—more than he had expected—on advice and guidance from Putin, his war-savvy predecessor and mentor. The shock was so strong that Medvedev publicly called Georgia's offensive "our 9/11."[30]

With its servicemen under attack and dying, Moscow had no option but to order an armed response. It was powerful, but limited: mostly tank columns, artillery fire, and some aerial bombardment. Its message—for Washington as much as for Tbilisi—was: Red lines are real, and they mark the border between peace and war. Russian forces did not merely engage another country's military. They fought against a quasi-ally of the United States, which during the previous four years had equipped, trained, and advised the Georgian military.

Russia's counterattack was the first case of Moscow using force against a foreign adversary and invading a neighboring country since the Afghan war (1979–1989). As such, it was fundamentally different from both Chechen campaigns and engagement in post-Soviet conflicts, from Transnistria to Tajikistan. Despite the conventional accusations, the Russian military action against Georgia, while being resolute, was also deliberate, careful, and measured. This systematic counterattack thus resulted in major damage to Georgian military capability and infrastructure, went beyond the zones of conflict in South Ossetia and Abkhazia proper, and occupied for weeks the Georgian towns of Gori, Poti, and Senaki, to humiliate Tbilisi and let it feel its defeat. Yet even though the Russian intervention was styled after the 1999 NATO war against Slobodan Milosevic's Yugoslavia, Moscow did not bomb Georgia's bridges, roads, TV transmitters, or government ministries. Very tellingly, it was careful to keep intact all the pipelines from the Caspian. The number of civilian casualties was small.[31]

Like the West with regard to Milosevic after the start of the 1999 Kosovo conflict, the Kremlin after the Tskhinvali attack branded Saakashvili a criminal, refused to deal with him, and did not hide its desire to see him leave office. Yet whatever Putin may have told French President Nicolas Sarkozy about the proper punishment to be meted out to the Georgian leader, he resisted the temptation to go after him to Tbilisi. The Russian hope appeared to be similar to the West's a decade ago: that the Georgian people, like the Serbs before them, would draw the consequence from their leader's misadventure and would remove him from power. Saakashvili, Moscow hoped, would be ousted by his own people, just as Milosevic was by the Serbs in 2000, fifteen months after the Kosovo war. After that, the Russians would prefer to put Saakashvili on trial (as Milosevic was), though few believed that scenario to be realistic.

By roundly defeating a U.S. friend, the Russian leadership aimed to undermine Washington's credibility as a security patron of pro-U.S. governments in the CIS. The effect was palpable. In the wake of the Caucasus crisis, most Poles worried that Russian tanks might roll in, their country's NATO membership notwithstanding. The Baltic states fretted, too; the United States, their protector, was far away while Russia was a direct neighbor.[32]

Even more important, the United States seemingly demonstrated its unwillingness to put itself in danger to defend a friend, while Russia has shown it had no such problems. Cold War analogies notwithstanding, Georgia in 2008 was no Germany of 1948. The Russian leadership thought that it had won a psychological advantage over Washington, and declared, vaguely, a "zone of privileged interests" along Russian borders.

Russian leaders could not believe that what they had was not a premeditated proxy attack, but rather an administration that had become dysfunctional on the Georgia issue. Thinking that they were fighting against a U.S. proxy, they also believed that Washington would probably not take the defeat of its client for an answer. Thus, when President Bush, in an effort to "do something," used the U.S. Sixth Fleet to ferry humanitarian supplies to Georgia, it looked highly ominous to Moscow. The Russians expected the United States to start resupplying the Georgians with arms and military equipment for a war of revenge, or even more. Dmitri Rogozin, Russia's ambassador to NATO, later revealed that Moscow feared a direct U.S. military intervention in the South Caucasus.[33]

In those circumstances, Moscow's recognition of Abkhazia and South Ossetia, two weeks after the end of hostilities, and during the U.S. Navy's humanitarian operation in the Georgian Black Sea ports, could be seen as a policy of deterrence. Of course, emotions had been running high in Moscow ever since the U.S.-led diplomatic recognition of Kosovo's independence in April 2008. Russia's recognition of Abkhazia and South Ossetia looked like natural "retaliation," punishing a U.S. friend. However, Moscow refrained from such a step both immediately after the Kosovo recognition and after the Tskhinvali attack. The Kremlin took the fateful step three weeks after the start of the conflict, when hostilities had long ended.

A lot can be said here about the fog of war. To a rational observer, the Russian leadership's logic might have appeared as follows: Georgia has been beaten, but the United States, which had instigated the hostilities, will not take no for an answer. Thus, a war of revenge was likely. The only way to deter such a war was to deploy sizable forces in both enclaves. The requirement for deployment was a formal request from the government in place. In order for the request to be considered, the government making it should be formally recognized: *Voila!* However, this rational politico-military-legal calculus, if it existed, had to be placed in a highly charged emotional environment dominated by deep-seated resentment, heady triumphalism, a high degree of uncertainty, and fear of things to come.

The Russian military action in Georgia briefly reversed the tide of post-Soviet Russian foreign policy. It had long been unhappy with the post–Cold War developments in Central and Eastern Europe and the former Soviet Union, such as NATO's eastern enlargement, Western military campaigns in the Balkans, and U.S. military deployments in former Warsaw Pact nations and ex-Soviet republics in Central Asia. Moscow, however, was at first powerless to do anything about these developments, and then it lacked a good cause to resist. Georgia's action changed that by delivering to Russia a just cause for going to war.

Russia turned revisionist as well. It embraced a revision of the post–Cold War order, which it refuses to recognize. The Kremlin resolved to give the United States no more advantages in the territory that Moscow had claimed as constituting, in Medvedev's words, its "sphere of privileged interests."[34] It also sought to reverse Western gains made in the previous years, which culminated in 2004 in the dual enlargement of NATO and the European Union and the color revolutions, which had replaced the early post-Soviet regimes with more pluralistic and Western-oriented ones in Georgia, Ukraine, and, initially, in Kyrgyzstan. In responding forcefully to the Georgian action, Putin and Medvedev demonstrated that they would not shy away from possible confrontation with the United States.

In the run-up to war, it was the prospect of NATO membership for Georgia that played the key role in Russian considerations and practical actions. Moscow saw NATO membership for any of its ex-satellites or former provinces as both a symbol of U.S. political influence and a potential platform for the U.S. military to use as a pressure instrument against Russia. Stopping NATO's eastern advance beyond the 2004 lines—that is, beyond the Baltic states—thus became its overriding foreign policy and security goal.

What this all betrays, importantly, is that the Russian security circles continued to assume, after 1991, that the United States was thinking seriously about one day striking militarily against Russia. True to this view, the territories vacated by Soviet power at the end of the Cold War had to remain as a kind of strategic no-man's-land, a buffer between Russia and NATO, which Russian generals still eyed with suspicion.

This was essentially a zero-sum approach. By preventing NATO enlargement, and with it, U.S. military deployments and installations, Russia meant to confirm the CIS as a zone of Russian privileged interests. Moscow's "privilege" did not claim a reconstitution of the historical empire, or an intention to establish a Warsaw Pact–like system of tight control. Rather, Moscow wanted to exclude any outside influence in the post-Soviet region that would threaten Russia's own. This stance called for neutrality of the new states (at minimum), security alliances with some, unencumbered access for Russian business interests, and strong Russian cultural influence across the board.

In early 2007, Moscow was still offering a deal to Georgia: full withdrawal of Russian troops, normalization of bilateral relations, and assistance in conflict resolution for Abkhazia and South Ossetia, in exchange for Georgia's nonalignment; in other words, a non-NATO status, and a legal obligation not to deploy third-country forces in its territory once the Russians had left. Tbilisi rejected this outright.

Beyond the CIS, Moscow sought to counter the formation of a united Western front against it. It tried to play the European Union off the United States and NATO by letting Sarkozy, conveniently in the chair of France's EU presidency, clinch a cease-fire deal in Georgia, thereby establishing Europe, rather than the United States, as the principal Western mediator and Russia's main partner in the Caucasus. Within the Union, Russia reached out to the major countries of continental Europe—France, Germany, Italy, and Spain—to thwart the Russo-skeptics, led by the United Kingdom, Poland, and Lithuania.

The Russian leadership showed willingness to take the Western media flak and sit it out. Over time, it relished the fact that early Western reporting of the Caucasus war, which put the onus on Moscow and de facto exonerated Saakashvili, was exposed as biased. The Tagliavini report, made public in 2009, apportioned responsibility for the war more evenly. The symbolic delay in the start of EU-Russia negotiations over a new partnership agreement did not last long. The NATO-Russia dialogue, likewise, was suspended only briefly. The Bush administration's decision to put the G8 format on hold was overruled by the need to convene the G20, in which Russia duly participated. The election in November 2008 of Barack Obama to the White House closed a chapter gone sour in U.S.-Russian relations and offered the prospect of a fresh start between Washington and Moscow.

To make crystal clear their message to Washington about the dangers of trespassing on other people's turf, Russian leaders embarked on a token military demonstration in the Western hemisphere. Its strategic bombers and ships practicing off Venezuela were designed to put the U.S. government in an uncomfortable position of watching a foreign power play in its backyard. Even though this "toy" show of force did not impress many people in the United States and won Moscow no friends, from the Kremlin's perspective, it was worth it; an important point had been made.

In a more lasting move, Russia created new realities on the ground, by formally recognizing Abkhazia and South Ossetia, something it had been avoiding for more than a decade and a half. Among the many reasons for recognition, perhaps the most important one is the pragmatic need to deploy regular Russian forces in both enclaves in order to deter Georgia and the United States from trying to retake them. Today's Russia is ruled, at the top, by avowed legalists who insist on their actions being covered by the Russian Constitution. Under the Constitution, deployments of Russian troops abroad require consent of the legal foreign authorities; hence, granting recognition was the only way to satisfy the domestic constitutional requirements. Other factors—from the need to show strength and determination in the North Caucasus, to the nod to the military that its sacrifice was not in vain, to letting off the pent-up frustration caused by the Western recognition of Kosovo despite Russia's pleas—certainly played some role.

The importance of the Russian action is not only that it is basically irreversible. Moscow has assumed the right to decide for itself what is right and what is wrong in the affairs of the world, something that the Soviet Union claimed but which the Russian Federation abandoned from the start in favor of common values and principles within the international community. With the war between Russia and Georgia, Russia challenged not only the wisdom but also the moral authority of the West, which it saw as self-serving. At the same time, Russia came up with its own interpretation of what constitutes, in this particular case, genocide, humanitarian intervention, and responsibility to protect. In other words, Moscow took international law into its own hands, where its interests were directly affected.

Despite the Kosovo analogy, Russia's military action and diplomatic recognition of Abkhazia and South Ossetia had more in common with Turkey's move in Northern Cyprus. Moscow had to accept that even its few close allies within the Collective Security Treaty Organization (CSTO), a security pact that unites Russia with Armenia, Belarus, Kazakhstan, Kyrgyzstan, Tajikistan, and Uzbekistan, and its friends in the Shanghai Cooperation Organization (SCO)—above all, China—decided against following its lead on recognition.[35] Yet the Russian leadership was richly compensated for this by a surge of patriotism and nationalism at home, reminiscent of the broad public support given to Putin in the fall of 1999 as he was taking on Chechen terrorists in the Caucasus amid the apartment house bombings in Moscow. To an outside observer, the Putin-Medvedev tandem had come through a major crisis with flying colors, and the younger of the two had received his baptism of fire. Within six months, another crisis—this time, financial—was upon them and the rest of the world, putting Georgia and the Caucasus on the back burner.

The talk of a new Cold War was shrill but short-lived.[36] The relationship was reset by the incoming Obama administration in the United States as part of a more general reset of U.S. foreign policy. Neither Russia nor its neighbors featured there as priorities. The process of NATO enlargement was put on hold, with Ukraine and Georgia told they were not ready, which was true. Russia likewise was a non-priority, but potentially it was a help in dealing with the real priorities, in Afghanistan and Iran. Moscow responded cautiously, but positively, to the U.S. reset, but it felt initially it had won a reprieve, at most. Russia's relations with the West remained volatile, for some time, and the geopolitical future of the other countries that emerged from the Soviet Union was unclear.

Then, the "reset" began to yield first fruit. In April 2010, the New START Treaty was signed. By the end of that year, the "123" agreement on U.S.-Russian nuclear energy cooperation entered into force, and the World Trade Organization (WTO) accession by Russia looked like a done deal. In addition to the rail link, Russia opened an air corridor for the United States to ferry goods and rotate its forces in and out of Afghanistan. Moscow joined Washington in a United Nations Security Council resolution that imposed new sanctions on Iran and went a step further, canceling its own sale of the S-300 air defense system to Tehran. In November 2010, President Medvedev came to the NATO summit in Lisbon in a very different mood, and with a different purpose, than Putin two-and-a-half years previously. The post-Soviet space did not look like an issue any more. There was only Georgia, successfully bracketed, so as not to spoil the progress made.

No Single Space Anymore

What is clear today is that, twenty years hence, there is no "post-Soviet space" anymore. The Soviet Union passed away abruptly. Although the precise date can probably never be fixed, the crucial final milestones in 1991 were August 19–22 (the putsch and its defeat, culminating in the formal banning of the Communist Party of the Soviet Union); December 1 (Ukraine's independence referendum); December 7–8 (the Belovezhskaya accords); and December 25 (Gorbachev's resignation).

The 2000s saw the next phase of geopolitical restructuring, the disappearance of the *former* Soviet Union as a useful notion. No precise date can be given, but again the milestones are clearly discernible: Russia's market pragmatism (2003); Georgia's Rose Revolution (2003) and Ukraine's Orange one (2004); the end of gas subsidies (2006); the Russo-Georgian war and its aftermath (2008); the public row between Moscow and Minsk (2010). Perhaps most importantly, thinking about the former imperial space *en bloc* is disappearing from the Russian mind, which now treats the new countries rather discretely.

The "post-Soviet space" has ceased to be a minimally usable concept in discussing geopolitics. New states have not only survived but have also established themselves. New generations with no direct experience of the Soviet Union have entered productive age. Old links—economic, political, defense, human, cultural—have frayed, and new ones reflecting post-imperial realities have been created. People born after 1985 find it hard to believe that countries as diverse as Estonia and Turkmenistan used to be part of the same state. After the *former* Soviet Union, what?

In lieu—literally—of the former Soviet Union, three new regions have formed. One is what can be termed New Eastern Europe, composed of Ukraine, Belarus, and Moldova. Another region is the South Caucasus, with Armenia, Azerbaijan, and Georgia and the breakaway territories of Abkhazia, Nagorno-Karabakh, and South Ossetia. Finally, there is Central Asia, consisting of Kazakhstan and the four states of what used to be called, in Soviet times, Middle Asia. Even if the empire is gone and cannot be re-created in a different form, all of its former constituent parts are living side by side. The Baltic states are in NATO and the EU, but two of them,

Latvia and Estonia, have sizable Russian populations. It was possible to move the bronze statue of a Soviet soldier from the Tallinn city center, but many of the local Russians are there to stay. Many old links remain, and many new ones are being created.

Russia is no longer synonymous with Eurasia, but it has not folded into Europe, as many Western analysts expected. Russia has not disintegrated, but neither has it integrated into the West. The imperial élan gone, Russian leaders define their country as a "great power," and this is broadly supported by the public, but what is the meaning of that term in the early twenty-first century? Russia's interests in the neighborhood are real, but a privileged zone in that area is a chimera. Moscow's current zone of influence extends only to Abkhazia and South Ossetia. The Russo-Belarusian union, promulgated in 1999, has long looked stillborn and is now recognized as a fiction; a customs union among Belarus, Kazakhstan, and Russia is a practical measure that, over time, can be the nucleus of a meaningful economic integration, but not some zone of influence.

Post-imperial Russia did not experience a rebirth as a nation-state, like post–World War II democratic Germany or the republican Kemalist Turkey. It did not shrink to a small fragment, a souvenir of past imperial glory, like post-1918 *Deutsch-Oesterreich*, which became the Republic of Austria. It did organize a Commonwealth of Independent States, which has nothing in common with the Commonwealth except for the term itself; it has promoted a *Russophonie*, in the image of *Russkiy Mir*, but essentially its post-imperial agenda is different from all others because, having ceased to be an empire, Russia has remained a great power.

Not *too* great a power, though. The multipolar world that Moscow started to call for in the late 1990s has finally arrived, but Russia's position in it is that of a relatively minor pole. True, today's Russian Federation occupies all the space between the European Union and China—something the Tsardom of Muscovy achieved in the seventeenth century. However, with just 2 percent of the global GDP and about the same share of the world's population, Russia, by its own standards, does not feature at the very top of the international hierarchy. With the category of transition economies abolished by the World Bank statistics, Russia has formally joined the rank of developing countries.

Whatever happens to Russia, whether it modernizes or not, there will be no new incarnation of its historical empire. Today's Russia is post, rather than neo-imperial. Such a Russia the world has not yet seen. As Thomas Graham, one of the best analysts of contemporary Russia in the United

States, has noted, it is no longer pushing outward, but looking inward: a seminal reversal of historical pattern.[37] Maybe Russia is, indeed, an island in the middle of a huge Eurasian landmass, as Vadim Tsymbursky, one of the most original and powerful brains in Russia, argued. And, as he added, by going back in terms of the physical space it occupies, Russia can reactivate an alternative to its imperial development. An island, actually, has infinite connections compared with even a huge place hemmed in by its land neighbors.[38]

In the last two decades, Russia's foreign policy has gone through a remarkable evolution. From immature attempts at integration into and with the West, it went on to assert itself as an independent great power, only to discover its glaring deficiencies. Having then adopted a foreign policy of promoting domestic modernization through close links with Europe and North America, it has been careful at the same time to hold the balance between the East and the West, North and South. It resembles a makeweight on the geopolitician's scales: a swing state.

1

IMPERIAL EXIT AND POST-IMPERIAL CONDITION

When Russians—and many other post-Soviets—discuss the Soviet Union, they do it differently than most people in the West. The latter view it as an empire at minimum, and often as an evil empire, to use Ronald Reagan's famous formulation. Ordinary Russians seldom view the USSR as an empire *par excellence*. To them, it stands above all for the communist regime, which some reject as totalitarian and murderous, while others look back on its paternalistic aspects with nostalgia.

As to the imperial element, Russians prefer to see the USSR as a "big country," which used the resources of the center—mainly the Russian Republic and Ukraine—to develop the borderlands: a core function of an empire. This "social" interpretation of the Soviet Union is still strong,[1] including in its non-Russian parts, such as Ukraine.[2] It is a fact, however, that it was only by the late 1950s that the Soviet population's living standards reached the level it had enjoyed in 1913. All things considered, it was World War I and the Bolshevik Revolution that grew out of it that deserve to be called the greatest catastrophe in Russia's twentieth-century history.

PUBLIC PERCEPTIONS

Leonid Brezhnev, who died in 1982 after eighteen years as head of the Soviet Communist Party, is now remembered vaguely but generally fondly, with the emphasis on the Soviet welfare state, science and technology, education, culture and the arts, and, although not in the first instance, the military. Gorbachev started with inspiration and ended with disillusionment. Yeltsin's years are generally—and unfairly—associated with crisis and chaos. At the end of his term, in the late 1990s, 40 percent of Russians said in a poll that they would prefer to live in the USSR, against the 45 percent who preferred contemporary Russia. Thus, the Russian people see the Soviet Union much more as a way of life than as a superpower or an empire.[3]

It is no wonder that, when the going was hard, they felt sorry for what they had left behind. A decade after the fall of the USSR, 73 percent of Russians regretted its passing.[4] Still, the end of the Soviet Union has not registered in the Russian collective mind as the most tragic event of the century by far. And, for the vast majority, the disintegration of the Union is not the most important problem now.

Only around 15–16 percent of those polled favored restoration of the USSR in 1998, 2004, and 2009. The support for a new voluntary union state based on the CIS first dropped from 34 percent to 28 percent, and then to 13 percent in the respective polls.[5] A purely Slavic state of Russia, Belarus, and Ukraine was favored by 13 percent. A seemingly "easy" Russo-Belarusian merger had a minuscule popularity of 2–3 percent. The share of those who preferred the Russian Federation to go it alone increased to 28 percent by 2004 from 25 percent in 1998.

The trend is clear: In 1995, restoration of the USSR and Russia's *Alleingang* was each favored by 23 percent of those polled. By 2004, the ratio was 2–1 in favor of the stand-alone Russian state. There was also far less of a difference between the near and far abroad than there used to be. The share of "imperial nostalgics" has dropped from 25 to 15 percent—but even there it is the economic and humanitarian concerns, not the power factor, that dominate.[6] The people who reject today's Russia do so not because it is not big enough for them, but because it is not quite their own.[7] They feel alienated. Even Vladimir Zhirinovsky, a mirror of Russian nationalism, publicly eschews the word "empire"[8] and cautions that Russia would unite with new states or territories only if doing so were deemed advantageous to Russia. He argues that Russia absolutely needs to pursue its self-interest with respect to the former borderlands.

TERRITORY AND BORDERS

Starting from the mid-1980s, Russia has gone through a four-dimensional crisis. It let go of its governing ideology-cum-political system, communism; its centrally planned economic system; its superpower foreign policy of Cold War confrontation; and the imperial state. While the first three issues dealt with the legacy of the 1917 Bolshevik Revolution, the last crisis ended more than four hundred years of Russia's imperial history. Now that the empire itself was history, what has remained of Russia? Witte's famous dictum had to be rethought.

The present-day Russian Federation is roughly three-quarters the size of the old Soviet Union. With the former borderlands in the west and south now independent states, the core of the "old country"—historical Muscovy, or simply Russia, as it is often called east of the Urals; Siberia, its most important resource base; and key outposts: St. Petersburg and Kaliningrad on the Baltic coast; Novorossiysk on the Black Sea; Astrakhan on the Caspian; and the entire Pacific seaboard from Vladivostok to Petropavlovsk-Kamchatsky to Chukotka, plus the Arctic coast from Murmansk to the Bering Strait, and the islands—continues to be in Russian hands. The Russian contiguous empire has shed some weight, but it retained a strong and solid platform for building a Russian nation-state.

Moreover, the dismantlement of the USSR has been a positive development *for Russia*. It drew the line, for the first time, between the country and its former empire, which is now referred to as the Commonwealth of Independent States. It relieved Moscow from the need to keep the Balts and Moldovans under control. It released Russia from quasi-colonial responsibilities in Central Asia and the South Caucasus. Finally, it created a basis for close and equitable relations between the Russian Federation and the Soviet Union's other bigger republics, Ukraine, Kazakhstan, and Belarus. Viewed from Moscow, the territorial settlement was rather generous toward the new states and created no real irredentist claims. For their part, the Russians have rather quickly adjusted to the emergence of new states in the former borderlands. Today, most of these former imperial Russian possessions engender scant public interest in the Russian Federation.

Furthermore, and very important, Russia itself has been able to live within the 1991 borders that had been branded "unnatural," "ahistorical," and, by extension, unsustainable by a number of nationalist commentators.[9] As pointed out earlier, these borders do have parallels in history. The Russian Federation, composed of the territories that did not secede after two imperial collapses—in 1917 and 1991—can be well termed the hard core of the historical empire, that is, the otherwise elusive metropolitan area. Thus, for more than three centuries what people sometimes referred to as "new" Russia—the Russian Federation—has been in fact an alternative-in-waiting to the imperial expansion.[10]

Here, it is important to note that the only parts of the present-day Russian Federation that were not part of the 1650 Tsardom of Muscovy are the North Caucasus in the south; St. Petersburg and Vyborg in the north; Transbaikal, the Maritime Provinces, and the Pacific islands in the east; and Kaliningrad in the west. Today, all these regions, with the exception of St. Petersburg, are geopolitically vulnerable, albeit for different reasons. Since 1991, Russia has lost no more territory, though it went through border adjustments, which fixed its new frontiers.

BORDER ADJUSTMENTS

Rather than keeping its new borders open in the hope of extending them at the right moment,* the Russian Federation embarked on a policy of fixing them in treaties and on the ground. In three takes—under Gorbachev, in 1991; under Yeltsin, in 1996; and under Putin, in 2004—Moscow managed to solve the most serious border issue by far, fixing the 4,355-kilometer boundary with China. By 2008, the demarcation of the border was complete.

In exchange for Beijing's agreement with the border—which, to many in China, is still the product of "unequal treaties" of 1858 and 1860 between St. Petersburg and the Qing dynasty—Russia conceded that the border would follow the high-water channel in the middle of the Amur and Ussuri rivers. The Soviet-era claim that both rivers, all the way to their Chinese banks, belonged to Russia, was dropped. Thus, Russia ceded to China two-and-a-half islands with a total area of 375 square kilometers. This created mild commotion nationally: 52 percent of Russians politely disagreed with the handover,[11] and some street protests took place along the Chinese border. The residents of Khabarovsk in particular were unhappy to see China advancing to within a few kilometers of the city center. However, no trouble followed.

Putin later called this deal the biggest foreign policy achievement of his eight-year presidency. With good reason. Unless the border issue was resolved, the Chinese could, over time, claim ownership of some 1.5 million square kilometers that Russia received under the 1858 and 1860 treaties.

---

* The Soviet Union did exactly this, by forming a Moldovan republic next to Romanian-occupied Bessarabia; a Karelian republic on the borders of Finland; or indeed the Belarusian republic, which one day would be able to claim western Belarusian lands that belonged to Poland.

Putin and others in the Russian leadership, watching China's rise, understood that it was folly to leave the entire border issue open as the balance of power between the two countries was changing heavily in China's favor. Moscow also expected that, for several decades, Beijing would stay rational and be primarily focused on domestic economic and social development.

In contrast to the China deal, Russia refused to accommodate Japan's claims to the four islands in the Kuril chain. The most Putin was prepared to do was to return to the 1956 Moscow declaration, ratified in both countries, and hand over two smaller pieces of territory, Habomai and Shikotan, which add up to a mere 7 percent of the area claimed by Tokyo.

Japan's position, unlike China's, is inflexible. Putin's 2000 attempt to reach a deal with Prime Minister Yoshiro Mori at their meeting in Irkutsk fell through. The politics of Japan make it next to impossible for any Japanese cabinet to agree to a territorial compromise: The four islands are essentially an indivisible claim. Their symbolic significance as a vestige of Japan's humiliation after World War II far outstrips their practical importance, significant as it is in terms of fish and seafood resources. In this situation, Moscow's attempts at compromise, such as joint economic exploration of the islands, have been flatly rejected.

Russia has no incentive to move: Japan is not a threat, real or potential, and economic cooperation with it is dictated by the economic conditions on the Russian side, not by the status of the islands, controlled by Moscow since 1945. In 2010, Medvedev became the first Russian leader to ever visit the southern Kuril Islands, all Japanese protests notwithstanding.

Russia was more successful in signing border treaties with its new neighbors Ukraine (2003), Kazakhstan (2004), Azerbaijan (2010), and the three Baltic states: Lithuania (1997), Latvia (2005), and Estonia (2007: still unratified). It was also able to agree with Kazakhstan (1998) and Azerbaijan (2002) on the division of the shelf in the northern Caspian, pending a general agreement on the Caspian Sea that is being blocked by Iranian and Turkmen claims. The Caspian's unresolved legal status prevents building a pipeline across the lake to transport Turkmen gas via the Caucasus to Europe, much to the advantage of Gazprom, the Russian energy giant.

Russia has come up with claims of its own, in the Arctic.[12] In a well-publicized move, a Russian undersea capsule in 2007 planted a small titanium tricolor on the ocean floor on the North Pole. At the same time, Moscow filed a legal claim with a UN commission to some 1.2 million square kilometers of the Arctic continental shelf. If it is internationally recognized as Russia's economic zone, it may add 30 percent to Russia's natural gas deposits. Also, the Northern Sea Route along Russia's Siberian coast—heretofore of limited importance as requiring the use of ice-breakers and lacking coastal infrastructure—may become commercially viable as the shortest link between the Atlantic and the Pacific. The warming of the Arctic and the rising importance of energy supply are driving Moscow's policies in the region.

Russia's burst of activity in the High North initially evoked concerns in the West, particularly in Canada. However, Moscow was later careful to allay those fears. In 2010, after forty years of negotiations, Russia agreed with Norway on a 50–50 deal on the disputed maritime area in the Barents Sea. For political reasons, the Russians are also determined to keep their coal mine settlements in Spitsbergen, allowed under the 1920 treaty. Interested in international recognition of its interests, Moscow made it very clear it will seek a legal or negotiated solution to the territorial issues in the Arctic.[13]

TERRITORIAL STATUS OF THE NEW STATES

Not only have all former Soviet republics survived, which was not a given in 1991, but they have largely kept their territory.

Other former Soviet republics have mostly consolidated their territory now as independent states. Very important, Ukraine has kept the territory of the Ukrainian Soviet Socialist Republic, which was put together by Lenin, Stalin, and Khrushchev. Fortunately, there was no question of official Polish, Czech, or Slovak claims on the territories, now in Ukraine, which the Soviet Union annexed in 1939 and 1945. The Soviet-era land border between Ukraine and Romania was sealed in a treaty signed in 1997. However, the issue of the continental shelf in the Black Sea remained unresolved until 2009 when the International Court ruled that Ukraine's Snake Island was in fact a rock, not warranting an economic zone around it. Kiev had to accept this judgment.

The issue of Crimea was much more important, and volatile. In 1954, Khrushchev transferred the largely Russian-populated peninsula from the Russian republic to the Ukrainian republic, to mark the three hundredth anniversary of what was officially called at the time "Russo-Ukrainian reunification." As long as the Soviet Union existed, this hardly mattered much, the more so since Sevastopol, a "closed city" as the headquarters of the Soviet Black Sea Fleet, was administered directly from Moscow. The issue, however, became very emotional amid the dissolution of the USSR. Indeed, the Crimea was the only territory outside of the perimeter of the new borders of the Russian Federation about which most Russians, irrespective of their political orientation, felt strongly.

In 1991, Yeltsin chose not to insist on the restoration of the peninsula to Russia, in exchange for Ukraine's renunciation of the portion of the Soviet nuclear arsenal deployed on its territory.[14] In 1993, the anti-Yeltsin Russian Supreme Soviet (parliament) laid claim to Sevastopol, arguing, on the strength of its Soviet-era special administrative status, that the city had not been handed over to Ukraine with the rest of the Crimea. The Kremlin ignored that claim. In early 1994, pro-Russian irredentists and separatists won the presidency of the Republic of Crimea, constituted within Ukraine since 1991. This was probably the most dangerous moment for the territorial unity of Ukraine. The tension subsided quickly, as Yeltsin defeated the Supreme Soviet in October 1993 and, in December 1994, moved against the Chechen separatists. Lacking Russian support, the Crimean republic presidency was abolished in 1995 and its status reduced to an autonomy the following year. As Leonid Kuchma, Ukraine's second president (1994–2005), later observed, had it not been for Yeltsin's principled position in 1993–1994, a war might have erupted between Russia and Ukraine over the Crimea.[15]

In 1997, Russia signed a treaty with Ukraine recognizing the borders that existed at the time of the breakup of the Soviet Union, thus confirming Crimea's status within Ukraine. Since those boundaries within a unitary Soviet state had never been demarcated, this still allowed for disputes, but on a micro-level. An example of that is the almost comical standoff in 2003 over Tuzla Island/peninsula in the Kerch Strait, which links the Black Sea with the small and virtually landlocked Sea of Azov. However, Russian commentators[16] were warning, darkly, that in the case of Ukraine's NATO accession, "every hillock, every ravine" along the border could become a flash point.

More seriously, Ukraine's internal cohesiveness was put to the test at the time of the Orange Revolution, when a number of regional and local authorities in eastern and southern Ukraine—unhappy about developments in Kiev—established a coordinating body to oppose the policies of newly elected President Viktor Yushchenko, deemed to be a representative of western Ukraine. This brought into stark relief the different geopolitical situations of western Ukraine, leaning toward Central Europe, and of the country's eastern and southern regions, which culturally feel closer to

Russia. These different identities actually threatened to tear Ukraine apart in case the country was confronted with a clear choice, such as NATO enlargement.

When President Putin told NATO leaders at Bucharest in April 2008 that Ukraine was "not even a state" and would "break apart,"[17] he was probably highlighting the brittleness of Ukraine's unity, which would not survive a serious test. This is not to say that Moscow had no strong views on the subject. It was clear then that Russia would support Ukraine's unity only as long as the country stayed neutral. Kiev's accession to NATO would lead Moscow, at minimum, to support Crimean irredentists. As if to underline this point, Crimean separatism suddenly became an issue again in 2008 after the Bucharest promise of NATO membership to Ukraine and Georgia and the war in the Caucasus. It died down quietly in 2009 when the NATO option receded, and it became totally docile with the advent of Viktor Yanukovych's presidency in 2010.

Between Russia and Belarus, there are no border posts or documents checks. Minsk, however, has not so much preserved its territory—as in Ukraine's case, Poland laid no claim to the territories lost in 1939—as asserted its sovereignty vis-à-vis Russia. In the 1990s, many analysts felt that Belarus, lacking a proper identity and nearly totally Russophone, would not survive as an independent state and thus simply fold into Russia. If Moscow had wanted a merger then, it would have been there for the asking. Alexandr Lukashenka, who became Belarusian president in 1994, was determined to reunify Belarus and Russia, with himself as Yeltsin's successor. This option was firmly rejected by the Russian elite, which was not interested in more territory, only in power and resources that it did not wish to share with a provincial parvenu.

The Russo-Belarusian Union State, proclaimed in 1999, formed a single customs territory on paper, but it did not lead to the creation of a new federal state, or even a confederation. In 2003, Putin laid down Moscow's conditions for a merger: essentially, *Anschluss* on the model of West Germany in 1990 absorbing the six East German *Laender*. Thus, Belarus received an offer to join the Russian Federation as six *oblasts*. This was totally unacceptable to Lukashenka as well as the bulk of the Belarusian elite, who for a dozen years had been enjoying the taste of their own nationhood and the opportunities it gave them.

Since then, Russo-Belarusian relations have been going from bad to worse, with the result being Belarus's moving farther away from Russia, from which it had been initially almost indistinguishable. Thus, paradoxically, Lukashenka, apparently the most Soviet of all post-Soviet leaders, became the father of the Belarusian state. By going east and being rebuffed, he achieved what the Belarusian nationalists sought by reaching out to the West in the early 1990s and failing miserably. Belarus is politically independent from Russia, de facto as well as de jure, even if it flies a version of its Soviet-era flag, rather than a remake of the colors of the medieval grand duchy of Lithuania, as the nationalists preferred. Economic dependence, however, is still strong.

Lithuania, Estonia, and Latvia, which were let out of the Soviet Union immediately in the aftermath of the 1991 Moscow coup, kept their Soviet-era territory intact. There was no question of Poland reclaiming Vilnius (Wilno) or Germany seeking Klaipeda (Memel), which they held in the 1920s and 1930s. Both regions were restored to Lithuania by Moscow as the Soviet Union annexed eastern Poland in 1939 and defeated Germany in 1945.

Alongside Ukraine, Lithuania stands out as a major beneficiary of Stalin's territorial rearrangements in Europe's east. When Lithuania in 2004 joined the European Union, Russia and the EU managed to negotiate arrangements for civilian and military transit between Russia/Belarus and Kaliningrad across the Lithuanian territory. The bargaining was hard, but the agreed-upon formula has been working without serious problems ever since.

The only territorial issues in the Baltic states were the relatively small border areas* that used to belong to Estonia and Latvia during the period between the two world wars. When the Baltic states were annexed by the Soviet Union in 1940, these areas were transferred to the Russian republic and are mainly Russophone by now. After the breakup of the USSR, there was no reason to claim them back, for such a step would have only compounded the problem of ethnic balance in the two Baltic states, where the titular ethnic groups held a bare majority. Riga and Tallinn were ready to accept the realities.

The snag was, however, that the interwar configuration of borders had been part of the 1920 treaties between the Baltic states and Russia, which recognized the independence of Latvia and Estonia. In the eyes of Riga and Tallinn, this recognition was a major argument in support of the claim that in 1940 the Soviet Union occupied the two states, and that Russia—as the successor state to the USSR—bore responsibility for that. This, in turn, was

---

* Pytalovo/Arbene in Latvia and Ivangorod and Pechory in Estonia.

unacceptable to Moscow, which delayed ratification of the border treaty with Latvia and has left the Russo-Estonian treaty unratified to this day.

The Transnistrian conflict notwithstanding, Moldova has managed to preserve its sovereignty in the face of neighboring Romania. An interesting parallel can be drawn here with Belarus and Russia. The first wave of unionism, a movement to join Romania, occurred in the immediate aftermath of the breakup of the Soviet Union. The second wave rose after Romania had joined the European Union in 2007. This was enhanced in 2009 after Moldova's liberal and democratic parties won the elections and formed the bulk of an Alliance for European Integration. Whereas many older Moldovans did not preserve the best of memories from the interwar (1918–1940) and World War II (1941–1944) periods when Moldova was officially part of Greater Romania, the younger generation of Moldovans wanted to be European, though not necessarily Romanian. The country's elite was divided, but the majority were more interested in running their own small state than in competing for position among Romania's provinces.

Pro-Romanian trends in Moldova stoked separatism in Transnistria. Since the Left Bank of the Dniester de facto broke away from the rest of then-Soviet Moldova in 1990, in part as a reaction to pro-Romanian unionism, the self-styled Dniester Moldovan Republic (PMR, in Russian) has acquired all the attributes of a sovereign state. Yet despite political and military support and material assistance given to Tiraspol, Moscow stopped short of formal recognition of the PMR. This was especially reaffirmed after the Russo-Georgian war of 2008.

The situation in the South Caucasus was much more serious. Georgia has fared worst, on all counts. It lost control over much of Abkhazia and South Ossetia in the early 1990s. For more than a dozen years, Tbilisi's control over the province of Ajara was also tenuous at best. In 2004, President Saakashvili managed to bring Ajara back to the fold, without firing a shot, but with Russian acquiescence. Moscow—which since 1878 had kept a military garrison in Batumi, Ajara's capital, guarded the nearby Georgian-Turkish border and had business interests in the province ruled by a local strongman—did not resist or even protest the restoration of Tbilisi's authority.

However, when Saakashvili tried to follow suit with a swift action in South Ossetia, he was rebuffed by the Ossetians and lost Putin's confidence. His next misguided attempt, in 2008, to enforce Georgia's authority over the former region, provoked a war with Russia, which Georgia lost *and* which pushed Moscow to formally recognize the breakaway territories. Even though Russia has been joined, in more than two years, by only Nicaragua, Venezuela, and Nauru, Tbilisi can hardly expect Moscow to withdraw its recognition. This constitutes a major trauma to the Georgian elite, who cannot accept the loss of the provinces.

However, as in the case of Moldova, this is actually a phantom pain: From Day One of their formal independence, neither Tbilisi nor Chisinau has been in full control of its Soviet-era territory. Abkhazia's separation from Georgia is as much a product of the disintegration of the Soviet Union as is Georgia's separation from the USSR. This fully applies to Azerbaijan, too.

Azerbaijan lost control over Nagorno-Karabakh in the early 1990s and has emerged as a sovereign state without its Armenian-populated enclave. Yet Baku is adamant that its 1991 Soviet borders are restored de facto. The compromise agreement negotiated in Key West, Florida, in 2001 by Presidents Haydar Aliyev and Robert Kocharyan fell through due to the unwillingness of the Azeri elite to follow their president in agreeing to horizontal relationship between Baku and Stepanakert, Karabakh's capital, in a nominally common state. Azerbaijan's loss is Armenia's gain, of course, though for diplomatic reasons Yerevan maintains that Baku's conflict is not with Armenia proper, but with the self-proclaimed Republic of Nagorno-Karabakh.

All countries of the South Caucasus have been watching developments over Kosovo. The former Serbian territory's recognition in 2008 by the major Western powers as a sovereign state is held up by the supporters of independence for the breakaway regions. A contrary example, of course, is the Turkish Republic of Northern Cyprus, which has existed since 1983 but is recognized only by Turkey.

Kazakhstan has been able to consolidate its borders with its major neighbors, Russia and China. Its border with China was the site of armed clashes in the 1960s and 1970s. Talks with China began in 1991, when the Soviet Union still existed, and were completed in 1996. Since then, Kazakhstan has had a properly fixed, and demilitarized, border with China.

Kazakhstan's border with Russia was sealed in a treaty in 2004. It is the longest land border in the world, running for more than 7,500 km (4,600 miles). This is also a border that lacks any other natural features than steppes. It comes close to a number of Russian industrial centers and communication lines that link European Russia to Siberia and the Pacific coast: Astrakhan, Volgograd, Saratov, Samara, Orenburg, Chelyabinsk, Tyumen, and Omsk. On the Kazakh side, majority Russian populations exist in many cities and towns: Aktobe (Aktyubinsk), Petropavlovsk-Kamchatsky,

Pavlodar, and Ust-Kamenogorsk. Since independence, Russo-Kazakhstani relations have been generally good, and only a handful of Russian nationalists resent the fact that the lifeline connecting European Russia and Siberia, "the backbone of Russia," is being made vulnerable by its proximity to "a Muslim country."[18]

Other Central Asian states have also kept their territory, making the borders among them drawn arbitrarily by Stalin in 1924–1925 look permanent. Tensions exist in the densely populated Fergana Valley, where the territories of Uzbekistan, Kyrgyzstan, and Tajikistan meet. Kyrgyzstan and Tajikistan fixed their borders with China in 1996, together with Kazakhstan and Russia. The expectation, entertained in the 1990s, that Afghanistan might break up—spawning ethnic Uzbek and Tajik states adjoining Uzbekistan and Tajikistan—never materialized. Turkmenistan, too, has survived in its Soviet-era physical shape. It not only kept its borders intact, but effectively sealed them. Thus, borders in Central Asia, which seemed artificial and unsustainable at the time of independence, have solidified and gained an air of permanence. The issues are within the borders of the new states, not along them.

INTERNAL DIVISIONS

In the aftermath of the imperial collapse, besides managing the border issue, the Russian Federation has been at pains to stabilize itself internally but eventually confounded those who had expected it to follow in the path of the Soviet Union. Unlike the fifteen constituent republics of the USSR, all 20 autonomous republics of the Russian Federation have stuck together.

This was not easy. Yakutia claimed ownership of its vast natural resources; Karelia, economic sovereignty; Komi, Bashkortostan, and others asserted the primacy of their constitutions over federal legislation; Tatarstan, Dagestan, and Ingushetia claimed the right to conclude international treaties and to pursue their own foreign policy; and Tuva, the right to make war and peace.[19] In Soviet days, regions were allowed to keep only 15–20 percent of their collected revenue. By 1999, the trend had reversed, with the federal government getting only 45 percent, on average. Tatarstan, by a special arrangement, kept 75 percent for itself.

This process of creeping territorial disintegration, evident in the late 1990s, was arrested in the following decade. The 1990s version of a "Russia of the Regions" was rendered inactive through a process of centralization pushed by Putin from 2000 on. Regional constitutions and legislation were aligned with the federal constitution. Special treaties establishing semi-confederal relationships, such as with Tatarstan or Bashkortostan, were abrogated. The once-powerful Federation Council—the Russian parliament's upper chamber consisting of popularly elected governors holding real power—was reformed into a docile institution largely made up of regional lobbyists. Federal districts were established, administered by Kremlin-appointed representatives—a kind of governor-general, each of whom presided over several regions. In 2004, governors lost their popular mandates and became presidential appointees. With the abolition in 2007 of single-member constituencies in the lower house, the Russian Federation became de facto a unitary state. And in 2010, the title of a president to describe the head of a republic within Russia was legally abolished.

The main challenge to the authority of the Russian state in the 1990s, coming from Chechen separatism, was met by military force and a policy of Chechenization. As a result, the ten-year war—dubbed "endless" by many—was stopped. Two visions of Chechnya—one devastated by the war and the other rebuilt after it was over—dramatically reduced the appetite for separatism across the North Caucasus. The new, and current, challenge is extremism, which uses religious rather than nationalist slogans and terrorism as its preferred method. The Russian federal authorities are yet to respond to that challenge. So far, their own policies and their local clients are part of the problem.

Today, the North Caucasus is drifting away from Russia, rather than breaking away. Territorial integrity, the Russian government's principal concern, is not being threatened directly. Instead, the region is becoming something like Russia's "inner abroad." Despite such exhortations as "the Caucasus is the foundation on which Russia rests,"[20] the reality is just the opposite. Chechnya is essentially self-governing, linked to Russia by a personal union—no more, no less—between its strongman Ramzan Kadyrov and Russia's leader Vladimir Putin. With Putin's backing, Kadyrov is virtually unrestrained in both his actions and his pronouncements, including on foreign policy issues. Chechenization is, in effect, Kadyrovization. While Chechnya is ruled with an iron fist (but a Chechen one), off-limits to the federal authorities, the neighboring republics of the North Caucasus are unstable.*

---

* More on Chechnya and the North Caucasus in chapter 2.

While, historically, Russia's most hard-fought colonial war was waged in the North Caucasus, Moscow's first conquest outside the ethnic Russian area was Kazan, annexed by Tsar Ivan in 1552. This annexation of what is present-day Tatarstan was the beginning of what later became the traditional (Muscovite) empire. Today's Tatars complain about the Russocentric view of history[21] and insist on their own historical turning points. Descendants of an ancient state, they celebrated the millennium anniversary of their capital, Kazan, in 2005, and five years later established a holiday to mark the beginning of Islamicization (which is defined as 922*) in what is now the Russian Federation.[22]

In the wake of the Soviet collapse, the Tatars—who were more numerous than all the residents of the Baltic republics combined—opted for sovereignty and an associated status within the federation. Yeltsin compromised, but Putin's unification drive put an end to that. However, though Tatarstan and its neighboring republic of Bashkortostan have lost their "special relations" with Moscow once codified in separate treaties, both are well integrated with the rest of Russia, relatively prosperous, and calm. In 2010, both republics saw off their first presidents, which happened in a smooth and orderly fashion.

The non-Muslim ethnic homelands have gone down the same road. Tuva, briefly an independent country (1921–1944), dropped its claim to the right to secede; Yakutia, the largest republic within the Russian Federation (3 million square kilometers, about the size of India, but with a population of only 1 million, or 0.1 percent of India's) has agreed to Moscow's formula for sharing its mineral wealth with the Russian Federation. Other regions rich in natural resources, such as Tyumen, have had to agree to budget transfer schemes that allow Moscow to redistribute the national income. Resource separatism, prevalent in the 1990s, is now a thing of the past.

Physically, Russia opened up. The new borders have turned many Russian regions that had been lying deep inside the country into border areas. This creates both new opportunities and new challenges. The optimists point to openings for trade, investment, and imports of labor. The pessimists respond with a litany of concerns about new vulnerabilities. Some of them suddenly remembered that the British Royal Navy in 1854 could easily reach places like Kronstadt in the Baltic, Solovki in the White Sea, and Petropavlovsk in Kamchatka, and that the Germans in 1942 showed

---

* This was the year when Volga Bulgaria, in present-day Tatarstan, embraced Islam.

up at Port Dikson on the Taimyr Peninsula. Now, the hazards are deemed to be economic rather than military.[23]

The thing is that Russia's borders with the EU countries, the United States, and Japan work as great divides: Depressive Russian regions lie next door to well-developed foreign territories. Thus, Kaliningrad is surrounded on land by EU members Poland and Lithuania; Leningrad Oblast and Karelia adjoin Finland along a broad front; Chukotka lies across the 90-mile-wide Bering Strait from America's Alaska; and the Kurils can be seen with the naked eye from Japan. A former Kremlin official fretted that once the Kurils become part of Japan's zone of influence, Sakhalin, Kamchatka, and Chukotka may be next.[24] Strangely, a similar concern was expressed by the Russian Foreign Ministry with regard to Estonia and its influence on the Finno-Ugric ethnics in Russia.[25] In 2008, these sensitivities led to a Russo-Estonian diplomatic row during an international summit gathering in Khanty-Mansiysk,[26] revealing a deep-seated insecurity.

Meanwhile, the borders on Belarus, Ukraine, and Kazakhstan are barely distinguishable, topographically or linguistically. Many Russian *oblasts* have long developed close ties to their Kazakh and Belarusian neighbors, which are sometimes more important than the links to other Russian regions. Understandably, Moscow has an interest in keeping the borders with those countries open. In the Caucasus, however, apart from the high mountains that separate the Russian Federation from its neighbors, ethnically Russian-populated territories—except for the Greater Sochi area—end well before the borders with Georgia and Azerbaijan. The republics of the North Caucasus, Abkhazia, and South Ossetia work like a buffer between Russia and other countries. Southern Russian territories such as Stavropol and Krasnodar form another buffer, between the restless North Caucasus and the core Russian lands.

The Russian government has worked to secure these fringe territories. Moscow sent Roman Abramovich, a prominent oligarch, to be governor of Chukotka (2004–2008), which he had to sustain, if need be, with his own companies' financial resources. Even when Abramovich was relieved as governor, he continued to be tied to the province, now as a provincial legislator. In 2007, Putin personally, and successfully, made the case for Sochi as the venue for the 2014 Winter Olympics. Three years later, he spearheaded another successful campaign to win the 2018 FIFA World Cup, to be held in thirteen cities across the European part of the country. The Russian Federation also won the right to host the 2013 University Games in Kazan and the 2012 summit of the Asia-Pacific Economic Cooperation (APEC).

The Russian government insisted on holding the APEC summit in Vladivostok, rejecting polite suggestions that it would be better to convene the event in the significantly more developed environment of St. Petersburg.

What makes Russia a world power, in geographic terms, is the fact that it extends from the Euro-Atlantic to the Asia-Pacific. It is the fate of eastern Russia, Siberia, and the Far East, rather than the fate of the North Caucasus, which will determine the geopolitical future of the country. Siberia is sometimes called "Russia's principal colony," an imperial crown jewel, on a par with India within the British empire. However, as Vadim Tsymbursky pointed out, "Russia did not annex Siberia—instead, it was being built by Siberia."[27] This is why a Russia without Siberia would be no Russia, but Muscovy. Since the late twentieth century, this is being more clearly understood.

General Secretary Gorbachev, in his 1986 Vladivostok speech, called for the country's integration with the Asia-Pacific. As president, Putin called the Far East "Russia's strategic survivability reserve for the twenty-first century."[28] In December 2006, the Russian National Security Council looked into security challenges of the region, such as depopulation, fraying of links with European Russia, and "disproportions" in foreign economic relations. Reviving an idea that it could not realize in the 1990s, the Russian government vowed to build a space launch center, Vostochny, in the Amur region, to replace Baikonur, now in Kazakhstan. The infrastructure gap is huge. Until very recently, one could not travel by road between the European part of Russia and the Far East. In August 2010, Putin, in a publicity stunt, drove a Russian-made car from Khabarovsk to Chita, virtually opening road transport between two regional capitals of the Far East. For Russian Far Easterners, it has become easier, cheaper, and more comfortable to travel to China, South Korea, or Japan than to Moscow or St. Petersburg.[29]

Immediately after the Soviet Union's collapse, many Russian people feared Chinese demographic aggression and occupation of the thinly populated areas. Twenty years later, what is not feared in Russia is China's expansion. The Chinese have filled their niche in Russia's immigration mosaic and do not venture much outside it. Interestingly, some Russian pensioners now choose to cross the border and settle in neighboring Chinese towns, where the cost of living is lower and life is more secure.

At the same time, the successive federal development programs (1996, 2002, and 2006)—the most recent of which amounted to just under $25 billion—have been only modestly successful, although some of Russia's best-known government-owned companies—Gazprom and Rosneft, Russian Railways, and others—are involved. Even the massive funding of Vladivostok's infrastructure in the run-up to the APEC summit will help only if the port city really develops into a hub for Russian companies doing business in the Pacific Basin.[30]

As for St. Petersburg itself, it has received the official seat of Gazprom, with its taxes; the Russian Federation Constitutional Court; the headquarters of the Russian Navy; and the headquarters of the new Operational-Strategic Command "West." All of these organizations left Moscow only reluctantly, and under pressure from the Kremlin. Russia's "Northern Capital" has also been played up as a venue for major international jamborees: the city's tricentennial in 2003, accompanied by the EU-Russia and CIS summits on its margins; the G8 summit in 2006; and countless bilaterals. Started on the Neva, the Petersburg Dialogue has become the main forum for Russo-German exchanges among politicians, civic leaders, and experts. Since 2007, the Russian leadership has been keen on making the St. Petersburg International Economic Forum—built on the Davos World Economic Forum model—a major annual international event, eclipsing in particular the London-Russia Forum.

Happy to show foreign leaders the vastness of their country, the Kremlin has been taking the twice-yearly EU-Russia summits to various parts of Russia, bringing top-level diplomatic dialogue to such formerly inward-looking cities as Kazan, Samara, Khanty-Mansiysk, Khabarovsk, and Rostov. In 2009, Yekaterinburg, the informal capital of the Urals, hosted in quick succession summits of the Collective Security Treaty Organization, the Shanghai Cooperation Organization, and of Russia, India, and China. The same year, President Medvedev started an annual international political forum in Yaroslavl, an ancient town 175 miles northeast of Moscow and until recently a complete backwater. In 2010, Astrakhan was chosen to host the next Caspian summit. From Soviet days, Sochi, as the vacation residence of Kremlin leaders, has been a venue for many informal summits. In post-Soviet times, particularly under Putin and Medvedev, this role has been greatly expanded. Sochi, like Krasnoyarsk and Irkutsk, has also become a venue for a regional economic forum, with international participation.

The new territorial unity of Russia has come at the expense of federalism, which has survived in little but name. A number of authors[31] point to the revival of the imperial syndrome in Russia. However, it is impossible to run such a big and diverse country from one center. The reality, since the demise of the Soviet Union, is that Russia—politically reunited—has become socially decentralized. Even as the authorities have sought to consolidate political control, they were eager to "uplift" the regions in terms of social and economic development.[32] Moscow still stands out, but more as the political and financial center of the country and a gateway to the globalized world. In terms of actual living standards and quality of life, the gap between the capital and the provincial centers is much narrower.

Indeed, all regional capitals are "little Moscows" vis-à-vis their regions. They all boast at least some decent housing projects, well-stocked stores, increasingly better quality restaurants, high-speed Internet connections, and universities. Around those centers, new regionalism has been developing. Each region has acquired a sense of identity, relying on its past glory and historical ties to European business, like Novgorod the Great; or on natural resources, like oil-rich Tyumen; or some special geographical position, like Vladivostok.

With the opening of borders, the world has started to look very different to ordinary Russians. Not all roads pass through Moscow anymore. Dozens of airports around Russia have received the status of international gateways. With flights from Novosibirsk to Dubai and from Irkutsk to Hainan, the traditional east-west axis has been complemented by the north-south one. The traditional Eurocentric view is also changing. Viewed from Pacific Russia, Moscow is distant and uncaring, while China, South Korea, and Japan are close and offer real economic opportunities.[33] This is not a case for separatism, but certainly a need for managing diversity.

Russian regions may all be uniformly subordinated to the authority of the Kremlin, but they are very different economically, socially, and politically. According to the UN Human Resources Index, Moscow is close to the Czech Republic in terms of development and personal income, while Ingushetia and Tuva are closer to Mongolia and Guatemala. Moscow's life expectancy is 71 years, Tuva's, 56. And Muscovites earn about three times as much as the residents of Kiev.

Seen from Russia, the New Eastern Europe is three very different countries, with interesting domestic divisions. Ukraine, unlike the Russian Federation, is a unitary state under its constitution. Yet, it is a country of many distinct regions. Its two poles are the east (Kharkiv, Donetsk) and the west (Lviv), with the center (Kiev) usually aligning with the former, and the south (Odessa and the Crimean Peninsula) with the latter. The two poles and their coalitions represent also two external policy vectors, with the center-west leaning toward the EU and the south-east toward Russia.

The 2004 Orange Revolution put the unity of Ukraine to a test, making the losers take steps toward separatism. In a similar fashion, Kiev's tensions with Moscow had an immediate impact on Crimea, especially Sevastopol. Moscow politicians started offering suggestions in favor of the "federal-ization" of Ukraine. This was interpreted in Kiev as a tactic designed to dangerously weaken the unity of the Ukrainian state, paving the way to its breakup and the absorption of its eastern and southern regions by Russia.

With the advent of the Party of Regions in 2010 as the dominant po-litical force in Ukraine, and the self-destruction of the opposition, the dis-cussion of federalism has died down. Kiev, in particular, strengthened its control over Crimea. So much for the Party of Regions' supposedly pro-Moscow leanings. However, the repeal of the 2004 power-sharing com-promise and the restoration of the presidential republic enshrined in the 1996 Ukrainian Constitution notwithstanding, Kiev has been careful not to alienate the regional elites. Managing them, it has avoided a clash with western Ukraine and has weakened pro-Russian separatism in the Crimea. Ironically, while the democratic and nationalistic Orange Revolution and the policies of President Yushchenko put Ukraine's territorial unity in ques-tion, the *revanche* of the oligarchs from eastern Ukraine has strengthened it.

Belarus, too, has its own "west," with palpable Polish influence, but the regional differences are nowhere as strong as in Ukraine, and the country is much smaller. Essentially, it can be taken as one unit. In tiny Moldova, by contrast, the gulf could not have been wider between the two banks of the Dniester, which have been living apart since 1990. As in the other two cas-es—Ukraine and Belarus—this has a lot to do with prior separate existence of the regions. Ukraine's western lands were long part of the Habsburg and Austro-Hungarian empires and Poland; western Belarus belonged to Poland between the two world wars; and, while, during the same period, the bulk of present-day Moldova was held by Romania, Transnistria stayed within Soviet Ukraine.

The South Caucasus is only a little less diverse, ethnically, than Russia's North Caucasus. Since 1989, this has resulted in conflicts, even wars. It is in that part of the former empire that the exit from imperial rule has been accompanied by particularly violent conflict. Russia became embroiled in most of these conflicts, often seeking to use the divisions to its advantage, as in Georgia, but that has only made the situation even messier.

So far, post-imperial Central Asia has escaped large-scale conflicts, with one exception: Tajikistan. There, civil war raged from 1991 to 1997, with the Russian military's involvement, and resulted in the triumph of the

Moscow-backed southern Kulyab clan over the northerners from Khujand (Leninabad), who dominated the power structures of Soviet Tajikistan. A third group, in the mountainous Pamir region of Gorno-Badakhshan, established a de facto autonomy.

Today, Tajikistan is still a fragmented society with very weak national identification.[34] Since the end of the civil conflict, Tajikistan has been recentralized under the authoritarian regime of President Emomali Rakhmon, but interregional rivalries have not disappeared. Rakhmon's eventual departure is likely to reopen the painful issue of regional balance in Tajikistan.

Kyrgyzstan, the smallest of Central Asia's new states, also finds it hard to forge unity. The north-south divide is both political and cultural. It remained just beneath the surface during the fourteen-year reign of Kyrgyzstan's first president, Askar Akayev (1991–2005), and has been evident ever since. Both the 2005 and 2010 "revolutions" in Kyrgyzstan put the unity of the country at stake. The outburst of violence in the southern Kyrgyz city of Osh in the summer of 2010 brought Kyrgyzstan to the verge of a civil war, but Russia stayed away. One hope is that the adoption of a new constitution in 2010, replacing the presidential republic with a parliamentary one, would result in a more representative government. But the Kremlin has publicly expressed concerns that a parliamentary system would make Kyrgyzstan completely ungovernable.

It is the larger Central Asian states, such as Uzbekistan and especially Kazakhstan, whose domestic unity is of central importance to Russia. Kazakhstan is a vast place with a sparse population. Its northern regions, adjoining Russia's southern Urals and southern Siberia, had a predominantly Russian urban population. After 1991, Moscow gave no hint of support to the ethnic Russian irredentists who wanted to secede from the new state of Kazakhstan and join Russia. To consolidate the newly born republic, President Nursultan Nazarbayev in 1997 moved the capital from Almaty to the remote town of Astana (formerly Tselinograd and before and after that Akmolinsk, Akmola), situated in the middle of the northern territories. In this masterful stroke, he at once moved Kazakhstan closer to Russia physically and consolidated Kazakhstan's control over its Russian-populated regions.

Apart from the north, Astana has to deal with the two other important regions: western Kazakhstan, where most oil fields are situated, and southern Kazakhstan, where the former capital, Almaty, is still functioning as Kazakhstan's premier business capital. The western regions have relatively small populations, even by Kazakh standards; there is no separate identity and little risk of separatism. Southern Kazakhstan is the country's link to

Middle Asia. It lies within a couple hours' drive from Kyrgyzstan's Bishkek and is fairly close to the Uzbek border. It is there that Kazakhstan's multi-ethnic, multilingual, not overly religious nature comes into direct contact with the distinctly Muslim cultures of its neighbors, who have been going through a period of political turbulence.

Uzbekistan is a country of several potential centers of influence: Tashkent, the capital; Samarqand and Bukhara, the ancient centers of power, learning, and religion; and the overpopulated Fergana Valley, with its Islamic revival, are all important stages of activity. In 2005, an uprising broke out in Andijan that was suppressed by the authorities with a heavy loss of life. Distant and almost forgotten, there is also Qaraqalpaqstan, the ancient Khorezm, an autonomous republic that adjoins the fast-shrinking Aral Sea.

With the issue of political succession looming ever larger, the stability of Uzbekistan cannot be taken for granted. By contrast, Turkmenistan, ruled by very harsh authoritarians ever since its independence, shows little sign of internal divisions. Founding President Saparmurat Niyazov's idea was to destroy the remnants of the tribal structure in Turkmen society and to create a single Turkmen nation with a single sultan-type leader. So far, this has proven doable.

NATION BUILDING

In an abrupt reversal, the breakup of the Soviet Union transformed the imperial question into an ethnic Russian one. After the previous imperial collapse in 1917, and the bloody civil war that followed, 2 to 3 million Russians were driven away from their country, which had been taken over by the Bolsheviks. Another few hundred thousand—in the Baltic states, Poland, Finland, Bessarabia, and Manchuria—found themselves outside of the Russian state due to border changes. After 1991, some 3 million ex-Soviet citizens emigrated, mostly to Europe, Israel, and the United States. At the same time, the number of ethnic Russians who were abandoned—or freed—by the state, which had allowed its borderland provinces to opt out, was about 25 million, around a fifth of the total number of ethnic Russians in the world.

Yet this did not lead to conflict. Alexander Solzhenitsyn's famous November 1990 clarion call to "reorganize Russia"[35] on the basis of the Russian Republic, Ukraine, Belarus, and northern Kazakhstan was widely heard—the newspaper *Komsomolskaya Pravda* distributed no fewer than 27 million copies of the brochure—but not heeded. The Russian government rejected irredentism. The nationalist discourse of a "divided nation," though loud and ubiquitous, does not guide the practical policy. Despite a clear rise in xenophobia and extremism, Russian ethnic nationalism remains a marginal force. The "post-imperial" or "supra-ethnic" element among Russians is still dominant.

Seen from a different angle, Russia's population is much smaller than the Soviet Union's, but it is much more homogeneous. Ethnic Russians made up just about half of the Soviet population of 1989. In 1913, only 43 percent of the empire's population were ethnic Russians, but the empire officially regarded all Eastern Slavs—including Little Russians (Ukrainians), White Russians (Belarusians), and Great Russians (now simply Russians)—as a single ethnic group. This was one of the underlying causes for the breakup of the Soviet version of the empire. However, the current share of ethnic Russians in the population of the Russian Federation is about four-fifths. The Russian Federation, having emerged from an empire, has a good chance to build a nation-state.[36]

Unlike in other post-imperial cases—Kemalist Turkey; post–World War I and pre-*Anschluss* Austria; or present-day Serbia and Croatia, or virtually all other new independent states of the former Soviet Union—the Russian nation-state is not being constructed on the basis of ethnicity.[37] This has much to do with the very low level of national consciousness among ethnic Russians. In pre-Petrine Russia, their identification was mostly with the Orthodox religion; within the empire, it was mostly with their localities, which left the vast number of peasants cold to the First World War and the empire's fate.[38] In Soviet days, some citizens identified with the ruling ideology, and others with the high culture that openly or tacitly rejected that ideology; and most identified themselves with the victory over German Nazism and the achievements of Soviet science, arts, and sports. State borders were, for Russians, the only real dividing lines; *within* those borders, there were almost no clearly marked ethnic territories. For most Russians of that period, the whole Soviet Union was a "home," as a popular song went. And it echoed Witte's maxim.

The empire was always bigger than the ethnic Russian nation. In the post-imperial days, building a post-imperial Russian civic nation is a first-order agenda item for the country. From early on, President Yeltsin started using the word *rossiyane*, "Rossians" (from *Rossiya*, the Russian for Russia) when referring to the citizens of the country. Two decades later, the word—first coined in the reign of Peter the Great but not much used after the eighteenth century—has become a common and accepted description. However, in reality, *rossiyane* are not there yet. Russia's populace is still unstructured. As it stands now, Russia is a country and a state, but not yet a nation.

For some observers, this is a mission impossible. Present-day Russia, they argue, is still an empire, only smaller. The Russian Federation, in that view, is the "third and last" form of the historical Russian empire. The Russian mosaic is bound to fall apart just like the Soviet one did before. As the sociologist Natalia Tikhonova pointedly asks, it is not clear why a civic Russian nation can now be composed of such ethnicities as Russians, Tatars, Dagestanis (three dozen ethnic groups in that category), and Yakuts, if it could not form on the basis of Russians, Ukrainians, Belarusians, and Kazakhs.

One can argue, of course, that numbers matter, as do ambitions and such things as capacity for leadership and willingness to be led. The ethnicity mix, however, is not the issue. It is not necessarily easier to build a common nation with Ukrainians than with Udmurts. The crucial point is that a civic nation can emerge only after a society has gone through the stages of modernization.[39] There can be no civic nation without institutions: the rule of law, property rights, market mechanisms, social solidarity, and values. At present, all these ingredients are sorely missing. A nation's most comprehensive expression is participatory democracy. Thus, a modern Russian nation can be the result of only a successful all-around modernization.

In Soviet days, most ethnic Russians—virtually all of whom lived in the borderlands—identified themselves as Soviets. By contrast, only a tiny proportion of Armenians or Estonians felt themselves to be Soviet first. When the USSR broke up, national (ethnic) mobilization was the natural path for most new states. Zviad Gamsakhurdia, Georgia's first president (1991–1992), essentially declared all non-Georgians to be second-class citizens. This had tragic consequences, especially in Abkhazia and South Ossetia. Moldova's first post-Soviet leadership imposed strict language rules that alienated many Russian speakers. Latvia and Estonia became the only two states of the former USSR that denied citizenship rights to those not born there before 1940, when both countries were annexed by the Soviet Union, or their successors. This, of course, excluded most ethnic Russians, Ukrainians, Jews, and others who had moved to the Baltic republics in Soviet times.

Russia was slower to move in that direction. The main reason is not that the Soviet communist state suppressed Russian nationalism. It also suppressed the nationalisms of Ukrainians, Estonians, and Chechens, with little result. The fact that post-Soviet Russian elites are focused on material wealth and, in this sense, are quite cosmopolitan, carries some, but not enough, weight. There is a sense that an ethnic Russian nation might spell the end of the present Russian state. Even though more than 50 percent of Russian residents find the slogan "Russia for the Russians" attractive,[40] an ethnic Russian nation in a country with so many ethnic homelands organized as republics with their constitutions, national languages, and aspirations is a sure way to a new disaster.

Ironically, while ethnic Russians, despite the growing xenophobia and outbursts of ultranationalism, are still largely reluctant to identify themselves with an ethnic nation, the situation with other nations within the Russian Federation is just the opposite. The Tatars, Chechens, Yakuts, and others are very ethnically conscious. The three dozen tiny groups in Dagestan, while calling themselves Russians (*rossiyane*), are extremely particular about their ethnic communities.

What the rise in xenophobia, the upsurge of chauvinism, and the spread of anti-foreign violence also tell is that there is no appetite whatsoever for a new edition of the empire, only residual nostalgia for the old days. Politicians sensed that. Dmitri Rogozin, who started his political career in the early 1990s as a co-founder—with the late General Alexander Lebed—of the Congress of Russian Communities (an organization that sought to unite ethnic Russians in such places as Crimea, Kazakhstan, and elsewhere in the "near abroad"), put his gear in reverse a decade later, when he campaigned under the slogan, "Moscow for the Muscovites." This was the essence of the message of Moscow's anti-Caucasus riots of December 2010, which were echoed in other parts of the country. This change of slogans illustrates as well as anything the passage from the imperial to the national.

The Congress of Russian Communities had no future. In general, Russians abroad assimilate easily by accepting the dominant groups' rules of the game. They form no diasporas. By the same token, however, while they accept, within Russia, the ethnic homelands' "specifics," they resent immigrants in the large metropolitan centers who do not accept the local rules of behavior. Those who do can be accepted as fellow Russians. To be considered Russian, one must Russify: speak the language, learn the ways and habits of the Russian people, and follow them, at least in public. During the Moscow clashes in December 2010—which pitted young Muscovites against the people from the Caucasus—a Dagestani youth told the ethnic Russian crowd that he, too, was a *rossiyanin*. "Why then do you folks carry knives about you?" was the response.[41]

Significantly, there is no imagined community of fate in today's Russia. The end of the Soviet Union was the end of the big macro-community. People used to be bound, almost physically, hand and foot, by tradition in tsarist times; by the official ideology, the police state, and impregnable borders in Soviet times. In present-day Russia, atomized society is not really bound by any barriers, official or conventional. The more successful the people are, the wider the distance between them and the rest of the population. The elite rise, but they do not lead, and do not care to. The private definitely trumps the public. Seen from virtually any level of society, the state is too corrupt to inspire national consciousness.

Having gone through the trauma of the sudden collapse of the state with all its systems—political, economic, societal, and ideological—Russian people have learned to prioritize their private lives and not to worry too much about such things as the color of the national flag, the delineation of the borders, or the composition of the government. What have survived are family ties, local and personal connections. Once communal in spirit and fiercely patriotic, Russia has definitely gone private. On the contrary, the public space, once all-embracing, is being decidedly neglected. Like in a typical big-city apartment block, the apartments are usually refurbished and generally well-kept; by contrast, the staircase is dirty and the elevator creaky, and no one seems to care.

There is no outside threat that is felt to be serious enough to lead to the emergence of defensive nationalism. In 2009, only 37 percent of those polled felt an external military threat, as compared with 49 percent in 2000 (after Kosovo) and 57 percent in 2003 (after Iraq). For 52 percent of Russians, no such threat exists.[42] The Kremlin actually agreed: Military reform was delayed by two decades and did not start until 2008, and military modernization was pushed to the 2010s agenda.

No wonder that "sacred" defense of the motherland has receded into the background. The Russian people would agree to pay moderately for security and defense, but they resent being engaged themselves in military actions. Even those who see the threat are absolutely not prepared to sacrifice anything, least of all their lives, for the benefit of the world as a whole (only 14 percent agree with the former "internationalist duty," as exercised in Afghanistan), even for their own country (33 percent). Only 57 percent say they would be ready to defend Russia against foreign aggression, which they clearly consider highly unlikely at the present stage. However, 88 percent say they would defend themselves and their families. Eighty percent put their own interests first, as against 6 percent for state interests.

The Kremlin has been working, in its own way, to correct that attitude. Yeltsin and his associates talked at length about a "national idea" but found none. Putin was more systematic. He developed modern Russian conservatism, anti-communist and anti-liberal at the same time. Its key values are the authority of the state; undivided political power; economic power rooted in and subordinate to political power; traditional values of the established religions (above all, the Russian Orthodoxy); patriotism; strategic independence in foreign policy; and great-power status. In order to keep the power status, the conservatives even support modernization—on the condition, of course, that it not erode their hold on power.

The conservatives' attitude toward democracy is interesting. They clearly do not see democracy as a value, but they have uses for democracy's attributes as a legitimizing instrument. Putin learned one thing from the experience of his two predecessors, Yeltsin and Gorbachev. Both of them started as immensely popular but soon lost popularity and had to relinquish power. Gorbachev also lost the state he had been entrusted with; Yeltsin nearly did so. Putin's insight was that in order to keep power, one had to win and preserve overwhelming popularity. This he did, and this he provided for Medvedev. The other insight was that this popularity had to stay personal: no ruling party, or government institution, would be able to attract it from above, and no serious opposition group would be allowed to bid for it from below. Thus, an atomized society beholden to personalized power works, for the time being, as a recipe for stability in post-Soviet Russia.

It is not all about vote rigging, though accusations abound. Nor is it all about control of the major TV channels, though it is essential, even vital, for the preservation of power by the ruling elite. This is much more about making strategic popular moves, such as slashing budget expenses on all items, save pensions, which have been rising.[43] Pensioners vote more actively than does any other segment of the population. Thus, popularity was essentially achieved by means of catering to the paternalistic demands of those groups that are wedded to the traditional system of governance, which predates the Soviet Union but was immensely strengthened by the communist regime. However, that, in turn, means continuing with the imperial state, which becomes less and less adequate to Russia's increasingly globalized environment.

Should Russia resume its move toward democracy, the "national question," and thus the issue of territorial integrity, may rise again. Separatism may resurface, and not only in the North Caucasus. During the 2010 census, some residents of Kaliningrad chose to describe themselves as "Kaliningraders" rather than Russians. At the same time, there is a possibility that the ethnic element may prevail over the supra-ethnic one in the Russian psyche. Democratization will put pressure on both internal and external borders.[44] If the pressure is too high, and these borders start moving, this will be a major threat to security along a vast area.

Nation building in the Baltic states, in comparison to Russia, was more straightforward. Estonian, Latvian, and Lithuanian elites proclaimed the restoration of their countries' independence, which had been taken away by the Soviet Union during the occupation that started in 1940. The constitutions that had operated until 1940 were again in force; private property restored to its rightful owners; citizens of 1940 and their descendants received citizenship; those who came afterward had to undergo a process of naturalization. And since 2004, the citizens of the Baltic states became citizens of the European Union. From the Soviet Union to the EU in less than fifteen years: quite a metamorphosis!

All residents of Lithuania were automatically granted citizenship. However, this was not the case in Latvia and Estonia. Hundreds of thousands of people, mostly ethnic Slavs, did not go through the naturalization process. What is more interesting is that many of those who did go through the process and who did receive citizenship feel excluded from the realm of politics and public administration. In practice, Latvia and Estonia are in the process of becoming bi-communal societies, with only one ethnic community being synonymous with the "nation."

Belarus exhibits many of the features common to Russian society, minus those rooted in the empire.[45] Belarus is a small, landlocked country in an Eastern European neighborhood. The Belarusian nation is still in gestation. It will not be defined by the language—Russian is the dominant medium. Nor will religion be a marker: Most Belarusians are Orthodox, but the patriarch sits in Moscow; a sizable minority are Roman Catholics.

Unlike the Russians, Belarusians were never touched by the imperial élan. Unlike the Ukrainians, they never developed a particularly strong sense of nationalism. They have a reputation of being quiet, hardworking people, closely tied to their unpretentious land, and they do not venture far from it. In the post-Soviet era, the determining factor for Belarus will be its geographical position in Eastern Europe. With such neighbors as Poland, Lithuania, and Ukraine, Belarusians cannot help but feel European.

Ukraine has faced a difficult task of forging a nation, given the diversity of the Ukrainian regions brought together within a common territory in Soviet times. Yet it was helped in other ways. Sharing many societal problems with Russia, Ukraine had an advantage in not being Russia, with its harsh climate, vast expanses, ethnic and cultural diversity, and imperial mentality. Indeed, post-Soviet Ukraine has emerged as a non-Russia. Not yet having defined what Ukraine is, Ukrainian leaders and elites highlighted independence—from Russia—as the most important value.

Two decades on, one should register a qualified success on the path of Ukrainian nation building. Absent major crises, which would create intolerable internal tension—one example of which would be a clear choice between Russia and "the West"—Ukraine will stand and not fall. The longer it can avoid such impossibly clear choices, the stronger it will become, eventually gaining immunity from the impact of life-threatening external factors.

Moldova is a torn country or, better said, a country that has not yet attained national unity and cohesion. Its unity has not been lost; rather, it is still to be gained—through tireless efforts and some luck. Two historical facts about Moldova stand out. One is that historical Moldova was a medieval princedom straddling the Prut River, which now forms the border between the Republic of Moldova and Romania. Both historical capitals of Moldova—Iasi and, before that, Suceava—are in present-day Romania.

When Moldova merged with Walachia into a single Romanian state in 1859, the present territory of the Republic of Moldova—then known as Bessarabia—remained under the control of the Russian empire, which had annexed it in 1812. During the entire crucial period of the formation of the Romanian nation-state, Bessarabia was not part of it. It was occupied by Romania and joined with it from 1918 to 1940, and again in 1941–1944, only to be reattached to the Soviet Union each time.

In 1940, almost the entire population of Chisinau left for Romania. The rest were mostly peasants, hardly imbued with pan-Romanian consciousness. Of the past nearly 200 years, the descendants of present-day Moldovans spent only one generation in Romania, compared with over six generations inside the Russian/Soviet empire.

The other fact is that Transnistria had never been part of either Moldova or Bessarabia but was attached to the Soviet Moldovan republic in 1940. Thus, Moldova faces a double problem as it seeks to establish itself as a nation. Moldovans need to distinguish themselves from their kith and kin in neighboring Romania, and they need to be able to integrate with Transnistrians, who broke away from them a generation ago, in September 1990, almost a year before the USSR collapsed, and who are ethnically and culturally different from them—and generally abhor Romanians.

Georgia's situation looks more complex, but in fact could be simpler, though hardly easier. Unlike Moldova, Georgia did have a brief experience with modern statehood. It proclaimed its independence in 1918 amid the Russian Civil War, which was recognized by the Bolsheviks in the 1920 treaty, but then was overrun by the Red forces, led in part by Georgian Bolsheviks, in 1920. After 1991, as Georgia opted out of the Soviet Union, the Abkhaz and the Ossetians opted out of Georgia, chasing ethnic Georgians out of their enclaves.

Now that Abkhazia and South Ossetia have escaped Tbilisi's control, Georgia has the option to focus on the development of what is sometimes referred to as "core Georgia." Achieving important results in the socioeconomic area, combating corruption, and consolidating the Georgian nation in the process would not only improve the Georgians' living standards but also heal their wounded pride and bolster their standing in the South Caucasus.

Like Moldova and Georgia, Azerbaijan is reeling after a loss of territory in the Armenian-populated enclave of Nagorno-Karabakh and the adjacent regions. As in Georgia, the blessing in disguise is the homogeneity of the rump state and a chance to build a nation on a solid basis of common ethnicity. Azerbaijan's problems with nation building are external; by being external, these problems actually assist nation building within the country. It helps that, thanks to the Caspian oil and gas, Baku has acquired substantial financial power to deal with the problems of socioeconomic development. At the same time, the sense of power and independence—also from foreign donors—enhances the Azeri elites' self-image and motivates them to press for the return of Karabakh. This heightens the danger of war with the Armenians.

Armenia is de facto united with Nagorno-Karabakh, an unrecognized state, in a single entity. Thus, the national dream of the 1980s has come true, and a modern version of Greater Armenia is already in place. The problem is that it is not accepted by the international community. The issues facing the Armenian nation today have everything to do with economic and social development. Armenians have gained the territory that the Azeris have lost. Yet Azerbaijan has the oil, the money, and international clout, making it impervious to outside pressure. By contrast, short of natural resources, sitting away from transit routes, landlocked Armenia depends very much on the support of the Armenian diaspora in the United States, Europe, the Middle East, and Russia.

Kazakhstan's problem, at the time of independence, was that the titular ethnic group was a minority in its own land. Throughout the twentieth century, the share of Kazakhs in Kazakhstan was decreasing: from 67 percent in 1911 to 57 percent in 1926 to 39 percent in 1938 to 30 percent in 1959. In 1989, just before the breakup of the Soviet Union, it stood at just under 40 percent of the republic's population. In that situation, "Kazakhization" of Kazakhstan became a major policy goal.

By 2009, the ethnic balance was reversed, essentially as a result of a higher birthrate among the Kazakhs and emigration of the Russians and other ethnics. The share of ethnic Kazakhs, however, rose to 63 percent, while the share of ethnic Russians decreased just as sharply, from 38 percent in 1989 to 23 percent two decades later. Many other non-Kazakhs—such as Germans, Ukrainians, and Belarusians—left the country, which led to a 10 percent net loss of the general population.

Kazakhization also included appointments of ethnic Kazakhs to senior government and administrative positions and the renaming of Russian-built cities. The ethnic balance corrected, Kazakhstan became more relaxed about other issues, such as the use of Russian as an official language. However, an ethnic Russian who in 2010 dared to express his wish to run for president of Kazakhstan was heckled by Kazakh nationalists. This is a sore point: In 1986, habitually peaceful Kazakhstan was rocked by riots at the news of a Russian apparatchik being appointed to lead the Kazakh branch of the Soviet Communist Party.

After 1991, Kyrgyzstan was essentially busy achieving a similar goal: all power to the indigenous ethnic group. Again, mass emigration of non-Kyrgyz residents—mainly Russians and other Slavs, and Germans—helped. After that, the only real competition was from the Uzbek community in the south of the country. Interethnic frictions in Osh in the summer of 2010 led to pogroms there and the mass exodus of Uzbeks to neighboring Uzbekistan.

Since independence, Uzbekistan itself did not feel as threatened by outsiders as Kazakhstan and Kyrgyzstan. Tashkent's nation-building efforts focused on the revival of the country's dominant position in the region. With Bukhara, Samarqand, Khiva, Khorezm, and much of the Fergana Valley all in its territory, the Uzbek government "appropriated" the great conqueror and empire-builder Tamerlane (1336–1405) as the historical father figure of the new nation.

Tajikistan, where national consciousness remains comparatively weak, and which pushed out almost its entire ethnic Russian population during the civil war of the 1990s, sought to make use of the Persian Samanid dynasty (ninth and tenth centuries), which built an empire in Central Asia and Iran, as the precursor of the modern Tajik state. Monuments were built to commemorate the ancient rulers, and the Tajik ruble was duly replaced by the somoni.[46]

In Turkmenistan, a different pattern prevailed. Instead of glorifying old dynasties or emirs, the last Communist Party leader in the republic, Gorbachev-appointee Saparmurat Niyazov, built himself into a father of the Turkmen nation and received the official title of Turkmenbashi, a version of Ataturk. A cult of personality ensued, unseen anywhere in the former Soviet Union since the death of Stalin, and comparable only to the situation in North Korea. In 2001, Turkmenbashi wrote a book, *Rukhnama*, which contained the official view of Turkmen history and the nation's aspirations, as well as a set of very conservative values. The book was ordered to be endlessly studied by the entire population—until Niyazov's successor stopped it and replaced Turkmenbashi's writings with his own more current, if less ambitious, ones.

ECONOMY

Post-imperial Russia experienced a stunning contraction of its economy—by 43 percent of real GDP. It did not reach the precrisis 1990 level until 2007, on the eve of the global financial crisis. Between the two dates, Russia lost the equivalent of seven 1989-size GDPs.[47] Having barely transformed the Soviet command economy into a very crude and primitive version of a market, Russia survived a major crisis in 1998–1999, provoked by its sovereign default, and climbed back, aided by a spike in oil prices. During the 2000s, it was growing so fast that by 2007, its GDP, in dollar terms, had surpassed its 1999 level no less than seven times! The ambition of the Russian government, enthused by the 2001 Goldman Sachs "BRICs" report, was to climb up two notches, to the Number 5 position in the world, by 2020. And then the global crisis broke out.

By the time it struck, in 2008, Russia's GDP, in purchasing power parity terms, was already seventh in the world, which finally justified, ex post facto, its seat on the G8. That comported with the self-image of the Russian leadership as a big-league player. They resented being repeatedly told, throughout the 1990s, that their economy's size was about the same as that of The Netherlands and their entire budget the size of New York City's.

When Putin, in late 1999, set the goal of catching up with Portugal, in per capita GDP terms, by 2015, many Russians were stunned: They were not ready to compare their country to Portugal—or Holland, or the Big Apple, for that matter. Now things were more or less back to "normal," and the City of Moscow's budget was in the same order of magnitude as New York's or Tokyo's.

Still, the 2008–2009 world economic crisis hit Russia harder than any other major economy. In 2009, Russia's GDP dropped by almost 10 percent. It now expects to reach its precrisis (2008) level in 2012.[48] Numbers tell only part of the story. More important, post-Soviet Russia has a wholly different kind of economy—essentially capitalist, even if not really free, suffering from appalling corruption and sorely lacking guaranteed property rights and the rule of law.

It is also different in other terms. It would be a caricature, of course, to say that the Soviet Union had a relatively small civilian sector within an essentially militarized economy, but there was something to this. Defense was a priority; consumers were not. Since 1991, with virtually no orders coming from the Russian government, Russia's military-industrial complex has dwindled and degraded. Except in the field of strategic nuclear systems, military modernization was put off for two decades. Russian defense enterprises started delivering to foreign forces: Chinese, Indian, Iranian, and others. It is only in the 2010s that Moscow will start buying Russian arms in earnest, to the tune of $600-plus billion over ten years.[49]

Russia's financial power was extremely low during most of the immediate post-imperial period. In 1992, Russia had foreign exchange reserves sufficient for only a few months of imports; by 2000, they had reached $12 billion.[50] The influx of the oil money was largely used to pay back the sovereign debt, which equaled 100 percent of the GDP in 1999 and dropped to 10 percent by 2006; to build currency reserves; and to create a stabilization fund, which substantially cushioned the blow of the global economic crisis. The money Russia earned in the 2000s was not used for foreign policy projects, including in the neighborhood. Just the opposite: Russia stopped subsidizing energy exports to the former Soviet republics and sought to collect Soviet-era debts from Moscow's ex-clients in the Middle East and Africa.

Russia's energy power is sometimes compared to its nuclear arsenal. It is credited with enormous leverage vis-à-vis its European customers. In reality, Russia is extremely dependent on just one factor—the price of oil—and thus is vulnerable to its fluctuations. The energy export proceeds—which were extremely low in 1999 (-13 percent of the GDP below the average long-time level)—came to be abnormally high in 2006 (+12 percent GDP, due to above-average prices).[51] The post-crisis oil price levels are close to being historically "normal"—and are thus wholly insufficient to help Russia realize its government's ambitions. Hence the idea of modernization.

Neither the post-Soviet collapse nor the subsequent revival of the Russian economy had much to do with severing or restoring economic links with the former republics or ex-satellites. Even though the Soviet Union had a highly integrated economy and the COMECON was a closed trading block, the liberalization of foreign commerce immediately deprioritized those markets in favor of the developed countries, above all Western Europe. There was little that Russia and the new countries with their antiquated technology and dysfunctional economies could offer one another. The share of CIS partners in Russia's foreign trade decreased dramatically.* The COMECON countries were all but forgotten in the 1990s. The only major complaint came from the defense industry, which depended on enterprises in the former republics for components.

Beyond the CIS and COMECON, the Soviet empire, economically, was a consumer of Soviet arms and equipment—mostly sold on credit, which was mostly never repaid—and of Soviet technological assistance. With the Soviet Union and its superpower ambitions gone, there was no political or ideological reason to pursue those relations, and no resources for that, either. Africa, Asia, and Latin America all sank below Russia's economic horizon in the 1990s. This started to change in the 2000s, but Russia's comeback to those regions is now driven by economic, rather than strategic or ideological, reasons.

Where Russians once traveled abroad mostly in tanks, as the popular Soviet joke had it, more and more of them today travel in business suits, or with bathing suits in their suitcases. Russia has entered the global business community with two dozen large companies, mostly energy and metals. These are supported by the government ("what is good for Gazprom is good for Russia"), but they can also be used by the government.

In the New Eastern Europe, Ukraine has essentially traveled the same road as Russia, transforming its Soviet-style economy into a version of the market one.[52] Belarus, by contrast to both Ukraine and Russia, has kept the Soviet economy with some modifications.[53] Moldova's domestic economy has essentially collapsed, with much of the industrial capacity remaining in Transnistria, and the Russian and Ukrainian market for Moldovan agricultural products growing much tighter. Faced with these conditions, Moldova began to export workers.

---

* More on this in chapter 3.

In the South Caucasus, there was no regional pattern, except for the end of the Soviet economic model. Azerbaijan has been able to build an energy-based economy; Armenia has an economy largely based on foreign grants. Georgia has managed to use its location to profit from the Caspian oil and gas transit; and it has attracted foreign grants, especially since the war with Russia. It has also made a serious effort to attract foreign investors.

For Central Asia, as for the South Caucasus, the imperial Russian and Soviet periods were a time of modernization. Modern industry, agriculture, secular education, and public health and welfare all appeared in the one hundred to one hundred and eighty-year period when the territories of the present Central Asian states were part of the Russian empire/USSR. The breakup of the Soviet Union led to a serious drop in the new states' GDP. In 2000, only Uzbekistan came close to its 1990 GDP levels (95–97 percent); Kazakhstan and Turkmenistan were at 75 percent; Kyrgyzstan, at 70–73 percent; and Tajikistan, ravaged by the civil war, at 37–40 percent of its Soviet-time high of 1988.[54]

Essentially, the countries of post-Soviet Central Asia followed the same path of economic reform as Russia, Ukraine, and others. They privatized the economy, introduced the market, and diversified economic ties; the economy also experienced primitivization, de-industrialization, and the disproportionate rise of the energy sector.[55] Kazakhstan has been the most successful reformer; Uzbekistan has been able to soften most of the economic shock; Turkmenistan was able to profit from its energy riches. Kyrgyzstan and Tajikistan have fared worse.

GOVERNMENT

Land empires are usually authoritarian; the unity of the territory does not allow for a happy cohabitation of a parliamentary democracy in the metropolitan area with colonial rule in the rest of the empire. The tsarist government in Russia was a traditional autocracy. It made an exception only for Finland and, briefly, for Poland. The Soviet government was thoroughly totalitarian.

The Russian Federation has a democratic constitution, adopted in 1993, and has all the formal institutions of a democracy. It is also structured as a federal state. In reality, however, Russia is an authoritarian political regime, even if moderate and generally noncoercive. It is also de facto a unitary state, but it is dependent on the regions' tacit acceptance of the arrangement.

In the twenty-first century, no Russian modernization is possible without modernizing the political system away from an imperial state and toward some form of genuine democracy.

In the former Soviet Union, only the three Baltic states—members of the EU and NATO—are functioning democracies. At the other end of the spectrum, several states in Central Asia are ruled by harsh authoritarians. Russia is somewhere between those two camps, although certainly closer to the latter.

Ukraine, Moldova, and Georgia, on the contrary, are closer to the democratic group. Of the three, Georgia's democratic credentials are the flimsiest. The country is definitely more pro-Western than democratic. The charismatic leader of the 2003 Rose Revolution, Mikheil Saakashvili, has strong support, especially in the countryside. His governing style, however, is more authoritarian than democratic. The opposition—disunited and bickering among themselves—is often harassed and is impotent to present a credible alternative. Saakashvili's Georgia is hardly the "beacon of liberty for this region and the world" that President George W. Bush called it during his 2005 visit to Tbilisi.

Even the adoption of a new constitution in 2010—which turned Georgia into a parliamentary republic—is dismissed by many skeptics as a means to perpetuate Saakashvili's personal rule beyond his second presidential term, which expires in 2013. However, if Saakashvili finds a different way of steering Georgia's modernization and allows a genuine opening in the political system, Georgian democracy can become functional.

Ukraine's 2004 Orange Revolution was a significant step toward democratic government. It resulted in genuinely free elections; an independent judiciary; and a free and vibrant media, including television. Though the Ukrainian political scene has long been dominated by powerful alliances of moneyed interests, the level of official corruption remains high, and the role of parliament, upgraded in 2004, was curtailed again in 2010 in favor of the president. Still, Ukraine stands as a major example to the rest of the CIS—and in particular Russia and Belarus—that a rules-based system of genuine political pluralism does not have to wait for decades, or even generations.

Ukraine's political transformation of the mid-2000s initially represented a clear break with the form of government practiced in Russia and—to various degrees—in much of the rest of the CIS. Sadly, much of this precious capital was wasted in 2005–2009 in the personal power struggle between President Viktor Yushchenko and Prime Minister Yuliya Tymoshenko, the two Orange leaders. Meanwhile, reforms in Ukraine took a back seat to the pursuit of vested interests. The election of Viktor Yanukovych, defeated in 2004–2005 and victorious in 2010, represents a major test of maturity and endurance for the Ukrainian political system. Focusing on improving Ukraine's economic performance is a must, but consolidating power beyond the point when power transfer becomes unimaginable would have tragic consequences for Ukraine.

Yet Ukrainian political culture is pluralist, and definitely not tsarist. Independence, and then the Orange Revolution, represented a material shift of the Ukrainian political system toward democratic Europe. A democratic Ukraine's natural orientation is the European Union. When Ukraine will have made substantial progress in the way of modernizing—which is to say, Europeanizing itself—it will have a major impact on Russia, challenging Moscow to redefine its own positions vis-à-vis both countries. To many Russians, Ukraine is—for better or for worse—a Little Russia. These Russians are watching closely across the border, and they care a lot.

Moldova's case is very interesting. Since the turn of the 2000s, it has been the only CIS country with a parliamentary form of government—similar in that sense to the Baltic states. Due to a political impasse, it went from 2008 to 2011 without a president altogether. More significantly, it also went through several power transitions: in 2000 from the agrarians and liberals to the communists; in 2008 from the communists to a liberal coalition. The most amazing thing about Moldova's politics perhaps is that the most democratic of all CIS countries is also one of the poorest.

In the mid-2000s, the Kremlin's reaction to the color revolutions in Ukraine, Georgia, and Kyrgyzstan was negative. At best, they were treated as U.S.-instigated attempts to supplant Moscow's influence in its neighborhood with Western domination. At worst, the Ukrainian case was interpreted as a dress rehearsal for a regime change in Moscow. As a Kremlin official put it, the good cop in the West seeks to place Russia under external control, while the bad cop seeks to destroy and dismember it.[56] In either interpretation, democracy was viewed as a mere tool of Washington's expansionism in what used to be Russia's imperial territory.

The Kremlin certainly played on the fears of other post-Soviet authoritarian rulers to become victims of some other color revolution. It was not alone making that case: Georgia's deposed President Eduard Shevardnadze wrote a letter to Central Asian heads of state warning them about sharing his fate. Yet the notion of an *authoritarian internationale* as an informal Moscow-led association of undemocratic former Soviet leaders is a big exaggeration.

Not a single autocrat who feared domestic opposition thought that the best way to protect his power would be to accept Moscow's protectorate. Here, Lukashenka of Belarus is the best example. There was never a conscious strategy by the George W. Bush administration to replace the authoritarian leaders of the post-Soviet states with genuine democrats. Some of those leaders, like Uzbekistan's President Islam Karimov, were key U.S. allies in the war on terrorism, as it was known then. Others, like Turkmenistan's founding despot, Turkmenbashi, or Azerbaijan's Aliyev dynasty, sat atop energy wealth and were courted by the West.

Over time, Moscow found, with surprise, that it was easier to deal with democratic-leaning pluralist regimes in Kiev, Chisinau, and—for a short while—even in Tbilisi than with the authoritarian governments, even those formally allied to Russia, as was the one in Minsk. Elsewhere in the former Soviet Union, governments were authoritarian, although the degree of authoritarianism varied from relatively mild forms in Armenia, Azerbaijan, Kazakhstan, Kyrgyzstan, and Tajikistan to harsher regimes in Belarus and Uzbekistan. Turkmenistan stands out as a quasi-totalitarian polity.

MILITARY POWER

While the Soviet Union, on the eve of its dissolution, boasted 207 divisions, the Russian Federation, two decades later, had to be content with only 85 brigades, former Soviet defense minister Dmitri Yazov bitterly complained.[57] Post-Soviet Russia has gone through one of the most stunning demilitarization processes in history. In less than five years, it withdrew forces from eastern Germany, the Czech Republic, Poland, Hungary, the Baltic states, Georgia, Azerbaijan, and Mongolia. It closed bases in Cuba and Vietnam. It allowed the troops stationed in Ukraine, Belarus, and Kazakhstan to become the national armed forces of those countries. It slashed its own military, from over 3 million to about 1 million people.

Since the passing of the Soviet Union, the dominant currency of international power has changed. Military strength is still important, but it takes a back seat to economic, financial, science, and technological power. The soft power of attraction trumps the hard power of coercion. Russia has taken note, and allowed its military to degrade for almost two decades. What is emerging as a result of the military reform begun in 2008 is a force no longer focused on waging large-scale wars: this is a revolution in Russian military thinking.

Foreign deployments are the palest of shadows of the recent past. As of 2010, Russia kept the larger part of the former Soviet Black Sea Fleet in Sevastopol—about 40 ships—most of them very old; a token army presence—a little over 1,000 strong—in Moldova (Transnistria); a few thousand troops in Abkhazia and South Ossetia; a division-size force in Armenia; an understrength mechanized division in Tajikistan; and a small air base in Kyrgyzstan. Apart from that, Russia has small noncombat contingents manning assets in Belarus (communications facilities), Azerbaijan (a radar station), and Kazakhstan (a space launch center).

The military-industrial complex is a fraction of the Soviet-era behemoth. In 1992, the government of Yegor Gaidar drastically slashed its defense budget, virtually stopping orders for arms and equipment. During the decade and a half that followed, the succeeding governments essentially allowed the military forces and the defense industry to fester. It effectively stopped all military exercises above battalion level. The *Kursk* submarine sank, and its crew could not be rescued. The war in Chechnya, which was initially a disaster, became the emblem of the collapse of the once-mighty military force.

Things have changed since then. In the early 2000s, the Russian military eventually prevailed in Chechnya. The 2008 war against Georgia lasted just five days. After that war, military reform started in earnest. Large-scale military exercises resumed, pilots began to fly, and sailors put out to sea again. Despite the economic crisis, Russia in 2009 embarked on a major multiyear rearmament program. Yet for the first time in recent history, the 2010 Russian military doctrine has completely eschewed major wars. Russia does not plan for a major conventional war against NATO in Europe, or against China in Asia.

This change has had far-reaching consequences for the Russian armed forces. Under the current reform, the overall reductions of some 200,000 positions are smaller than they appear to be: often, it will be positions, rather than actual people, that will be reduced. The number of units, however, is being cut drastically: from 26,000 in 2007 to 6,000 in 2010 and to 2,500 by 2020.[58] This has produced some protests by those who see the reform as nothing less than the wholesale destruction of the Russian Army.

The changes are drastic indeed. In 2010, the system of military districts introduced in the 1870s was abolished. Instead of six districts and seven armies, the Russian armed forces are now organized into four regional commands: West, with headquarters in St. Petersburg (which also hosts the headquarters of the Russian Navy); South, with headquarters in Rostov; East, with headquarters in Khabarovsk; and Center, controlled from Yekaterinburg.

The former separate headquarters of the army, navy, and air force/air defense are being transformed into elements of the General Staff. The General Staff, long the all-powerful body that overshadowed the Ministry of Defense (MOD)—people referred to the MOD in Soviet times as just one of the floors of the General Staff—has lost its political autonomy through direct subordination to the civilian minister, while the ministry, populated by civilian managers, has risen in stature and importance.

All the failings and reductions notwithstanding, Russia is the dominant military power by far within what used to be the Soviet Union. With Ukraine, Belarus, and Kazakhstan having given up the Soviet strategic weapons in their territories, Russia is the only post-Soviet country with nuclear weapons. It still has forces deployed in a number of places across the former empire. In the 2008 war, the Black Sea Fleet protected the Abkhazian coast from possible Georgian landing operations.

A number of other countries have reduced their forces as much, proportionally, as Russia. Ukraine, which used to host 450,000 troops in Soviet times, keeps only 180,000 under arms. Belarus, once the most heavily militarized part of the Soviet Union, has just about 50,000 troops. Moldova has actually sold its air force (the MiG-29s went to the United States) and keeps only a tiny army, which consumes a puny 0.4 percent of GDP. Georgia, meanwhile, made a huge investment in its military before the 2008 war.[59] Azerbaijan is another big military spender. In Central Asia, Kazakhstan has built a small but effective army.

Russia may have started, at long last, to reform its military, but it is far from clear what the role of its military will be. So far, several things are more or less established:

1. Russia does not regard large-scale war in Europe as likely. Moscow sees military power as only a marginally useful political instrument in Europe. "Missiles in Kaliningrad" has become the standard answer to any U.S. military plans that the Russian leadership sees as threatening or destabilizing. In principle, Moscow is ready to move toward demilitarizing its relations with all European countries. However, the U.S. presence and role as a European power is a complicating factor for the Russian leadership.

2. Moscow still considers U.S. military power as a threat. It does not know very well how to manage the situation in which balancing the United States—in terms of non-nuclear military power—is impos-

sible, and accepting U.S. leadership—some say hegemony—is un-desirable. The Russian leaders are wedded to the country's strategic independence, but they see it eroded by advances in U.S. military power and technology. A solution may be found along the lines of a degree of strategic collaboration—for example, on missile defense—which would transform the strategic relationship between the two countries and make U.S. superiority irrelevant, as among friends. Failing that, Moscow would have to respond to U.S. missile defense efforts by reenergizing its nuclear deterrence posture.

3. Russia's strategic relations with China are based on political cooperation and tacit deterrence—both strategic and pre-strategic. Moscow has de facto dismissed Japan and South Korea as potential adversaries, and it regards the U.S. presence and role in East Asia more favorably than in Central and Eastern Europe. For a somewhat different reason than in Europe, Russia's leaders do not foresee having to wage a large-scale war in Asia either. The challenge to Russia is being posed by other people's conflicts, starting with the Korean Peninsula. In the years to come, Sino-American relations will test Moscow's capability to think and act strategically.

4. In the near and medium term, the most serious military challenges to the Russian Federation are likely to emerge in Central Asia and the Caucasus. Russian forces may be called in to deal with incursions of armed jihadi groups from abroad (such as Afghanistan); ethnic and local conflicts in member states of the Collective Security Treaty Organization; domestic political disturbances threatening regional stability; and other disorder. The Russian military will continue to be involved, at least indirectly, in managing the security situation in the North Caucasus. Farther afield, Russia seeks to strengthen its military relationship with India and is closely observing developments in Afghanistan. Still, the Afghan syndrome remains strong enough to preclude, in the next several years, direct Russian military involvement in that country.

5. In 2008–2009, Russia used force against Georgia, went through a period of tension with Ukraine, warned about missile deployments in Kaliningrad, and sought to impress Estonia with military exercises. The Russian brinkmanship that led to the Georgia war

and the other conflicts have worked against Russia's best interests. Rather than inspiring respect for Russia and its interests, they have created an image of a bully bent on imperial *revanche*—something for which Moscow neither planned nor had the spirit and resources to carry out. With its European neighbors and Kazakhstan, Russia's goal has to be forming a security community, which excludes the use of force and its threat in principle.

INTERNATIONAL POSITION

Since 1991, Russian leaders have seen their country as the continuation state of the Soviet Union. As such, they accepted the USSR's international obligations, made Russia responsible for the entire Soviet debt, and appropriated Soviet property abroad. Crucially, Russia managed to retain the Soviet Union's "scepter and orb": the nuclear weapons arsenal and the permanent seat on the United Nations Security Council.

Today's Russian Federation is well-connected internationally. Russia did not become a member of either NATO or the European Union, as some hoped in the 1990s, but it joined the Council of Europe (1996) and the prestigious G7, which became the G8 in 1998. The following year, Russia acceded to the Asia-Pacific Economic Community; in 2005, it became an observer at the Organization of the Islamic Conference (OIC). Alongside China, it informally chairs the Shanghai Cooperation Organization (SCO). In 2010, Russia joined the Asia-Europe Meeting (ASEM) and is on track to participate in the East Asia Summit. Russia's long saga of accession to the World Trade Organization (WTO), begun in 1993, may be finally nearing consummation. After that, Russia will strive to become a member of the Organization for Economic Cooperation and Development.

The other ex-republics promptly joined the United Nations and the Commission on Security and Cooperation in Europe (CSCE), now known as the Organization for Security and Cooperation in Europe (OSCE). Kazakhstan even chaired the OSCE in 2010. The Baltic three are integrated in the European and Atlantic institutions; those in Eastern Europe and the South Caucasus acceded to the Council of Europe; and the Muslim countries to the OIC and the Organization for Economic Cooperation (which also includes Iran and Turkey). In addition to the Baltic states, only Ukraine, Moldova, Georgia, and Kyrgyzstan are members of the WTO.

The former Soviet republics are only very loosely linked to one another by means of the Commonwealth of Independent States, created in December 1991 in the same breath as the Soviet Union was dismantled. Today, the CIS is essentially institutionalized summitry for leaders and high-level officials, and visa-free travel for ordinary citizens. After Georgia dropped out in 2009, the CIS counts eleven participating states, one of which— Turkmenistan—has gone from being a member to a self-styled observer (the CIS charter does not provide for such status). Consequently, its top leader does not attend all events, and it imposes visas on travelers.

That Russia and other CIS countries have so far failed to construct effective international institutions to manage their relations parallels their failure to establish such institutions domestically. Russia, as the biggest country by far and the natural leader, bears prime responsibility for that failure. Ironically but also tellingly, the CIS countries' individual relations to outside states and organizations are better structured and organized than the relations among the ex-"sister republics." The latter remain messy and nontransparent; agreements, for instance, are often signed, but not fulfilled.

The root cause of this negligence may be the mutual tacit dismissal of the CIS as something "substandard." For many in Russia, the new states are not yet quite states. Interestingly, Moscow's political relations with them are still managed by the Kremlin chief of staff, rather than the foreign minister. For many in the new states, the CIS is a holdover from the imperial era, a club in which they are less equal than the former hegemon. There are practical issues, of course, that make periodic CIS gatherings worth the leaders' while, but neither Russia nor the other ten countries have their hearts in it.

This situation is probably beyond repair. By contrast, smaller post-Soviet arrangements have fared somewhat better. Among them are the Eurasian Economic Community—whose members include Armenia, Belarus, Kazakhstan, Kyrgyzstan, Russia, and Tajikistan—and the Collective Security Treaty Organization (1999), with all of the above countries, plus Uzbekistan. The more exclusive Customs Union (2010) has only three members, of which only Russia and Kazakhstan have actually joined; Belarus' participation is hampered by, outwardly, its grudges against Russia, and more fundamentally by the essentially unreformed nature of the Belarusian economy. There is an organization that does not include Russia and was an antithesis of sorts to the Russia-led CSTO: the GUAM Organization for Democracy and Economic Development, uniting Georgia, Ukraine, Azerbaijan, and Moldova.

Thus, the countries of New Eastern Europe and Georgia are leaning toward Europe; the countries of Middle Asia are being drawn into the Muslim world. Armenia and Belarus; Azerbaijan and Kazakhstan; and Russia itself are somewhere in the middle. Russia is Euro-Pacific; Kazakhstan, like Turkey, is Eurasian; Armenia and Azerbaijan are too locked in a conflict with each other to move forward; and Belarus will be able to define its future once its dictatorial present is history. The next chapter will examine the geopolitics of post-imperial Eurasia more closely.

CONCLUSION

The Russian Federation is not an empire, either in its domestic constitution or in its foreign policy aspirations. It is neo-tsarist domestically, and it wants to continue as a great power on the international scene: a subtle but crucial change. There is no urge to re-conquer or reintegrate lost lands. Over time, the severed limbs ache less and less. There is, of course, an interest in the neighborhood, but it is about "soft" domination, not "hard" control.

Great power was once part of the baggage from the past, alongside communism. Liberals fought hard against the notion. "Great country" was touted as a substitute.[60] Years have passed. Can there be a democratic great power? Some 85 percent of Russians believe that Russia is a great power, and as many believe that Russia will be respected only if it manages to become an economic powerhouse. Many Russians still expect their country to become one of the leading powers in the world. However, to the vast majority of them, this is not the most pressing need. Quality of life, a modicum of domestic order, and fairer treatment by the authorities are all more important to them than the state's status in the international arena.

Russian rulers have found other, more personal, ways to riches and glory than national aggrandizement. But, as this group becomes richer, it also becomes more ambitious. The winners are thinking globally. Focusing exclusively on the former Soviet Union makes little sense to them: The world is wide, and opportunities may be better in faraway lands. Still, the former imperial borderlands are low-hanging fruit, not to be ignored. As to the losers in Russia's transformation, they are certainly less happy and are more concerned about such issues as illegal aliens. Their motto is: Russia for the Russians. Again, this is a post-imperial attitude.

The new states have proved themselves viable. Even though the frozen conflicts in Moldova and over Nagorno-Karabakh persist, and Georgia's two breakaway regions have been recognized by Russia as independent states, not a single country in the former Soviet territory has turned into a failed state. Nation building has advanced everywhere, with a sense of national identity forming, often for the first time in modern history. In economic terms, all new states are middle- to low-income developing economies, and they have all joined the global market, usually as producers of energy or other raw materials, or agriculture.

In terms of political regimes, the relatively more democratic Ukraine and Moldova sit next to authoritarian Russia and Belarus; Georgia, whose democratic credentials have been oversold, but can still be saved, is a neighbor of autocratic Azerbaijan and Armenia. In Central Asia, Kyrgyzstan stands out as a relatively more free country, and Turkmenistan as the one with the harshest political regime; all the others—Kazakhstan, Tajikistan, and Uzbekistan—are authoritarian. Consequently, Kyrgyzstan is the least stable of the five, with its frequent domestic conflicts, and Turkmenistan looks, politically, like a frozen desert.

However, the differences in the political regimes do not make for sharp divisions between the relative "democrats" and the solid "authoritarians." There is no such thing as an *authoritarian internationale* headed by Moscow. Clan interests camouflaged as national ones are more important policy drivers, and pragmatism has become the modus operandi. In terms of the guiding light, geopolitics has replaced the old communist doctrine—a subject for the next chapter.

2

GEOPOLITICS AND SECURITY

The end of the Soviet Union meant the end of Eurasia as a unit. In the past, only the empire of Genghis Khan succeeded in creating a political space stretching from East Asia to Eastern Europe, and from the southern edge of the Siberian taiga to the deserts of Central Asia.[1] The Russian imperial/ Soviet version of Eurasia was on a similar scale as the Mongol one, and it also lasted longer. The present Russian Federation, now spanning nine time zones (reduced from eleven in 2010 by President Medvedev), *looks* like it can be a nucleus for a new edition of Eurasia, which remains a temptation for a number of people in Russia.

This is not new. After the Bolshevik Revolution, which had destroyed old Russia, a group of Russian intellectuals exiled in Prague developed the concept of Eurasianism.[2] After the end of the Soviet Union—which had built the most expanded version of the traditional Russian empire—neo-Eurasianism emerged, seeking ways to restore Russian imperial power.[3]

Yet Eurasia as another name for the Russian empire is gone forever.[4] In the age of globalization—with its new possibilities for instant communication and fast transportation, and the rapid modernization of formerly "sleepy" societies—the old distinction between Europe and Asia is being blurred. It means as little as the obelisk on the outskirts of Yekaterinburg in the Urals, which marks the Europe-Asia divide. A far better analogy would be the bridges in Istanbul, spanning the Bosporus and linking its European and Asian shores. Eurasia, for better or for worse, is becoming not only so much better interconnected, but also interdependent. Only Russia is merely an element of the highly complex picture, no longer its core.

Since the fall of the Soviet Union, the international setting has changed dramatically for Russia. European countries are economically and, to a growing extent, politically united within the European Union; militarily, they have long been united within NATO. China is an economic powerhouse, with an autocratic government and an increasingly modern military. The Muslim world, while it finds it difficult to modernize, is bubbling with energy. Turkey, Iran, and Pakistan have emerged or are in the process of emerging as regional powers, and one of them, Pakistan, already is a nuclear power. The pull that the other former Soviet states feel from each of these three centers is, especially in the adjacent regions, greater than Russia's. Indeed, Russia itself is being torn economically between the EU and China.

Geopolitics and security come first in our narrative, because that is where the leaders in Russia and the rest of the CIS traditionally place it. Their world is still primarily the world of states, and geopolitics is usually believed to be the heart of statecraft. If there were a place for philosophy in that realm, it would be called Realpolitik. Security, of course, is the principal preoccupation of all governments, but for authoritarian regimes, their own regime security comes first. Its importance is enhanced by the security background of many senior leaders.

RUSSIA'S GENERAL APPROACH TOWARD THE NEW STATES

On December 14, 1992, Andrei Kozyrev, the Russian foreign minister, took the floor at the meeting of the CSCE Council in Stockholm. He said:

> I need to amend the Russian foreign policy concept. . . . While still basically focused on entering Europe, we clearly realize that our traditions to a large extent, if not mainly, lie in Asia, which sets limits to our rapprochement with Western Europe. . . . The former Soviet space can not be considered as an area for full implementation of CSCE norms. This is essentially post-imperial space where Russia will need to defend its interests with all available means, including military and economic. We will firmly insist that the former republics of the USSR immediately join a new federation or a confederacy, and this will be a subject of some tough talking.[5]

The speech by the avowedly pro-Western Russian foreign minister produced consternation among his colleagues. Some thought there had been a coup in Moscow and that Kozyrev had been forced to make his statement. Soon, however, there was a sigh of relief. When Kozyrev spoke again, he said that Moscow's foreign policy was unchanged but that it would change if "reactionary nationalist forces" had their way.

Two decades on, the concept of what constitutes post-imperial space has evolved. Russia has not "entered Europe" in the sense Kozyrev meant, and the tradition of domestic power distribution has shown itself stronger than the democratic innovation that Kozyrev and others promoted. Moscow has also defended its interests with both economic and military means, as in its disputes with Ukraine and Georgia.

However, on the obviously crucial issue of reassembling the empire by means of a federation or a confederacy, the Russian leadership showed a surprising lack of interest. In other words, after the "Kozyrev line" had been repudiated, Moscow did many things he had warned about, but the Russian leadership did not end up doing something that, for Kozyrev, was the ultimate objective: an attempt to restore the empire. Why?

In a way, the Soviet Union was the victim of a power struggle at the heart of the empire, and of the socioeconomic discontent below. Ironically, this was similar to the collapse of the Russian empire in 1917. In both cases, it was not the forces of national liberation that won independence for the borderland territories, but the opposing forces in the imperial capital that released the bonds that had kept the empire together. This distinguished Russia from the old colonial powers such as France and Portugal, which fought doggedly to keep their overseas possessions and from the land empires of Germany, Austro-Hungary, and the Ottoman Porte, which suffered military defeat at the hands of foreign powers. Britain, too, dissolved its empire, but over a period of several decades; Russia's was set free at once.

This does not mean that, over time, national liberation would not have prevailed. It was clear even before 1917, for example, that Poland and Finland would gradually regain sovereignty. They would press for autonomy, in Poland's case, or enhanced autonomy, in the case of Finland, eventually achieving independence. Other cases, such as the Baltic states or Ukraine, are far less clear.

In late 1917–1918, proclamations of independence were often a desperate reaction to the Bolshevik coup and the extremist policies of the new communist authorities. By the same token, popular support for independence in the fall of 1991 in such places as Ukraine—including the Crimea, which had voted just six months earlier for preserving the Soviet Union in a new form—was a reaction to the self-annihilation of the central authority and the rapidly mounting economic hardships.

Since the loss of the Soviet Union was considered almost accidental in its immediate aftermath, many in Moscow in the early 1990s thought that the former republics-turned-independent states would "naturally" gravitate to Russia again, if only for economic reasons. *Don't worry, just keep waiting*: This was essentially a passive approach on Moscow's behalf, and it failed to accomplish much. Almost from its inception, the CIS has stood for countless summits and hundreds of agreements, most of which were never implemented. It mattered little: Throughout the 1990s, Moscow was heavily focused on its relations with the West and the lifeline that loans from the International Monetary Fund represented. The only notional achievement of the decade was the signing, in December 1999, of the treaty on Russo-Belarusian union, but even that was stillborn. Alexandr Lukashenka, the Belarusian leader who pushed the project, was denied the prize he had been actually seeking with his initiative: succession to Boris Yeltsin at the Kremlin.

Vladimir Putin, who succeeded Yeltsin, took a more active and pragmatic approach to the former Soviet republics. Unlike his predecessor, he felt no personal guilt for the destruction of the USSR. He did not enjoy CIS summits as a posthumous version of Politburo meetings, replete with outward signs of deference to Yeltsin on behalf of the actually sovereign leaders who sang praises to the Russian president only because they expected material favors from Russia in return. Yeltsin liked it—and paid for that, in terms of de facto energy subsidies, which kept gas prices to the ex-republics well below European levels. Putin wanted none of that.

Putin saw the newly independent states of the Soviet Union not so much as former parts of "Greater Russia" but as foreign countries, weak and dependent as they were. Rather than trying to bring them back to Russia—which he knew was both impossible and unnecessary—he resolved to advance Russian interests in each of them. Where Yeltsin's policies had been reactive and nostalgic, Putin's were no-nonsense and assertive. The Russian Federation was no longer an empire, caring for its subjects; it was a great power, ready to throw its weight around in pursuit of naked self-interest. Thus, Yeltsin's pseudo-integration was replaced by Putin's expansion.

There was an overarching idea, too. Around the time that Moscow's Western integrationist drive had exhausted itself, Putin embarked on a policy of building a Russian power center in a multipolar world order. The former Soviet republics were the natural elements of that project. In 2003–2004, a decade after Kozyrev's fake speech, something like "Project CIS" probably emerged in the Kremlin. It called for a major overhaul of gas export prices to all CIS customers, to bring them in line with the other Gazprom customers, including the Central European and Baltic states, which had been paying "real money" for the gas pumped from Russia. It also called for an economic union to serve as a basis for the political one in due course. Ukraine, in particular, was wooed to join a "single economic space" with Russia, Belarus, and Kazakhstan. It endowed the loose Collective Security Treaty, signed in 1992 essentially to divide up the Soviet military assets, with an organization (CSTO) that laid the foundation of a security alliance. The CIS as a whole was no longer an instrument; it was merely a playground, a space for Russian great-power activism.[6]

Within that space, Moscow did not aspire to Soviet-type control. Instead, it pursued more limited objectives. Topping the list was a general sense of geopolitical comfort. The new states were not pressed to join, against their will, Russia-led military blocs, but neither were they expected to accede to those—above all NATO, where Russia was not a member. Nor did Russia seek to expand its relatively light military footprint in the ex-borderlands, but then the new states were strongly advised against hosting other foreign bases. In the zones of ethnic conflict, Russia recognized the 1991 borders and did not intend to change the status quo on the ground, but it served warning that no side to those conflicts would be allowed to change that status quo either. (Saakashvili in 2004 ignored that and lost Putin; he did it again in 2008, and this time he lost South Ossetia and Abkhazia.)

In the economic area, Russia was much more relaxed, even taking competition over pipelines out of the Caspian as a hard reality, but it made it clear it would not tolerate meddling with its own export pipelines carrying Russian gas to EU customers. (Ukraine pretended not to hear, in 2006 and 2009.)* In more positive terms, the Russian government was focused on creating an economic base for a Eurasian power center, and it sought to turn Moscow into the financial hub for the region lying east of Europe and north and northeast of China. Finally, the Russian Federation hoped to maintain its cultural and linguistic preponderance in the neighborhood, and it gave support to its ally, the Russian Orthodox Church, in the church's efforts to keep its "canonical territory," particularly in Ukraine, intact.

The new approach was not totally unrealistic, but its implementation was often too crude to succeed. The gas wars against Ukraine resulted in material losses for Gazprom and severely damaged its (and Russia's) reputation in Europe and elsewhere. Keeping the frozen conflicts as obstacles to NATO's enlargement backfired when the conflicts led to high tension, and eventually, war, with Georgia.

---

* These crises will be discussed in detail in chapter 3.

The most serious setback came, however, as Russia tried to influence the 2004 presidential elections in Ukraine. This is where we will start— looking first at the Western flank of the former empire, before moving to the south, east, and, ultimately, the north.

THE WESTERN FLANK

THE ORANGE REVOLUTION IN UKRAINE

"The loss of former influence, particularly in the borders of the former Soviet Union, is a catastrophe" for Moscow, Leonid Kuchma, Ukraine's second president (1994–2005), later observed in his memoirs. It is, he declared, a "life-and-death matter" for the Russian leadership.[7] Well, this is an exaggeration. The loss of influence was a serious problem but not a catastrophe; and certainly it was painful, but not a life-and-death matter.

When Putin first tried to solve that problem, he might have inadvertently echoed Zbigniew Brzezinski's famous maxim, oft-repeated in Russia, that there could be no Russian empire without Ukraine. This was actually also Gorbachev's and Yeltsin's joint conclusion after the Ukrainian independence referendum of December 1, 1991: The Soviet Union was finally dead now that Ukraine had walked out of it. In Putin's thinking in 2003– 2004, for any mega-project to succeed in the former Soviet space, Ukraine had to be part of it.

Hence the Single Economic Space project crafted specially for Ukraine; positive discrimination on behalf of Ukrainian citizens in Russia; and Putin's single-minded support for Kuchma's prime minister and anointed successor, Viktor Yanukovych, in the 2004 presidential election. The Kremlin rejected more cautious suggestions to take a seemingly evenhanded approach by inviting, for example, Yanukovych on Tuesday; his rival ex-premier Viktor Yushchenko on Thursday; and spending the weekend with the flamboyant and exceedingly ambitious "gas princess," Yuliya Tymoshenko. The Kremlin, at the time, was not in the business of creating balances; it was going in to win and take all. And all the eggs were placed in one basket.

Putin, still very popular in Ukraine at the time, made a heavy personal investment into the election campaign on behalf of Yanukovych. Putin traveled to Kiev to be seen with Yanukovych at a military parade. Medvedev, then the Kremlin chief of staff, coordinated closely with his counterpart in Kiev, Kuchma's chief of staff, Viktor Medvedchuk. Kremlin-recruited political technologists, such as Gleb Pavlovsky, were at Yanukovych's side all the time.

The Kremlin used vast resources—financial, political, administrative, and human—to make sure that Yanukovych became president of Ukraine. One could think it was not an election in a neighboring country that was going on, but a battle for Ukraine. Moscow did not see the storm coming until it was too late.[8]

The Russian leadership was brusquely and suddenly jolted out of its complacency by the developments in the street, which later became known as the Orange Revolution in Ukraine. Pavlovsky, the Kremlin's best-known spin doctor, quipped immediately after the shock: "I had a contract from the Kremlin to win the election for Yanukovych, which I did, but we were faced with a revolution, and I had no contract to stop that."[9] Pavlovsky may have saved his skin, but his clients saw red. Putin took the Ukrainian fiasco as his worst foreign policy defeat ever. Medvedev brooded darkly about the dire implications of Ukrainian events to Russia.[10] The threat was no less than Russia's disintegration provoked by fissures within the elite: an "orange" scenario.

Russian government propaganda dismissed the Orange Revolution itself as a CIA operation that used democracy promotion for achieving geopolitical goals. At a minimum, this was to keep the Kremlin off-balance in the neighborhood and diminish Russian influence. At most, the goal was to use Kiev as a way station, a staging ground for projecting the revolutionary march on to Moscow and effecting regime change there as well. Thus, geopolitical concerns came to be very intimately intertwined with the need to preserve political power.

The state of near-despair did not last long. The threat turned out to be far less than what it had appeared to be. The House of Orange divided against itself, with Yushchenko and Tymoshenko soon becoming implacable enemies. By mid-2005, the popular revolutionary élan gave way to bitterness and apathy. In 2006, parliamentary elections returned a cabinet headed by Yanukovych. When Tymoshenko came back as prime minister the following year, her rivalry with Yushchenko ahead of the presidential elections led to the near-paralysis of power. The Kremlin became used to the perennial three-corner internal rivalry in Ukraine, with each of the three having a piece of power but none having all of it. It had digested the lessons of the Orange Revolution and was preparing to come up with its own technology of swaying Ukraine back to the Russian orbit. Then there was a bolt from the blue.

"The heart of the matter lies in U.S.-Russian confrontation," Leonid Kuchma opined in retirement, referring to the Orange Revolution as the maidan, or essentially mob rule.[11] When Kuchma was in power, he was much more nuanced. The 2003 Ukrainian law on national security called NATO membership the final objective of the country's Euro-Atlantic integration. As if oblivious to Moscow's attitude, Kuchma linked Ukraine's future EU and NATO membership to "good-neighborly relations and strategic partnership with the Russian Federation." He later claimed, improbably, that good relations with Russia were a condition for Ukraine's NATO accession. He also ascribed to his "balanced" policy the lack of strong reaction from Moscow to his sending a Ukrainian unit to serve with the U.S.-led coalition in Iraq. He even dreamed of Ukraine as a pro-Russian lobbyist in NATO![12] Was Kuchma just naïve or simply insincere? He wouldn't tell.

The Orange Revolution raised the specter of NATO moving across the red line. The newly elected Yushchenko, the Kremlin feared, would bring the country into the Atlantic alliance within a few years. Kremlin propagandists started talking about U.S. air bases on the Dnieper and the U.S. navy replacing the Russian Black Sea Fleet in Sevastopol. As the Kremlin later regained its composure, these fears subsided. The Russian leadership, moreover, grew confident it had found a way to manage the Orange and Blue (Yanukovych's color) princes and princesses. Then, in January 2008, the threat was suddenly back.*

But what was the nature of the threat posed by Ukraine's accession to NATO's Membership Action Plan? To put it simply: This step was generally considered to be the point of no return. All countries that had come that far eventually became members. As to Ukraine's NATO membership itself, Russian officials and opinion leaders advanced the following arguments, ranging from the highly emotional to the very specific.

Russia's "historical space" will be invaded. Since the mid-1990s, Russians have come to accept Ukraine as a separate state, but they still did not exactly consider it a foreign one. In the elite and to some extent also popular mind, Kiev remained "the mother of Russian cities." NATO accession would turn this part of Russian national patrimony into a Western bulwark against Russia.

Ukraine will turn against Russia. Most elite Russian voices were convinced—quite contrary to Kuchma's exhortations—that NATO and the West would turn Ukraine into an anti-Russian force, just like Poland. Be-

---

* See the Introduction.

hind that conviction was the view that the Ukrainian elite was imbued with a "Mazepa complex"—after the hetman who turned against Peter I and joined with Sweden's Charles XII in the famous 1709 Battle of Poltava—and thus essentially disloyal to Russia.

Ukraine will break with the Russian Orthodox Church. NATO membership would make it easier for Yushchenko to carry out his long-term project of formally separating the Ukrainian Church from the Moscow Patriarchate and creating a national Orthodox Church. Thus, Ukraine's cultural identity would be redefined.

The Russo-Ukrainian border will become analogous to the Cold War divide. A "true" border would emerge where for centuries there had been none. Visas would have to be introduced, and border controls instituted. Border demarcation would lead to countless disputes. Since Russia would have to consider Ukraine in NATO as a potential adversary, major troop redeployments would follow.

Russia will have to cut defense industrial links with Ukraine. There would be no question of continuing cooperation on a number of joint projects in the defense industry.

U.S. military power in the Black Sea region will displace Russia's. The Black Sea Fleet would have to leave Crimea. Instead, the United States would probably deploy its forces in Ukraine, from missile defenses to the Sixth Fleet. In that case, Putin warned at a 2008 news conference with Yushchenko in Moscow, Russia would have to "think the unthinkable," and target Ukraine with its nuclear deterrent.[13]

Despite the Kremlin's worries and veiled threats, the real problem with Ukraine's membership was not so much the position taken by Moscow as how the issue might play in Ukraine itself. In Berlin and to the west of it, NATO today mainly is about Afghanistan, but to the east of the German capital, NATO is still about Russia. True, it is also a certificate of belonging to the "West," but, apart from the Balkans, this, again, is seen as a security policy against Russia. As a relatively easier task than European Union accession, NATO is a bridge to Union membership. But since the EU does not guarantee the military security of its members, NATO has a distinct and unique role as a security umbrella.

In 2008, as well as now, all Central and Eastern European countries are more or less united, domestically, about NATO and Russia. Even in the Baltic states, local ethnic Russians, for various reasons, did not actively protest NATO accession. Belarusians have a generally benign view of Russia as a country and a people; most Moldovans would prefer to stay neutral and demilitarized; Georgians see the Russian state in stark adversarial terms. Ukraine is different.

Had Ukraine, too, been predominantly of one mind on the twin issue of NATO and Russia, the problem would have been far easier to solve. A Ukraine deeply suspicious about Russia would have required reassurance from the West, and Russia, too, would have required reassurance that Ukraine's accession posed no material threat. In other words, this would have been a replay of the Central European trio's (Poland, Hungary, and the Czech Republic) joining the alliance, perhaps writ large, in view of Ukraine's size and geographical proximity to Russia.

In reality, however, Ukraine is a cleft state. Ukrainians' slack support for the idea of NATO membership did not stem from lack of information about NATO, or even of interest. It was more an issue of identity. Even though the often provocative actions and statements by Russian politicians—like longtime Moscow Mayor Yuri Luzhkov—usually helped Ukrainians rally around their state,[14] they were not sufficient to produce Ukrainian-Russian alienation. Most Ukrainians do not want to be part of Russia, but they do not want to part with Russia, either. Add to this fractious politics at the top; the gap existing between the elites and ordinary citizens; the still strong interregional differences within Ukraine; the related competing views of national history and identity; and the large proportion of ethnic Russians. Any decision to go for NATO regardless of these fissures is an invitation to instability.

If Ukraine divided against itself, it not only would plunge into a deep political crisis that would render itself ungovernable, but also invite interference from outsiders—starting with Russia but not stopping there. Until the reset in U.S.-Russian relations under President Obama, there was no shortage in Russia of scare scenarios on that score. Ukraine was openly treated as a *casus belli*. The Kremlin was said to be considering Ukraine's accession to NATO as a decision to finish off Russia, give it a coup de grâce.[15] The prophets of doom talked about a restoration of U.S.-Soviet nuclear confrontation and a return in Moscow to revanchist anti-Western policies. Russia's domestic regime would grow harsher, and any thought of modernization would be abandoned. In a word, Russia would be ready to repeat Germany's post–World War I experience, with all its tragic consequences. Were the scaremongers bluffing? They were probably engaged by the Kremlin in the tactic of dissuasion, and thus were overstating the case rather than understating it, but the consequences would be dire.

In the 2010 presidential elections in Ukraine, Moscow enjoyed sweet revenge. Its tactic had changed. Rather than picking its favorite candidate, the Kremlin indicated whom it did not want as president: Yushchenko. Between the other two leading contenders, Moscow hedged its bets. Even as the United Russia Party was working with Yanukovych's Party of Regions, Prime Minister Putin was cultivating his opposite number, Tymoshenko. Yanukovych's victory soon paved the way to a major understanding on the most controversial issues, the gas price and the naval base lease. Both were resolved as a package: In exchange for a 30 percent discount on the gas price—worth $40 billion over a quarter-century—Russia was able to extend its lease of Sevastopol, due to expire in 2017, by twenty-five years.[16]

For some critics in Russia, this was too hefty a concession to Kiev. The fleet, they argued, was not worth it. Its three dozen ships, whose average age was twenty-eight years, were the oldest in the Russian Navy, more like a museum of former glory than a usable force. Others pointed to the slowness in construction of a new base in Novorossiysk; the symbolic value of a Russian military presence in Crimea; and, of course, an obstacle to Ukraine's possible future intention to seek NATO membership.

FROM FROZEN CONFLICTS TO THE FIVE-DAY WAR: GEORGIA

The issue of NATO membership, also promised to Georgia at Bucharest, was the underlying cause of Russia's conflict with Georgia. Of course, the strategic importance of Georgia to Russia cannot be compared to that of Ukraine. Moscow's real security agenda in the area has far less to do with traditional power balances and is dominated by extremism in religious wrapping, terrorism, and separatism.

During the Chechen war, part of the Georgian territory—the Pankisi Gorge—was used by Chechen fighters as a sanctuary. Seen from the Kremlin, the situation was similar in kind to that of al-Qaeda and the Taliban. In 2002, Russia issued a strongly worded warning to Tbilisi, using some of the language of the U.S. war on terrorism.

The Georgian government at the time was ambivalent about the Chechen war. On the one hand, Georgians, a lowland civilization, traditionally feared the mountaineers, who came down to plunder. They also suffered from separatism in Abkhazia and South Ossetia and had no natural sympathy for breakaway Chechnya. On the other hand, they blamed Russia for giving support to Abkhazia and South Ossetia and could not resist *Schaden-freude* when they saw their offender placed in a situation similar to the one into which Russia had placed Georgia.

During the Yeltsin period, Moscow's policy toward Georgia—by no means a priority even within the CIS space—was essentially subcontracted to the military and security services. Yeltsin would occasionally meet with Eduard Shevardnadze, Georgia's head of state from 1992 to 2003 and Gorbachev's foreign minister in 1985–1990, and Russian Foreign Minister Evgeny Primakov would try to mediate between the Georgians and the Abkhaz. But day-to-day affairs were handled by the officials at the Ministry of Defense and, increasingly, the Federal Security Service, who acted on behalf of Russia in both Abkhazia and South Ossetia.

The military and security services' attitude to Georgia was very much an extension of their attitude to Shevardnadze. The "Silver Fox," as he had come to be dubbed by the U.S. media, was intensely distrusted within the Soviet power ministries as someone who had conceded too much to the United States in the last years of the Soviet Union. Among his offenses: unnecessarily adding a missile system to the list of items banned under the 1987 Intermediate-Range Nuclear Forces (INF) Treaty; ceding to the United States a chunk of the Soviet Arctic while drawing the boundary in the Bering Sea in 1990; and signing agreements on Soviet troop withdrawals from Central and Eastern Europe with impossibly short timetables. For Shevardnadze's alleged betrayals, right-wing nationalist Soviet media and later Russian media named him an American agent of influence who swayed Gorbachev even more toward accepting U.S. positions on a wide range of issues.

Although Shevardnadze was installed as Georgia's leader with Moscow's support in early 1992 after an uprising had ousted Georgia's first president, Zviad Gamsakhurdia, and even though his life was probably saved by the Russian Defense Minister Pavel Grachev—who had flown Shevardnadze out of Sukhumi during the 1993 Abkhaz offensive—Russian officials later definitely played with the option of a regime change in Georgia. Shevardnadze was a target of several attempts on his life. After the second one, in 1995, he stopped actively seeking accommodation with Moscow and turned to Washington for support.

This led to a worsening of, but not a break in, relations between Russia and Georgia. Under Russian pressure, and U.S. prodding, the Georgian military mounted an operation in Pankisi, even as the Russian forces were consolidating their control over the mountainous part of Chechnya.

The Kremlin did not particularly regret the toppling of Shevardnadze in November 2003 in what became known as the Rose Revolution. What worried it was the uncertainty ushered in by the departure of the longtime leader. Putin sent Foreign Minister Igor Ivanov, himself Georgia-born, to Tbilisi on a fact-finding mission. This was the second "color revolution" Ivanov had come to observe at close range, after Serbia's in 2000. It appeared to the outside world that Moscow was mediating in its "sphere of influence." In reality, its envoy could do little beyond assessing the situation and establishing contacts with the new revolutionary leaders.

Putin himself established direct contact with Mikheil Saakashvili in early 2004. Their relationship was initially very close, with Saakashvili privately admiring Putin as his role model and clearly being deferential to him.[17] Putin thought he could do business with the young and energetic Georgian and, in April 2004, allowed him to reestablish Tbilisi's control over Ajara, an autonomous republic within Georgia that had been ruled by a local feudal lord since 1991.

Formerly strategically important, with its capital Batumi, Ajara hosted a Russian military base and the border guards who patrolled the Turkish border. In the post-Soviet period, the city of Moscow and its mayor's friends had acquired assets in Ajara. Putin, however, was prepared to concede all that in the name of a more solid relationship with Georgia. The Russian military garrison stayed in its barracks, and the feudal lord and his family fled to the side of the Moscow mayor.

For Saakashvili, however, this was only the beginning. His ambition was to restore Georgia's territorial integrity in its internationally recognized 1991 borders of the Georgian Soviet republic. Putin promised to help him achieve gradual conflict settlement, but Saakashvili was a young man in a hurry. In August 2004, he mounted a police operation to clamp down on smugglers in South Ossetia. As a result, fighting broke out. Before that move, Saakashvili could drive to Tskhinvali, the South Ossetian capital, and talk to its residents in the street. After the operation, all goodwill was gone, and the conflict that had been seemingly on the way to becoming history erupted with renewed violence. Putin was enraged. He lost faith in someone he had considered a partner. During the fall of 2004, Saakashvili repeatedly tried to place a call to the Kremlin. He was answered by silence.[18]

The Ossetian raid ended the happy interlude in Russian-Georgian relations. From then on, things deteriorated rapidly. Most unfortunately, Prime Minister Zurab Zhvania, a reasonable and thoughtful man, suddenly died in 2005. Saakashvili could no longer be restrained. Moscow had written him off and started to build pressure on him.

For some time, Russia had been distributing its passports among the residents of Abkhazia and South Ossetia. Alexander Voloshin, the Kremlin chief of staff, argued that this was being done on humanitarian grounds, in order to allow people to travel, but the Georgian authorities saw it as gross interference by Russia. In 2006, they seized several Russian servicemen, accused them of spying, and put them on public trial in Tbilisi. Under the circumstances, it looked like a step designed to provoke Putin, a former KGB officer, into overreaction.

Russian authorities saw the incident as both an injury and an insult. The Russian ambassador was called back to Moscow. Georgian wines and mineral water were embargoed. Air and sea travel was suspended, and postal services cut, which stopped direct remittances from Georgian guest workers in Russia. Some of those workers were accused of being illegal immigrants and were turned back. Ordinary people of Georgian descent in Russia—both guests and Russian citizens—were subjected to officially sanctioned harassment.

In other words, Moscow did a lot of things to hurt Georgians for the behavior of their president. It stopped short, however, of taking the one step—maybe the one anticipated in Tbilisi—to try to free the defendants by force (Russia at that time still had some troop presence in Tbilisi), and thus expose itself as an aggressor. In the end, the United States intervened, the trial was halted, and the defendants were handed over to Russia.

Strikingly, the incident did not stop the negotiated withdrawal of Russian forces from Georgia. By 2007, none were left outside of Abkhazia and South Ossetia, where Russia was allowed—under the 1992 agreements with Georgia—to deploy peacekeepers. In return, while negotiating with Tbilisi, Moscow sought assurances that, once Russian troops left, Georgia would not play host to other foreign forces or join military alliances. Saakashvili refused to enshrine a permanently neutral status in the constitution but told the Russians he did not intend to seek NATO accession.[19]

Russian objections to Georgia's NATO membership were essentially geopolitical. There was fear of a domino effect: With Georgia in, Azerbaijan would follow suit, and Armenia would be estranged from Russia and have to lean on the United States to help it manage Azerbaijan. Thus, Moscow would lose any leverage in Baku and a foothold in Armenia.

Moreover, the entire strategic energy corridor from the Caspian to Europe would be in Western hands, protected by the forces of the United

States, the dominant Black Sea and Caspian power. This would encourage those in the North Caucasus seeking separation in Russia: Georgia, Azerbaijan, and Turkey have all had a record of supporting Chechen separatists in the 1990s. Sochi, Russia's "third capital" after Moscow and St. Petersburg—in terms of the time Putin and Medvedev spend there—would find itself a mere thirteen miles from the border of a NATO member state.

Whether Saakashvili had changed his mind or had been insincere from the start is a moot question. In early 2007, Moscow made one final attempt to stabilize its relations with Tbilisi. When the Russian ambassador returned to Tbilisi, he proposed a deal to the Georgians. If Georgia agreed not to seek NATO membership and not to allow foreign forces on its territory, and if it declared permanent neutrality, Russia would assist in resolving the conflicts in Abkhazia and South Ossetia. There was no deal.

Once the two sides had reached a deadlock—and the prospect of NATO membership started to beckon in Tbilisi and loomed like a menace in Moscow—a war of nerves started. This was replete with frequent shootings and bombings in the conflict zones, reconnaissance flights by drones, spy catches and trials, and propaganda exercises. It looked as if both sides were provoking each other, playing essentially to the same Western gallery. The Russians were provoking the Georgians to reveal themselves as triggerhappy hotheads, unfit for any responsible club, least of all NATO. The Georgians hoped that Moscow's actions would expose Russia as a newer version of the Soviet Union: aggressive, brutal, and greedy. The upshot was the direct opposite of the Russian message: Russia was a clear and present danger; Georgia was a frontline state, as Germany was during the Cold War; and defense of Georgia was the defense of the Free World.

Russia mostly focused its message on the Western European members of NATO; Georgia, on the United States. In a way, both messages were heeded, as evidenced by the bizarre decision of the Bucharest NATO summit. The summit also provided a deadline for the final decision: the December North Atlantic Council ministerial meeting. What worried Moscow was that Georgia would not want to give up its breakaway provinces in order to join NATO; and NATO, for its part, would not want to accept a country engaged in two running conflicts with a neighboring nuclear power. So, if Georgia was seeking membership and NATO was willing to grant it, that only could have meant the restoration of Georgia's territorial unity by finding a means to exclude Russia from the game.

Russia's game was essentially that of deterrence. It aimed to bolster the separatist regimes in both Abkhazia and South Ossetia by sending them more and more powerful weapons and improving land communication and transportation links, such as the railroad. It held exercises in the North Caucasus with a view to restoring South Ossetia after it had come under attack. It maintained control over both enclaves, which it regarded as guarantees against Georgia's NATO membership; and it believed the United States was controlling the Georgian president. In early August 2008, the newly inaugurated President Medvedev went on a boat trip along the Volga, and Prime Minister Putin flew to the Beijing Olympics.

Saakashvili's calculus was to go beyond the usual provocations, strike first and fast, overrun Tskhinvali before the arrival of the Russian forces, and terminate at least one conflict on his own terms. Having gained the momentum, he would have been able to press for the internalization of peacekeeping in Abkhazia, place the Russians under pressure as ineffective peacekeepers, and rely on U.S. support to change the political status quo in Abkhazia even as he would have changed the military one in Ossetia.

The five-day war in August 2008* signified the lowest point in Europe's security levels since 1988, when Gorbachev started his military build-down and strategic stand-down. For Moscow, the war was not about Georgia as much as about the United States, with Georgia no more than a proxy. The Russian leadership never believed that Georgia's participation in the Train and Equip Program with the United States—or the dispatch of Georgia's military contingents to Iraq and Afghanistan—had any point other than getting weapons, training, and political support in preparation for a war to retake the two breakaway provinces.

Since the end of the conflict—negotiated with the participation of President Sarkozy of France, then presiding over the EU—the situation has become frozen again. No more hostilities followed; even minor incidents have been extremely rare. Russia has failed to obtain its allies' solidarity on the issue of Abkhazian and South Ossetian recognition. The countries with real or potential territorial issues—such as the Central Asian nations—flatly refused, but even those without them, such as Belarus, never delivered. The reason, clear if unstated, was the same: Not a single new state wanted to be seen as being Moscow's puppet. "Abkhazia and South Ossetia" was the independence test, which no country in the CIS thought it could afford to flunk.

---

* The five-day war between Russia and Georgia, as well as the events leading to it and its aftermath, is described in the Introduction.

Eventually, the loss of Abkhazia may be seen in Georgia as a blessing in disguise, allowing far more productive use of the country's energy and promising a far more homogeneous nation-state. Should a solution to the issue become possible, at some indefinite point in the future, it could be something along the following lines.

South Ossetia, unviable as an independent country and politically too costly to be annexed by North Ossetia—which is to say, the Russian Federation—goes for an "Andorra model." It becomes nominally independent, but de facto a Georgian-Russian condominium. The Russian forces will leave, and thus remove a potential military threat to Tbilisi, but Moscow will receive a formal *droit de regard* as far as the security of the Ossetian people is concerned. Tbilisi, for its part, will have a similar *droit de regard* vis-à-vis the Georgian population in the area. Neither Georgia nor Russia, however, will have military forces on the ground. A European Union police force will keep the peace in the area.

Georgia and Abkhazia will enter into negotiations to reach an understanding. Eventually, Abkhazia will give up the Georgian-populated Gali region, which will return to Georgia. In return, Georgia will give up its claim for the return of refugees who fled Abkhazia in the 1990s. After that, Tbilisi and Sukhum will agree on the border between the two and a set of confidence-building measures. This will allow trade, transportation, and economic links to be restored between the two countries. Finally, Georgia will recognize Abkhazia's independence.[20]

Even as Russia fought a war against Georgia and recognized its two breakaway territories, Moscow was at pains to show this was a special case, not a new trend. The Kremlin publicly mediated between Armenia and Azerbaijan, organizing several summit meetings between the two, the first one just a few weeks after the Georgia war.

The cease-fire around Nagorno-Karabakh, negotiated with Russian mediation in 1994, has been holding ever since without major incidents. However, the efforts of the so-called OSCE Minsk Group—with its Russian, U.S., and French co-chairs—to bring the two parties to closure have proven elusive so far. The closest the parties came to a deal was at Key West, Florida, in 2001, when Presidents Haydar Aliyev and Robert Kocharyan basically approved a formula for "horizontal" relations between Karabakh and Azerbaijan within a common state. Soon afterward, Aliyev had to back off, because even his closest associates refused to go along. Throughout the entire period since the end of hostilities, Russia has been a loyal member of the Minsk "troika," fully engaged in teamwork with the Americans and

Europeans. When it relaunched its mediation efforts after the 2008 Georgia war, Moscow did so in close contact with its partners.

Russia has been heavily involved in the conflict along the Dniester, between the Republic of Moldova and the unrecognized Dniester Moldovan Republic, usually referred to in the West* as Transnistria. In 2003, Moscow made an attempt to single-handedly resolve the issue by means of an agreement that would have federalized Moldova. The deal—negotiated by an ambitious Kremlin official, Dmitri Kozak—fell through, virtually at the last minute, when Moldovan President Vladimir Voronin, after consultations with Western countries, refused to allow a permanent Russian military presence in his country.

After this, the peace process languished for another five years, with the Kremlin visibly unhappy over the westward leaning of Voronin's Communist Party of Moldova in its foreign policy, even as the Moldovan president himself was becoming increasingly authoritarian in domestic affairs. At the low point of the Kremlin's self-consciousness and high water mark of perceived Western penetration of the former Soviet Union—the time of the Orange Revolution in Ukraine and again after the Ukrainian bid for a path to NATO membership—some not entirely academic quarters in Moscow played with the idea of a major geopolitical redesign of the northern Black Sea area, under which southern Ukraine, from the Crimea to Odessa, would secede from Kiev and form a Moscow-friendly buffer state, "Novorossiya"—New Russia.** As part of that grand scheme, tiny Transnistria would either be affiliated with that state or absorbed by it. The rest of Moldova could then be annexed by Romania.

These concepts never materialized. Eventually, the peace process was revived in the fall of 2008 after the Georgia war, and it was stepped up after the communists' loss of power in 2009.[21] With regard to Transnistria, as in the case of Georgia and—implicitly, with an eye to the Crimea—in Ukraine, Moscow was using the frozen conflicts as obstacles to NATO enlargement (for Georgia and Ukraine) or absorption by a NATO country (Romania, in the case of Moldova).

That prospect dimmed, it was ready to deal. In mid-2010, President Medvedev agreed with German Chancellor Angela Merkel to move for-

---

* The Russian equivalent is Pridnestrovye, which literally means "land along the Dniester."

** "Novorossiya" was the name of the northern coast of the Black Sea conquered from the Ottomans in 1768–1791 and annexed by the empire during the reign of Catherine II. Most of Novorossiya is in present-day Ukraine. The city of Novorossiysk, meanwhile, is on the Russian Black Sea coast, just north of the North Caucasus.

ward with Russia-EU cooperation on solving the Transnistrian conflict, as part of an effort of closer foreign policy coordination between the EU and Russia. As in the Caucasus, the EU is accepted as a partner, while NATO is not. Why?

THE BROADER NATO ENLARGEMENT ISSUE

Even the newest version of the Russian military doctrine adopted in 2010 refers to NATO enlargement as a threat to the Russian Federation.[22] Why such opposition to NATO, two decades after the end of the Cold War and after even President Medvedev referred to "NATO's aggressiveness" as a myth?[23] The story of Russia's attitudes toward the North Atlantic Alliance is one of illusion and delusion.

To many Russians, NATO is a code word for America in Europe, or more precisely the U.S.-led system of alliances and power infrastructure. Remarkably, there is no fear of Germany, or hard feelings toward it, which is striking, given the history of the twentieth century. Mikhail Gorbachev agreed to Germany's reunification. In that sentiment, he stood alongside President George H. W. Bush and the United States, but against the gut feelings of all major European countries: Britain, France, and Italy.[24] With the last Russian soldiers withdrawn from the former German Democratic Republic in 1994, the reconciliation is virtually complete.[25] Unthinkable two decades ago, German war cemeteries have appeared in many parts of Russia where battles were waged during World War II.

Two other major European NATO members, Britain and France, were Russia's allies in both world wars. France, in particular, is being credited as Russia's historical friend and ally. Napoleon's 1812 invasion and the Great Fire of Moscow are ancient history, provoking no adversity. Charles de Gaulle's withdrawal from NATO's military organization and his concept of a "Europe from the Atlantic to the Urals," as well as his passionate 1966 speech from the balcony of Moscow's City Hall, convinced the Kremlin and the Russian people that France was not an enemy. During the remainder of the Cold War, Paris received special treatment from Moscow.

The historical Russian view of Britain is more contentious, despite the absence of a major invasion of Russia by British forces. Britain nibbled at the extremities of the Russian territory, its largest incursion being in the Crimea during the 1853–1854 war that pitted much of Europe against Russia. Rather than an actual adversary, Britain has been more of a political competitor—

particularly in the Great Game in Central Asia and the Caucasus, or a close associate of the principal probable enemy, the United States, during the Cold War. Other major NATO countries, such as Italy and Spain, have either never been regarded in Russia as adversaries, or have dramatically improved relations with post-Soviet Russia, as Turkey has done.

Why, then, such strong opposition in Russia to NATO's enlargement? The point of departure is the end of the Cold War. Most Russians believe exiting from the forty-year confrontation was made possible above all by Gorbachev's policies of reconciliation and accommodation. Those of more democratic persuasion add that the Cold War was truly over once Russians rejected communism. And still others pointed to the dissolution of the Soviet empire and of the Soviet Union, dismantled under the leadership of the Russian elites. On all three counts, most Russians are convinced that ending the Cold War was their choice and their achievement. Of course, they needed partners: Reagan, Bush, Margaret Thatcher, Helmut Kohl, François Mitterrand, and others, and thus ending the Cold War was a common victory of Russians, Europeans, and Americans.

It was logical, from that point of view, to expect Russia's swift integration into the institutions of the West. When Yeltsin sent his first letter to NATO, in December 1991, he said that Russia was considering joining the alliance in the near future. To the Kremlin's dismay, there was no immediate response from Brussels. Instead, Russia and all other former Soviet republics and ex-members of the Warsaw Pact were invited to join the North Atlantic Cooperation Council (NACC). Moscow was clearly disappointed. Then, two weeks later, another letter was sent to NATO headquarters from Moscow, announcing that the previous message had contained a misprint: Russia was *not* considering joining the Alliance in the foreseeable future.

To many in the West, Russia was still too big and thus unwieldy, too chaotic and woefully unready, and still too ambitious. NACC, a consultative group with the basic mission of making sure that Soviet arms control commitments would be met by the successor states, was not exactly the "common European home" that Gorbachev had dreamed about. As to the "Europe whole and free" that George H. W. Bush had called for, Yeltsin and Andrei Kozyrev, his foreign minister, wondered whether that included Russia. In Washington in spring 1992, Bush flatly rejected Yeltsin's bid for a U.S.-Russian alliance as inappropriate now that peace was breaking out around the globe. Russia's hopes of adoption were being quickly dispelled. In the dramatic 1992 "dual speech" at Stockholm, Kozyrev warned of what might happen if Russia were not integrated.

When the United States in 1994 announced the Partnership for Peace (PfP) as the security arrangement between NATO and the former Warsaw Pact countries and ex-Soviet republics, including Russia, Moscow accepted the offer. For some time, it hoped that PfP would be an alternative to NATO enlargement and thus welcomed PfP in that form. It was soon to be sorely disappointed when the Clinton administration—answering the pleas for NATO membership from Poland, Hungary, the Czech Republic, and Slovakia and under pressure of interest groups in Washington—began to reconfigure PfP as a path to membership—for some countries.

Initially, Yeltsin was inclined to tolerate it, which he communicated to Poland's president, Lech Walesa, during a September 1993 visit. However, virtually the entire Russian defense and security establishment disagreed. In the absence of an alliance with the West, the only tangible positive result of Gorbachev's foreign policy was a wide buffer zone between Russia and NATO. Now this was going to disappear.[26] Yeltsin, who had to rely on the military to crush his communist and nationalist opponents in the Supreme Soviet, had to back off.

The Russian democrats, shaken by the December 1993 Duma election that resulted in a psychological revenge of the nationalists and communists, saw the Western move as a vote of no confidence in Russia's democracy, which is to say, themselves. They now started to warn that enlarging NATO without Russia—and they believed Russia should be the first country in the former East to join—would inevitably lead to the reincarnation of NATO's enemy image in Russia. Those who had taken part in negotiations on German reunification argued that the negotiating record indicated that Western interlocutors promised not to extend NATO's zone of responsibility beyond where it was in 1989. Thus, what the West was doing now was a breach of faith.

The conclusion was damning for NATO's reputation in Moscow. NATO not only refused to dissolve after the disappearance of communism and the Soviet Union and continued to function as a military alliance, but it started taking new members on Russia's borders. In the area of NATO's responsibility, Russia was the only potential adversary. Russians now saw that, in the eyes of the West, it was the Soviet Union that had lost the Cold War and that its principal successor state, Russia, had to put up with the consequences.

Central Europe, the original battlefield of the confrontation, was now being taken over by the victorious West as both war booty and a possible bulwark against a future resurgent Russia. The Russian Federation itself was at best on probation and still viewed with a lot of suspicion. This produced the first-ever near consensus within the Russian political elite: NATO's enlargement was against the Russian national interest. The basis for that consensus was essentially nationalistic. Russia's fledgling democracy, feeling deceived, deferred to the *derzhava* (great power).

Moscow staged a noisy, but hopeless, campaign in an effort to stop the enlargement. The campaign's effect on the West was minimal. If anything, it was counterproductive. Supporters of the enlargement were able to portray Russian opposition as proof of Moscow's residual imperial inclination and of its unwillingness to allow its erstwhile satellite states to freely choose their strategic orientation. The countries of Central Europe—which had benefited from Gorbachev's policies, had given a velvet feel to their exit from communism, and had more recently made common cause with Yeltsin "for common freedom"—now saw Russia as essentially unreconstructed. Yeltsin was just another tsar, and NATO was absolutely the right road to take.

Political consequences in Russia were more damaging. Many politicians and officials came to regard NATO's newly launched Partnership for Peace program as a ploy to put some countries on a fast track to membership, while keeping others, like Russia, within a meaningless framework, a school from which they would never be able to graduate. Between 1994 and 1997, the idea of Western integration was largely discredited, and a new reincarnation of Eurasianism was back. Nikolai Danilevsky's *Russia and Europe*, written in the bitter aftermath of the Crimean War, was reprinted in 1995 and became a best seller. Geopolitics, in a traditional Realpolitik version, was elevated to supreme statecraft. Alexander Dugin, heretofore an obscure and obscurantist writer, became *salonfaehig*. Phrases like "NATO forces at the gates of St. Petersburg, Smolensk" or "a new June 22 [a reference to Germany's 1941 surprise attack] is just round the corner" became commonplace in opinion editorials. In January 1996, Kozyrev, a symbol of now-defunct policies, got the sack.

Eventually, new Foreign Minister Evgeny Primakov and NATO Secretary General Javier Solana negotiated an agreement on the modalities of NATO enlargement which, NATO thought, would reassure the Russians. In May 1997, Yeltsin came to Paris to sign the Russia-NATO Founding Act. But it was too little, too late. The act had few supporters. Traditionalists saw it as a face-saver to cover Russia's capitulation. Some national liberals thought more could have been achieved by refusing to "accept" NATO's enlargement. Very few hoped that the breakthrough in Denver—Bill Clinton's agreement to include Russia in the G7 as a full political participant—

would overshadow the pain of Madrid, where the Central Europeans were invited to join NATO.

All this, however, was still an elite phenomenon. The wider public could not be aroused by abstract geopolitical constructs. While the early Balkan wars in Croatia and Bosnia produced only a moderate impact on the Russian public, NATO's use of force against Yugoslavia in March–June 1999 shocked most Russians. NATO—by now having just been accepted in its historical role of defender against Soviet communism—suddenly turned into an *offensive* alliance. NATO countries ignored Russian protests and admonitions against the war as unhelpful; they went ahead without seeking authorization from the UN Security Council, where Russia could have vetoed the use of force. Moscow could do nothing.

A popular Russian thesis at the time suggested that the difference between Serbia and Russia was that the latter had nuclear weapons, and thus was safe from Western invasion. Otherwise, it would share a similar fate. At the time, Western publics generally sympathized with the Chechens, as they did with the Kosovo Albanians. Russian Prime Minister Primakov, en route to Washington as the NATO air strikes were about to begin, abruptly ordered his plane back, in the middle of the Atlantic. The "Primakov loop," as it was immediately dubbed, became the symbol of a dramatic policy reversal.

The Kosovo conflict revealed the new geopolitics of Europe. Almost simultaneously, Poland, Hungary, and the Czech Republic* joined NATO. When the General Staff in Moscow—having ordered a Russian peacekeeping unit to redeploy from Bosnia to Kosovo—decided to send in reinforcements by air, Ukraine, Romania, and Bulgaria refused to give the Russians an air corridor. The small Russian party, which risked a military confrontation with NATO forces, was completely isolated at the airfield it had occupied; in fact, the Russians were at the mercy of the British army, which helped out with water and food supplies. Russia was given no "sector" in Kosovo, as it had desired.

Four years later, Russian peacekeepers left Kosovo, and Bosnia, altogether. Since then, Moscow has consigned the Balkans to the "Western (NATO/EU) sphere of influence." A full decade after the fall of the Berlin Wall, Russia's influence in Europe was physically reduced to the territory of the former Soviet Union.

---

* Slovakia was dropped from the first wave of enlargement because of its domestic political dynamic. It joined in the next wave in 2004.

After 9/11, Putin made a serious bid for an "alliance with the Alliance," to use the phrase coined by U.S. Ambassador to Russia Alexander Vershbow. Not only did Putin call President George W. Bush to express solidarity with America, but Russia did more than any other country to help the United States with the operation to oust the Taliban in the fall of 2001. Russian allies in Afghanistan, the Northern Alliance, formed the bulk of the force that captured Kabul. Moscow also supplied Washington with valuable intelligence and shared its own Afghanistan experience.

In a major departure from its own newly approved military doctrine, Moscow did not object to its Central Asian allies in the Collective Security Treaty Organization offering bases to the U.S. military for the purpose of fighting the Taliban. And Russia did not claim any special role for itself in the newly liberated Afghanistan, accepting U.S. predominance in the region. Just over two decades previously, it was Moscow's fear of U.S. influence in Afghanistan that provoked the Soviet invasion of that country and led to the ten-year war.

In 2000–2002, Putin was publicly hinting at,[27] and privately seeking,[28] NATO membership for Russia. The most he could get, however, was upgrading the NATO-Russia Permanent Joint Council (PJC) to a new NATO-Russia Council (NRC). The principal supposed change was that, from now on, Russia would be a co-equal member of the group, no longer confronted by the unified NATO "side." A solemn declaration on the principles of cooperation was adopted.[29] This did not work out as hoped.

Already by mid-2002, the Bush administration lost interest in pursuing close collaboration with Moscow, in order to focus on the Middle East. The 2003 invasion of Iraq led to further cooling of U.S.-Russian relations, which since that time and for the remainder of President Bush's eight-year term would only go downhill. Eventually, just as the PJC failed in 1999 at the time of NATO's war on Yugoslavia over Kosovo, the NRC was abandoned at the time of the Russo-Georgian war, nine years later.

The brief warming of Russo-NATO relations, however, did not stop the enlargement process, which made a quantum leap. In 2004, the Russian leadership accepted what in the 1990s had been deemed impossible by many, namely, the three Baltic states' membership in NATO. True, the Baltics, even in Soviet and imperial days, had been considered something of an "inner abroad." Equally true, Estonia, Latvia, and Lithuania were allowed out of the USSR with no strings attached immediately after the failed 1991 Moscow coup. In 1993, after some prodding from Clinton,

Yeltsin ordered the military to stop its foot-dragging and withdraw from the Baltics completely.

Yet seeing NATO territory extend to within 100 miles of St. Petersburg and having Kaliningrad as an enclave within NATO territory—some compared its position to that of West Berlin—was not easy. When in 2006 NATO held its summit in Riga—its first in former Soviet territory—people around Europe saw this as a symbol of changing times. However, where people in the West saw a triumph of democracy, quite a few in Russia focused on the geopolitical shift.

By contrast, Moscow was largely unperturbed by Romania's and Bulgaria's wish to join NATO. When they did join, in 2004, Russia made no complaints. Traditionally, the Russians had little respect for Romania's military, either as an ally or an enemy, and they have learned to take in stride Bulgaria's membership in anti-Russian coalitions in both world wars. However, from 2004 on, both the Baltic and Black seas had come to be dominated by NATO. Russia, the former hegemon, was reduced to small footholds in each area.

When in 2003 Russia redeployed forces from the Balkans and "conceded" the Baltics—under Putin, unlike in the Yeltsin period, there was no vociferous campaign protesting their membership, just clenched teeth—this regrouping was done to better consolidate Russia's few assets where it mattered most: in the CIS. Moscow was ready to renounce its claim on a role in its old sphere of interest: Central and Southeastern Europe, and the Baltics. But it resolved not to allow further Western encroachments into the territory it felt was its "historical space."

This resolve was put to the test in 2004, as Ukraine was engulfed by the Orange Revolution, whose leaders openly aimed at NATO membership; and again in 2008, as the Bucharest NATO summit promised membership, albeit at an unspecified date, to Ukraine and Georgia. By the end of George W. Bush's second term, another major irritant appeared: the prospect of U.S. ballistic missile defenses deployed in Central Europe.

The 2007 decision by the Bush administration to deploy ten interceptor missiles in Poland and a ballistic missile defense interceptor in the Czech Republic was intended to defend against a missile threat from Iran. Seen from Moscow, however, this had potentially serious implications. One was that the Central European site would be a third in an emerging global ballistic missile defense system, which Washington had been constructing since its withdrawal, in 2002, from the 1972 Anti-Ballistic Missile Treaty. The two other sites, in Alaska and California, were dealing with the North Korean threat.

Ominously for the Russians, Bush did not accept an offer—made by Putin in 2007 at their meeting in Kennebunkport, Maine—to cooperate on missile defenses. The Bush administration phased out joint exercises with Russia on defending against missile attacks and turned its back on the 2000 agreement to establish joint missile-launch monitoring centers. Moscow strategists imagined that at some point the new global system would achieve a capability against its own aging and shrinking strategic missile arsenal, and thus erode Russia's deterrence potential vis-à-vis the United States.

Another issue was the deployment area for the European site. Launched from their bases in Poland, U.S. interceptors would have a theoretical capacity to shoot down Russian missiles en route to North America.[30] Ten missiles, of course, would not make much of a difference, but if that number were expanded, they would. As to the radar, it would have made it possible for the United States to see very clearly the entire grouping of Russian strategic assets in the European part of the country. Finally, Russians were incensed about the site's being located in Poland and the Czech Republic—both among the more Russia-skeptical among NATO's members and the most reluctant to allow even a token permanent Russian military presence, as inspectors, at U.S. facilities in their territory.

While the Yeltsin round of Russian-Western strategic integration ended in 1999 amid the bombings of Belgrade, the Putin round perished in the 2008 Georgia war. A new round started with the arrival of Barack Obama as the forty-fourth president of the United States, and the reset in U.S. policy toward the Russian Federation. In November 2010, President Medvedev came to the NATO summit at Lisbon with a very different agenda than Putin took to Bucharest. NATO and Russia agreed to move forward on a number of cooperative projects. The most ambitious of them, missile defense coordination, has the potential to transform the very nature of their strategic relationship away from the adversarial Cold War patterns. The NATO-Russia relationship, however, has an important element: the situation, and perceptions, of Russia's neighbors.

THE FUTURE: NEW EASTERN EUROPE

New Eastern Europe is not only a new reality; it is a long-term reality. There is virtually no realistic scenario of the former Soviet republics' reabsorption into the Russian Federation. Their integration into a meaningful Russia-led economic union—even though Putin, in October 2010, said the

Customs Union was in principle open to all interested parties[31]—will largely depend on whether Moscow wants to become a motor for real integration, which means performing the role of a donor. This is not the case today, and achieving it would require a major change in Russia's foreign policy.

As to joining the European Union, this option can reappear only after the EU has overcome the consequences of the 2008–2009 economic crisis; fully digested the Big Bang membership expansion of 2004–2007, when it absorbed ten countries; mastered the challenge of governance among its nearly 30 members; and regained a sense of leadership and mission. Even then, the Balkans will remain a near- to medium-term priority, with Croatia on the doorstep of membership; Serbia and Kosovo next in line; followed by the rest of the region: Albania, Macedonia, and Montenegro. Conceivably, little Moldova could be taken on board in the long-term perspective. Turkey will probably not be allowed in, at least not in the foreseeable future. Ukraine is a long, long way off and, for the rest of the region, there is simply no visible prospect.

The Georgia war drew a line beneath a period in the history of Europe's east that was dominated by the reality and expectations of the enlargement of Atlantic and European institutions. It had been clear, even before Bucharest, that the safe limits of NATO's eastern march had been reached.[32] After 2008, this became widely recognized.[33] Simultaneously, the global crisis and its implications—in particular the confluence in 2009–2010 of financial, economic, and social issues in a number of European Union countries—made it clear that EU enlargement would, at minimum, take a long pause.

What also became clear was Russia's inability, and unwillingness, to turn what Dmitri Medvedev famously described, in 2008, as a zone of Russia's "privileged interests" into a major integration project. True, in mid-2009, Putin put the formation of a Customs Union of Belarus, Kazakhstan, and Russia on a fast track, which briefly put in doubt Moscow's interest in completing the WTO accession process.

However, it was soon revealed that it was only with Astana that Moscow would be able, for the time being, to proceed with meaningful economic integration. The (abridged) Customs Union became a reality by July 2010. By contrast, the Kremlin's relations with Belarusian President Lukashenka reached an all-time low in the fall of 2010. By that time, Russia had achieved an agreement with the United States and moved within reach of WTO membership.*

---

* The economic aspects of the Customs Union and WTO accession will be discussed in chapter 3.

Moscow's attempts to sway the new Ukrainian leadership to join the Customs Union fell flat. Yanukovych's first foreign visit, symbolically, was to Brussels. In Moldova, Moscow had to deal with a coalition that called itself an Alliance for European Integration. Georgia, thwarted in its government's hopes of early NATO membership, formally withdrew from the CIS by 2009 and continued to fly EU flags on all government ministries in Tbilisi. Azerbaijan continued to grow richer and increasingly more independent. In August 2010, Armenia strengthened its alliance with Russia, but only in terms of winning a Russian guarantee of all its borders, including the Azeri one.

Of the six countries, three—Belarus, Moldova, and Ukraine—can be collectively described as New Eastern Europe.* The three others—Armenia, Azerbaijan, and Georgia—belong to the South Caucasus. Twenty years after the dismantlement of the Soviet Union, all of them have established themselves as independent states. The difference between the two groups is more than geographical and cultural. The South Caucasus is not merely physically separated from the EU countries. Except for Georgia, there is no particular pro-European sentiment in the region. The countries abut Turkey and Iran and can be seen as much part of the Greater Middle East as part of a Greater Europe. By contrast, the members of the Eastern European trio are not only direct neighbors of the EU countries but also feel they belong in Europe. At the same time, they are intimately linked with Russia.

This reality is not easy to take by those who had spent the last two decades thinking in terms of "joining Europe." Ukrainian nationalists, or westerners, believe that either Ukraine integrates into the Western world or it will be a state in permanent danger of losing its independence. Hence, the issue of joining NATO is in reality an issue of Ukraine's securing its still fragile independence. When Yushchenko was president, he argued that "NATO membership and Ukrainian independence are synonymous."[34] Ukrainian nationalists prefer not to see this in terms of for or against Russia, but rather for or against Ukraine. They also call this a civilizational choice, in terms of horizontal or vertical organization. From that perspective, Russia's authoritarian trends actually aided Ukrainian nationalism by widening the gap between the two countries.[35]

Ukrainian easterners, on the contrary, believe that, as president, Yushchenko tried to build a *cordon sanitaire* around Russia. By turning Russia

---

* Abkhazia and South Ossetia are not included in that list because of the issue of status, and also due to their utter dependence, at present, on Russia. For related reasons, Nagorno-Karabakh and Transnistria are not considered as separate units.

into an opponent of Ukrainian interests, he caused enormous economic damage to Ukraine. His policies were single-mindedly anti-Russian: help Russia's enemies. Gone were the hopes, entertained under Kuchma, of Ukraine's regional leadership, creating a soft alternative to Moscow. In the easterners' view, Ukraine needs a multi-vector foreign policy: to NATO, partnership; to the EU, a free-trade area and association; to Continental Europe, specifically Germany and France, an alliance to reduce U.S. influence; to Russia, industrial cooperation, joining in Russia's and the EU's relationships with the United States.[36]

What became clear in the five years of Orange rule is that western Ukraine failed to become the foundation of a modern Ukrainian nation. Intellectually, westerners could only repeat, again and again, Hrushevskiy's lines from the early 1900s. Essentially rooted in village culture, they had little to offer to the large urban centers of the east: Kharkiv, Donetsk; the south: Odessa; or even to Kiev. Finally, it became clear that western Ukraine can only be a subculture within the emerging all-Ukrainian nation.

Belarusian President Alexandr Lukashenka, rather than playing the role of Moscow's loyal ally in exchange for economic privileges and political protection, chose complicated geopolitical maneuvering. The recognition of Abkhazia and South Ossetia became a test case. In 2008 and 2009, Minsk promised Moscow it would recognize the two enclaves as independent states, but it eventually balked, embarrassing and angering its patrons.

For Lukashenka personally, this issue may have been a test of how sovereign he himself was. Sensing that he could "sell" to the West his refusal to be a Moscow puppet, he engaged in direct contacts with EU officials. These contacts should have served as a counter-warning to Moscow: Belarus had other options apart from Russia. In the words of a Belarusian opposition politician, this was "dual blackmail."[37] To neutralize the Russian threat of withholding subsidies, Minsk reached out to Beijing, seeking credits.

As a sideshow, Lukashenka secured oil shipments from Venezuela to make up for a shortfall in Russian supplies and gave refuge in April 2010 to ousted Kyrgyz President Kurmanbek Bakiyev, who had angered Moscow by double-crossing it on a number of political and economic issues. His interference, verbally, in Russian domestic issues provoked the Kremlin into an unprecedented propaganda war against the Belarusian president in the run-up to the December 2010 elections in Belarus.

This was the first election since 1996 in which Moscow did not support Lukashenka. That, however, did not lead to victory for the opposition. Having portrayed Lukashenka as thoroughly unreliable and actually criminal, the Kremlin, nevertheless, had to work with Lukashenka and his government once the election was over. Moreover, the Belarusian elections themselves were hardly less free or fair than those in Russia or in most other CIS countries. This is nothing if not embarrassing. Moscow has lost a handle on Minsk, which, rather than buckling under pressure, is exploring an array of partnership options—from China and Venezuela to the European Union and the United States.

One day, the "last dictator in Europe" will certainly leave the scene. Absent, from now on, the Russian subsidies, Lukashenka will have left a country in worse shape, above all economically, than any of its neighbors. He will, however, have established Belarus on the map as a country and a state, and not a mere extension of Russia. Whoever succeeds him will take it from there. And the issue of Belarus's long-term orientation will come up again. The Belarusians will no longer be looking only to Moscow, but also to their immediate western neighbors in the former Soviet empire.

If Belarus has the harshest political regime in the New Eastern Europe, Moldova's is the most liberal. A parliamentary democracy since 2000, Moldova has seen constitutional power transfers from agrarians to communists, and then, even more stunningly, from communists to liberals. Of course, Moldova's importance to Russia is not to be compared to the importance of Belarus or Ukraine, but Moscow has been paying attention—in view of the frozen conflict in Transnistria, the gas pipeline that traverses Moldova en route to the Balkans, Romania's ambitions and aspirations vis-à-vis the kindred population of Moldova, and the ubiquitous issue of NATO enlargement.

It was those interests, rather than personalities and party affiliations, that guided Moscow's policies toward Chisinau. A man with a typical Russian name—Vladimir Voronin,* who until 1994 was a police general in Russia, and later rose to lead the Moldovan Communist Party—was first embraced as an ally by Moscow, then—when he refused to accept a Russian military presence as part of a conflict settlement plan for Transnistria—dismissed by the Kremlin as pro-Western and eventually dealt with pragmatically as one of several key players in the small world of Moldovan politics. Of all these players, the only one whom Moscow does not see as a partner is Acting President** Mihai Gimpu, known for his strident anti-Russian

* President of Moldova, 2001–2009.

** Since 2009.

rhetoric and pro-Romanian sympathies. All others—liberals, democrats, liberal-democrats, and communists—are welcome as partners, to the extent that they understand Moscow's interests. This is a pattern that has also emerged in Russia's relations with the former countries of the Warsaw Pact and the COMECON.

FORGOTTEN SATELLITES: CENTRAL AND SOUTHEASTERN EUROPE AND THE BALTICS

After the Georgia war, the Russian leadership made a sustained effort to improve relations with Poland. Long neglected and dismissed as almost genetically anti-Russian, Poland had become a major stumbling block in Moscow's relations with the European Union. A row over Polish meat exports to Russia led in 2005 to a suspension of negotiations of a new treaty between Russia and the EU to replace the 1994 Partnership and Cooperation Agreement (PCA). The PCA then expired in 2007 without a follow-up. Within both the EU and NATO, Poland, led in 2005–2007 by the Kaczynski brothers—President Lech and Prime Minister Jaroslaw—became both a recognized expert and a perennial skeptic on Russia: a damning combination. To make its point absolutely clear, Warsaw suspended government-level contacts with Moscow.

Moscow's early attempts to overcome the Polish obstacle by means of special relations with key EU member states, in particular Germany and France, came to naught. Poland would not budge, calling for EU solidarity with its member that had to deal with an authoritarian Russia. For both Angela Merkel and Nicolas Sarkozy, joining forces with Putin to lean against a former Soviet satellite was morally repugnant and politically suicidal, and thus unthinkable.

In the end, Moscow decided to address the Polish obstacle directly, taking advantage of an election that had produced a more moderate government. From 2008, the Russian Foreign Ministry was instructed to engage in extensive and serious consultations with its Polish counterpart. The Poles, amazed, sensed respect coming from their Russian counterparts.

In 2009, Putin himself decided to travel to Gdansk for a ceremony commemorating seventy years since the start of World War II. His trip was preceded by a rather conciliatory article written for the popular *Gazeta Wyborcza*. At the ceremony itself, Putin heard a lot of criticism of the Soviet Union's policies. On the margins of the event, however, Putin was able to establish rapport with Poland's new premier, Donald Tusk. At the beginning of 2010, Putin invited Tusk to jointly visit Katyn, the site of the 1940 massacre by Stalin's NKVD of 22,000 Polish officers and civilians.

The importance of Katyn in Polish eyes cannot be overestimated. During the April 7, 2010, joint visit, Putin knelt at the Polish memorial and clearly laid the responsibility for the mass killing on Stalin. Just three days later, the budding Polish-Russian rapprochement was put to a sudden and severe test.

Putin had invited to Katyn only Tusk, but not President Lech Kaczynski. This was in accordance with the diplomatic protocol—Putin, like Tusk, was prime minister. More important, while Tusk was considered a pragmatist, Kaczynski was seen as hopelessly anti-Russian. Kaczynski, however, could not abandon Katyn to his political rival, Tusk. On April 10, 2010, he set off for Katyn on a private visit, accompanied by scores of Polish dignitaries. Their plane crashed while landing at Smolensk, the nearest airfield to Katyn, killing all aboard.

This was the worst possible blow to the relationship. The Russian officials handled the tragedy surprisingly well. They were professional, respectful, open, cooperative, and deeply sympathetic to the bereaved families and the Polish people. Even though the remaining Kaczynski brother, Jaroslaw, the unlucky contender for the Polish presidency in the election held in the summer of 2010, and a number of his supporters suspect foul play—even, in the best conspiratorial tradition of Eastern Europe, a Putin-Tusk plot to get Kaczynski out of their way—the momentum toward an improved Polish-Russian relationship has been sustained.

A Polish-Russian reconciliation would need to be both deepened and made irreversible, as well as expanded to include other new members of NATO and the EU, in particular the Baltic states. Their relations with Russia have been strained virtually since Estonia, Latvia, and Lithuania were allowed to leave the Soviet Union in September 1991.

By contrast, relations with other ex-satellites, neglected during the 1990s, were strengthened in the 2000s as a function of Moscow's new interest in expanding and diversifying energy transit routes to Gazprom's main EU customers. Hungary, Romania, Bulgaria, and Slovakia were all offered roles in various Gazprom projects. In the same vein, the Russians also reached out to a number of ex-Yugoslav states: Slovenia, Croatia, and Serbia. The Czech Republic, conspicuously missing in Gazprom's projects, became a permanent home to the highest number of Russian residents, and—alongside Croatia, Montenegro, and Bulgaria—a favorite destination for Russian holidaymakers. Across Southeastern and part of Central Europe, Russia's business has become business and pleasure.

In military terms, the historically most important strategic direction is becoming increasingly stable. In 2009, led by the inertia of the previous period, Russia conducted Zapad-2009 military exercises, which operated based on an obviously unreal scenario of a NATO attack against Russia. With modernization at the heart of Moscow's current foreign policy, the old Western Front is fast evolving into an interface with the most developed part of Russia's neighborhood.

To take account of this sea change, in 2010, the Russian military reformers merged the Moscow and Leningrad military districts, Kaliningrad garrison, and the Baltic and Northern fleets into a single regional command headquartered in St. Petersburg. It still has numerous forces, but Moscow's strategic focus is now elsewhere. With the end of the Cold War and dissolution of the Soviet Union, the South's time has arrived.

In 1945 at Yalta, Stalin, in Tsymbursky's words, got "just what the Western world, as represented by its leaders, did not regard with certainty as its own"—Czechoslovakia, first abandoned by Britain and France at Munich in 1938; Poland, over which the same countries engaged in what they called *une drôle de guerre* with Hitler's Germany; and the Balkans, not considered to be "European" until very recently. Six-and-a-half decades later, the West has moved its borders to include all these areas within its expanded community. Moscow recognized that by 2003 at the latest, by ending its peacekeeping mission in the Balkans and deciding not to challenge the Big Bang dual enlargement of NATO and the EU. Three centuries of Russian politico-military involvement in Europe became history. The focus has shifted.

THE SOUTHERN FRONT

Even as the controversies in the West were turning increasingly political, real military dangers emerged in the south. The Operational-Strategic Command "South," in Rostov—which controls the former North Caucasus military district, the Black Sea Fleet, and the Caspian Flotilla, as well as some units from the abolished Volga-Urals district—has the toughest job. As in the nineteenth century, the Caucasus again has become Russia's restless frontier. As the Russian Federation sought to break out of the USSR, so did Chechnya out of Russia. When Chechen separatism was defeated, a new enemy arose: militant radicalism, raising the Islamist banner and using terror as the weapon of choice.

THE NORTH CAUCASUS

I discussed the Chechen conflict in an earlier book, *Russia's Restless Frontier*.[38] The Chechen war was fought to preserve a tiny bit of the former empire after the bulk of the empire had been set free. It was fought at the time when Russia's state power was at a nadir and essentially out of fear that unless the new borders of the Russian Federation were not seen as permanent, the federation would unravel, as the Soviet Union had just done. According to the domino theory, Chechnya would not only lead the rest of the North Caucasus out of Russia, but would also inspire the defection of the entire Muslim element, including Tatarstan and Bashkortostan.

The importance of the Chechen factor in the history of post-imperial Russia can hardly be underestimated. If the first Chechen campaign (1994–1996)—which ended in defeat for the federal government and Moscow's de facto recognition of Chechnya's independence—was a symbol of Russia's weakness and disorganization, the second campaign (1999–2001), which crushed Chechen separatism, became a symbol of Russia's recentralization—along more or less traditional lines. In the new narrative of the Kremlin, Yeltsin-era "chaos" was supplanted by Putin's "order."

Eventually, Chechnya was pacified, but at a high price. President Putin, against much advice, entrusted it to a former battlefield enemy, Akhmad Kadyrov, with whom he struck a personal deal. After Akhmad's assassination in 2005, the Kremlin allowed the Kadyrov clan, led by Akhmad's son Ramzan, to establish a dynasty and rule the place essentially as they wished. In 2009, after ten years, the formal regime of antiterrorist operation was lifted in Chechnya, and the situation in the republic was officially considered "normal."

The decision to recruit a former enemy as a partner for reconstruction was a momentous decision. Within a few years, Chechnya achieved a stunning degree of home rule. The policy of "national reconciliation" promoted by the Kadyrovs lured many of the former opposition fighters out of the mountains. The Russian forces deployed in Chechnya—essentially confined to their barracks—were safely isolated and rarely spoken of. The "East" and "West" battalions formed by the Russian military intelligence and composed of Chechens, but not necessarily Kadyrov supporters, have been disbanded.[39] At the same time, young conscripts from Chechnya were allowed to do military service at home.

Virtually no ethnic Russian residents of Chechnya who managed to flee the war in the 1990s have dared come back. In an effort to combat Islamist militancy, the Kadyrovs—Akhmad, the former mufti, and then Ramzan— have turned Chechnya into a mild version of an Islamic republic.[40] Grozny now boasts the largest mosque in Europe. Official guidelines have been established on what clothing is appropriate for Chechen women. Elements of Sharia law were introduced. More ominously, Chechen authorities have been de facto allowed to operate, with virtual impunity, across Russia in pursuit of their enemies.

As a result, Chechnya today is a virtual khanate linked to Russia by means of a personal union between Kadyrov and Putin. Except for formal independence, the goals once set by the late separatist leaders Dzhokhar Dudayev and Aslan Maskhadov* have been achieved. Over time, both these figures can yet emerge as national heroes, and join, in the Chechen pantheon, the nineteenth-century warrior leader, Imam Shamil.** What is known to the present generation of Russians as the "Chechen war" is being quietly refashioned in Chechnya as a struggle for national liberation. Be that as it may, for the first time in about 150 years, Chechnya is on its own, and Russia, satisfied with outward signs of loyalty, does not contest it.[41]

Even as Chechnya was proclaimed pacified, its neighbors—Ingushetia to the west and Dagestan to the east—erupted in violence. In 2009, the Ingush president was badly wounded in an assassination attempt, and the Dagestani interior minister killed. Speaking in Makhachkala, the Dagestani capital, Medvedev admitted that the problems in the North Caucasus were of domestic origin, not the result of foreign—Islamist, Western— meddling.[42] Both regions suffered from weak and corrupt local governments and clan strife.

---

* Dzhokhar Dudayev, a former Soviet bomber pilot and a major general in the Soviet air force, became the first president of the Chechen Republic, which declared its independence from Russia in 1991. He was killed by a Russian missile strike in 1996. Aslan Maskhadov, a former colonel in the Soviet artillery, became president in 1997. With Chechen separatist resistance overrun in 2000, he led a guerrilla war against Russian forces. He was killed by Russian special forces in 2005.

** Imam Shamil was the military, political, and spiritual leader of Chechnya and Dagestan, who led a long war of resistance against Russian conquerors. He was captured in 1859 and spent the rest of his days in exile, a de facto prisoner, in Russia.

In Ingushetia, the Kremlin in 2004 dismissed the republic's first president and Soviet Afghan war hero, Major General Ruslan Aushev, who had been deemed too close to the Chechen separatists. Instead, the federal authorities installed a former security service general, Murat Zyazikov. The second president was absolutely loyal but also deeply unpopular. He presided over pervasive corruption, police brutalities, and a wave of terror attacks. During his five-year term, more than 400 police officers were killed, and over 3,000 ordinary citizens wounded.[43]

As a result, Ingushetia was sliding deeper into chaos, and the Kremlin had to install a new ruler. An army officer, Colonel Yunus-Bek Yevkurov, Ingushetia's third leader, has been able to gain some personal popularity and respect and survived an assassination attempt, but he has proved unable to rein in corruption, tame the powerful clans, or reduce the appeal of Islamists who thrive on popular discontent.

In Dagestan, Moscow has had to manage a precarious balance among the three dozen ethnic groups. To its chagrin, the local rulers are mostly busy dividing up the federal budget transfers. As a cynical joke has it, "Dagestan never joined Russia voluntarily, and will not leave it voluntarily." In the meantime, the corrupt officials are losing authority, which passes more and more into the hands of religious leaders. As in Ingushetia under Zyazikov, the local police use brutal methods against the "Wahhabi" militants but fail to stamp out the militancy.[44] Shootings, bombings, and assassinations have become a daily routine in Dagestan. In 2010 alone, more than 180 police officers were killed.

In the words of Ivan Sydoruk, Russia's deputy public prosecutor in charge of the North Caucasus, the root cause of the appalling criminal situation in the region is deeply rooted corruption. The militants can purchase weapons and ammunition from military and police units. Thus, the weapon used in the assassination of the Dagestani interior minister had been "leased" from a military unit, and then returned there.[45] Russian authorities, however, focused almost entirely on the local governments, exonerating the federal bureaucracy.

The western part of the North Caucasus has grown more restive than it was in the late 1990s–early 2000s. The use of brutal methods of fighting extremism in Kabardino-Balkaria led to a radicalization of local protesters and initially moderate Islamists, which erupted in 2005 in an armed uprising in Nalchik, the capital. Kabardino-Balkaria has joined Chechnya, Dagestan, and Ingushetia as one of the hottest spots in the region. Islam is also becoming more radical in neighboring Karachaevo-Cherkessia. In Adygeya, there are rumblings of ethnic nationalism.

In this very fragmented and worrisome picture, the centrally located North Ossetia has rediscovered its historical role: to be the mainstay of Russian power in the region. North Ossetia is often rocked by terrorist attacks. Suffice it to remember the 2004 school seizure at Beslan, which led to more than 300 deaths. Also, the predominantly Orthodox republic finds itself in a territorial dispute with Ingushetia. The conflict was frozen by the Russian military in 1992, but it was never resolved. The 2008 Russo-Georgian war over South Ossetia and Moscow's subsequent recognition of the tiny enclave's independence further complicated matters. Ossetia's unification as an independent nation was briefly discussed as an option. It was later abandoned, but the future of South Ossetia remains an issue in two ways: the obvious non-viability of the Republic of South Ossetia and the temptation of independence it represents for the Russian North Caucasus.[46]

Against this background, Putin's successful bid, in 2007, to hold the 2014 Winter Olympics in Sochi is an attempt to shore up Russia's position in a vulnerable region. In late 2009, to deal with Russia's most serious domestic problem—in Medvedev's words—a new federal district was carved out to include the ethnic republics of the North Caucasus, thus separating them from the predominantly Russian lands staying within the rump Southern district. To head the new territory, the Kremlin in January 2010 appointed a successful business manager and a former governor of Krasnoyarsk, Alexander Khloponin.

"It was a typical behind-the-scenes advancement of a person lacking the appropriate experience, motivated by internal bureaucratic logic, rather then pressing national interest," Sergei Markedonov, a noted expert on the Caucasus, wrote.[47] The idea that stimulating economic development in the region was the best means of fighting the insurgency was basically right. The rate of unemployment among young men in the North Caucasus is appalling: 44 percent in Karachaevo-Cherkessia; 50 percent in Kabardino-Balkaria; 79 percent in Chechnya; and 84 percent in Ingushetia.[48]

Soon, however, the basic idea of preventing militancy by means of simply throwing money at the problem was confronted with the reality of rampant corruption at all levels. Even Chechnya, considered "pacified," became a target of terrorist attacks, including, in 2010, against the Kadyrovs' clan seat at Tsentoroy and the Chechen parliament building in Grozny. In 2009, after a break of six years, suicide terrorist attacks resumed in Moscow, killing scores of people in the metro. But the Russian government—while it passed a policy document, founded a new district, and appointed a new governor to head it—has yet to find an effective strategy.

The Russian officials and their local allies do not get it. Ramzan Kady-rov had long talked about 50–60 "shaitans" (devils) running in the mountains; the Dagestani police chiefs talked about a couple of hundred "irreconcilables" in the republic. Yet the very ability of these groups to perform their attacks on the scale and at the rate described suggests that they operate in a permissive, even friendly, environment. Blaming foreign "mercenaries," al-Qaeda, or the government of Georgia—as the Russian interior minister, his subordinates, or the Russian National Security Council chief does—points to their inability, or unwillingness, to see things straight.

The North Caucasus is now often referred to as Russia's "inner abroad." This is more than a catchy phrase. A number of observers call the North Caucasus a surviving bit of Russia's empire. This may have been the unintended message of the creation of the new district: the Southern district, with Rostov as its capital, is Russia; the North Caucasus district is the Russian Federation, or simply an imperial borderland. The Russian civilian administrators and military/police commanders look at the locals as an inferior class: primitive "natives," dangerous "aliens," who, depending on the circumstances, may also be a source of bribes. Even President Medvedev referred to "colonial attitudes" among the local officials.[49] The combination of arrogance and repression breeds radicalism and provides more recruits to the extremist cause. Ironically but sadly, public statements to that effect are branded by senior Russian officials as "support for terrorism."

A small surviving piece of empire the North Caucasus may be, but what is happening there now is the opposite of the processes that were under way in the nineteenth and twentieth centuries, as the area was being conquered, annexed, newly organized, its elites integrated and socialized, and the rest of the population assimilated to some degree and diversified through immigration.

Now, instead of moving in, Russia is on the way out. Ethnic Russians are leaving,* and the ethnic republics are becoming even more indigenous. The Russian army is still in the region, but it is essentially confined to barracks and occasionally attacked. The security forces are playing an unclear and complicated role. At times, they seem to act like Moscow's arm; at times, they apparently do the bidding of local interests with whom they are allied; at times, they play games of their own. The police forces, however, are very much part of the local landscape.

De-modernization is settling in. The courts of law still function under the double-headed Russian eagle, but outside of the courthouses lo-

---

* See chapter 4 for a detailed discussion of domestic migration in Russia.

cal traditions are reasserting themselves, and Sharia law is establishing its presence. Islam is on the rise, and within it the established structures are giving way to radicals and extremists who are often summarily referred to as "Wahhabis."

Thus, what has emerged in the North Caucasus is a string of very small ethnocratic polities, stretching from the Caspian almost to the Black Sea. They may be described, collectively, as "soft" versions of de facto independent Chechnya, but each has a distinct political culture of its own. All are formally linked to Russia, and this link is indeed a lifeline: The tiny statelets survive thanks to Russian federal subsidies. They could be best described as Russian protectorates, or loosely associated states, rather than full-fledged parts of the Russian Federation. On quite a few issues, they can well say "no" to Moscow.

In actual fact, two more areas currently belong to the same category: Abkhazia and South Ossetia. In each case, initial exuberance aroused by Russia's recognition of their independence was succeeded by bitter disappointment.[50] Ironically, today's Abkhazia, while more independent from Georgia, is at the same time more dependent on Russia. This leads to friction and even low-level conflicts, usually over money and property.

South Ossetia is very small, in just about every aspect: physical size, population, resources, even its political elite. Many senior positions in South Ossetia are thus filled by Russian officials, servicemen, or businesspeople. Its future looks uncertain: independence worth the name impossible; a return to Georgia unthinkable, after the August 7 attack on Tskhinvali; and, finally, annexation by Russia/North Ossetia would create a worse earthquake than recognition of independence—for it would be Russia's borders, not Georgia's, that would start changing in that case. With South Ossetia and Abkhazia directly under Russian control, Russia is physically present in the South Caucasus.

THE SOUTH CAUCASUS AND THE NEIGHBORHOOD

Russia's conflicts with Georgia and its position with regard to the Azeri-Armenian dispute over Nagorno-Karabakh have been referred to in these pages. While Moscow has failed to manage its relations with Tbilisi, it has been able to maneuver, rather deftly, between Baku and Yerevan. Armenia is Russia's formal ally in the Collective Security Treaty Organization, which hosts Russia's only remaining military base in the region—with the exception, of course, of Abkhazia and South Ossetia. In August 2010,

Russia received Armenia's consent to extend its troop presence until 2044. The mission of the forward base at Gyumri has been to keep in check all other players in the region: Georgia in the north, Turkey in the south, and Azerbaijan in the east.

This happened only months after a similar agreement with Ukraine, which allowed the Russian Black Sea Fleet to remain in Sevastopol until 2042. The pattern is clear: Russia is staking out its security perimeter, projecting the provisional post-Soviet arrangements into the mid–twenty-first century. In return, Russia has agreed to guarantee all of Armenia's borders, not just the ones with Turkey. This is a message to Baku: Do not think about using force to recover Nagorno-Karabakh.

There are other messages, too. In an act of geopolitical balancing in 2007, Moscow was offering arms to Azerbaijan, which remains de facto in a state of war with Armenia, its nominal ally. Baku, meanwhile, is very important in energy security and pipeline politics. In 2010, Gazprom offered to buy more Azeri gas, which again did not make Yerevan too happy.

Russia is prepared to tolerate its broad and highly profitable relations with Western oil majors; its close links with Turkey, whose flags can be seen in Baku almost as often as EU flags in Tbilisi; and its relations with the United States. However, Russia is unhappy about U.S. support for the modernization of Azeri and Kazakhstani navies. Moscow stands firm on the principle: The Caspian belongs to the Caspian states only, and outsiders should keep off, especially in the area of regional security. Russia countered the U.S.-proposed Caspian Guard venture with its own project, Caspian Force (CASFOR).

Coming from a much less favorable initial position vis-à-vis Moscow than Georgia (a fellow Orthodox country, with very close cultural and historical links to Russia), Azerbaijan—with its authoritarian regime—has managed Russia extremely well. Like Georgia, Azerbaijan acceded to the CIS only in 1993, and, again like Georgia, it never signed the CIS Collective Security Treaty. Russian forces left the country in 1993, except for a handful of personnel at an early warning radar station at Gabala that monitors missile and bomber activity in the eastern Mediterranean and the Middle East.[*]

Azerbaijan has also been able to complete the Baku-Tbilisi-Ceyhan oil pipeline and the Baku-Tbilisi-Supsa gas pipeline—both replaced the Soviet-era outlets that had run across southern Russia—without irreparably

---

[*] It was this facility that Putin offered to Bush in 2007 at Kennebunkport as a Russian contribution to the common missile defense project.

damaging its relations with Moscow. Azeri migrant workers in Russia are more numerous than Georgians, but they have not been subjected to Russian government-imposed restrictions. There is a visa-free regime between Russia and Azerbaijan. It is clear that Azerbaijan has long decided not to cross two red lines: seeking NATO membership and hosting U.S. military bases.

Since the nineteenth century and through the end of the Cold War, Russia regarded the South Caucasus—or Transcaucasus, as it was known then—as a forward base against Ottoman, and later NATO, Turkey. Since the end of the Cold War, the Turkish-Russian relationship has experienced a dramatic and positive reversal. Turkey has become Russia's important trading partner, in energy, construction, and even arms sales. It has also re-placed the Crimea as a favorite holiday destination for millions of Russians.

Russia appreciates Turkey's rise as a regional power at the strategic juncture of Europe and the Middle East, and does not see that as a threat to itself. In particular, Moscow respects Ankara's independent stance vis-à-vis the United States, as a NATO ally that can say "no" to Washington.** Neither does the moderate Islamism of the AK Party government evoke much concern in the Kremlin. Turkey's ascendance and independence fit well into the general Moscow concept of a multipolar world in which U.S. dominance is reduced.

Ankara's difficult relations with the European Union and the dimming prospect of EU membership add to Moscow's perception of Turkey as an emerging power center with which it needs to build solid relations based on self-interest. Much of that is linked to energy trade, where Turkey features both as a consumer of Russian natural gas and a regional energy transit hub.

Russian and Turkish interests, of course, are far from identical, but business competition is generally accepted in Moscow as a natural state. Where the Russians become more concerned is in cases of Turkish non-governmental organizations supporting separatism in the North Caucasus. With a sizable diaspora of nineteenth-century expellees from the region, collectively known as Circassians, Turkey is not always a passive observer of the developments in Russia's most volatile region. At the same time, Moscow does not object to Turkey's diplomatic initiatives to bring stability to the South Caucasus or its efforts in 2009–2010 to achieve historic recon-ciliation with Armenia. Russia has long acknowledged the 1915 massacre of Armenians in Ottoman Turkey as genocide, and this acknowledgment did not lead to a crisis in Russo-Turkish relations.

** For example, by denying the use of Turkish territory in 2003 for the U.S.-led invasion of Iraq.

In a similar vein, Moscow has acknowledged close ethnic, linguistic, and political ties between Ankara and Baku and has treated the development of those relations calmly. Gone are the fears—prevalent in the early and mid-1990s—of "pan-Turkism," which would aim to create a new Turkish empire from the Balkans to the Caucasus to Central Asia, where four of five new states are Turkic-speaking. President Turgut Özal, the ebullient exponent of those ideas, is long gone; Turkey has revealed the lack of resources for an enterprise as ambitious as the fears; and the new "neo-Ottoman" foreign policy conceived and implemented by Foreign Minister Ahmet Davutoglu is considered "normal" for a rising regional power.

In the nineteenth century, the Russian empire conquered much of the Caucasus from Iran. Repeatedly, parts of Iran were occupied by the Russian and Soviet forces, the last time in 1941–1946. For much of the Cold War, Iran—under the Shah—was a U.S. ally. The Islamic Revolution of 1979 confronted Moscow for the first time with the challenge of radical Islam.

After the dissolution of the Soviet Union, the new Russian leadership feared Iran's meddling in the former Soviet republics, in an effort to subvert the weak secular regimes there and replace them with a version of its own. This did not happen. Moreover, Iran actually joined forces with Russia in 1997 to help end the civil war in Persian-speaking Tajikistan. Most important, Tehran supported Moscow on Chechnya, when much of the rest of the Islamic world was turning anti-Russian. The Iranian leadership supported Moscow's bid to join the Organization of the Islamic Conference as an observer, which Russia was able to do in 2005.

In the South Caucasus, Iran did not seek to undermine nominally Shiite—but in reality very secular—Azerbaijan, and it engaged in active trade with Russia's ally Armenia, which faced an economic blockade from both Azerbaijan and Turkey. For Yerevan, this was nothing short of a lifeline. In the late 1990s and early 2000s, observers talked about Russia, Iran, and Armenia forming one geopolitical axis, with Turkey, Azerbaijan, and the United States forming an opposite one.

Moscow has been relatively unconcerned about Iran's activities elsewhere in the Middle East. It viewed the Tehran-Hizbollah connection as a means for Iran to get within striking distance of its regional adversary, Israel, also standing as a proxy for the United States. Moscow also viewed Hizbollah as a real player in Lebanon and in the broader Arab-Israeli context. This is true as well for Hamas, another of Iran's friends, which Moscow sees more as a political group with an unconventional military arm than as a terrorist organization. To send a message that Russia was more than a "piece of furniture" in the Middle East Quartet—which also includes the United States, the European Union, and the United Nations—it invited Hamas representatives to Moscow. On a visit to Damascus in 2010, Medvedev met with the organization's chief ideologue.

In the 1990s, Moscow became a major arms supplier to Iran. It also undertook to build a nuclear reactor in Bushehr when the German company Siemens had to abandon the project for political reasons. Completed after many delays, the Bushehr reactor will start generating electricity in 2011. The project is placed under International Atomic Energy Agency safeguards, with Russia supplying Iran with the fuel and taking spent fuel back. The United States and other countries regard it as proliferation-safe and hail it as a model for Tehran to emulate.

Not everything, however, is without controversy in Russo-Iranian relations. The breakup of the Soviet Union raised the issue of the Caspian Sea, whose status had been governed by the 1921 Soviet-Iranian treaty. Tehran did not agree to the Moscow-supported formula for dividing the Caspian and insisted on a larger share of the lake than Moscow or the others were willing to concede. Iran even used the threat of force with regard to Azerbaijan—something Russia viewed as trespassing on its turf—although Azerbaijan was not under Russian security protection. What seriously strained the relations was Iran's nuclear and missile programs.

Moscow saw those programs directed more at the United States, Israel, and Saudi Arabia, but did not like the prospect of an ideologically driven power possessing an arsenal of nuclear weapons and long-range missiles. Russia tried to mediate between Tehran and the West; it hoped that the Iranian leadership would be reasonable and reach out for a compromise with the international community. With Tehran recalcitrant, and Washington needing international support, Moscow in 2010 supported UN Security Council sanctions against Iran and imposed an embargo on heavy weapons exports to Iran. The future of Iran's standoff with the international community is a serious cause for concern in Moscow, not least in view of the potential impact of the military conflict between Iran and the United States/Israel on Central Asia.

CENTRAL ASIA[51]

Central Asia's five republics—Kazakhstan, Kyrgyzstan, Tajikistan, Turkmenistan, and Uzbekistan—did not secede from the Soviet Union: It was the Union that imploded and abandoned them. To their credit, all five survived on their own, even though none of them had any previous experience as a modern independent state, not even to the extent that the three South Caucasian countries have. Also to their credit, they did not openly challenge one another's borders, even though those borders had been drawn arbitrarily by the Bolsheviks in 1924–1925, without due consideration of the ethnic distribution map of what used to be Russian Turkestan.

The authoritarian post-Soviet regimes of new Central Asian states largely survived, and some have experienced transfers of power. Almost two decades after the collapse of the USSR, two of them—Kazakhstan and Uzbekistan—are still led by their founding presidents. One, Turkmenistan, features a second-generation leader who had seamlessly succeeded the "Father of All Turkmens." Another, Kyrgyzstan—the most liberal country of all—has gone through a color revolution of sorts and continues to experience tensions. Finally, Tajikistan is presided over by a leader who had emerged from a civil war. However, that civil conflict, resulting in about 100,000 deaths and hundreds of thousands of refugees, is the only conflict in the former Soviet Union that has been successfully settled through a reconciliation accord.

Since 1991, Russia has been on a slow-motion retreat throughout the region. Gradually, the new states have learned to live without Moscow and manage their affairs, domestic and foreign, on their own. Russia, however, continued to count Central Asia in its orbit. All five countries have remained in the CIS, although Turkmenistan has downgraded its participation to that of an observer. Four countries are members of the Collective Security Treaty Organization (again, Turkmenistan proclaimed neutrality in 1995), and three belong to the Eurasian Economic Community (EurAsEC; Uzbekistan has opted out). Two countries, Tajikistan and Kyrgyzstan, host small Russian combat forces. Finally, Kazakhstan in 2010 joined with Russia and Belarus to form a Customs Union, which is seen as a nucleus of a future Single Economic Space.

Virtually all security risks and potential threats in the region are of local origin. Kazakhstan's continued stability remains Russia's principal interest, even as the country is approaching the time when its founding president will have to pass on the baton. Kazakhstan's stability hopes rest with its reasonably numerous, extensively modernized, and structured elite, which has a big stake in the growing prosperity of the energy-rich country. It also is based on generally healthy interethnic relations in the country. For Moscow, Kazakhstan is not part of the problem, but a key part of any regional solution.

Central Asia is within the zone of responsibility of the newly formed Operational-Strategic Command "Center," with headquarters in Yekaterinburg. The only military ally Russia has in the area is Kazakhstan, whose forces are bigger than those of the Russian central command and are clearly the best in Central Asia. Kazakhstan and Russia are the only two countries that have contributed substantial contingents toward the CSTO Collective Rapid Reaction Force (KSOR, in Russian).[52]

Kazakhstan's neighbor, Kyrgyzstan, is almost the opposite. Since 2005, it has had two revolutions, chronic interregional tensions between its own north and south, and a major interethnic conflict. The country is poor, with few resources and warring clans in lieu of a national elite. It also suffers from Islamist radicalism and drug trafficking.

So far, Russia has abstained from active involvement in Kyrgyz conflicts. It preferred the Kyrgyz to resolve their disputes themselves, and then deal with the winners. It clearly did not want to stand between the Kyrgyz and the Uzbeks, risking being hit in the cross fire. But it also did not have sufficient resources, in terms of deployable military or police forces, and had incomplete knowledge and insufficient understanding of the local scene.

Moscow, however, became very involved in the issue of the U.S. air base at Manas, Kyrgyzstan. Initially, in the wake of 9/11, it acquiesced to the U.S. military presence. Then it opened its own air base at Kant, a dozen miles from Manas. In 2005, Russia initiated a call on behalf of Shanghai Cooperation Organization countries to wind up American military presence in Central Asia. It leaned on Kurmanbek's government, which had emerged from the "Tulip Revolution," to follow the Uzbek example and send the Americans packing. Bakiyev dithered. In 2009, Kyrgyz authorities received an aid package and an investment promise from Russia, which they reciprocated with a commitment to close down Manas. In reality, they negotiated a new agreement with Washington, which substantially increased the rent, and left the base under a different label.

Moscow felt deceived. By 2009, U.S.-Russian relations had been "reset," but Moscow wanted to be the decider on the U.S. base issue. Kremlin leaders would have probably agreed to extend the base lease, but they wanted it to be part of a U.S.-Russia deal, with Bishkek only a subcontractor: after all, Kyrgyzstan was Russia's CSTO ally. Instead, Moscow itself was left behind. Furious, Russia bided its time. When in the spring of 2010 Bakiyev faced a rebellion headed by his political opponents, Moscow relished the demise of his regime and swiftly recognized the new government, led by Roza Otunbayeva. By the end of 2010, Otunbayeva got a visit from U.S.

Secretary of State Hillary Rodham Clinton and extended the base lease by three more years.

Cautious about periodic Kyrgyz uprisings, Russia did become heavily involved in the early 1990s in the civil war in Tajikistan. The regime Moscow helped install in 1992 is still in power. Moreover, it grew stronger in the 2000s by effectively neutralizing the opposition after the power-sharing accord. However, by the early 2010s, signs of regime fatigue began to appear. This may have serious implications, given the country's proximity to Afghanistan and the uncertainty over which way the situation may develop there. In the wake of 9/11, the Tajik government was able to benefit from Western attention to the frontline state. If the U.S. and NATO forces leave Afghanistan, that could be a major reversal of fortune for Tajikistan.

Since the start of Gorbachev's perestroika a quarter-century ago, Turkmenistan has experienced virtually no public protests, not to speak of conflicts or clashes. Even the sudden death of its God-like first president in 2006 did not lead to instability. The regime, buoyed by the country's energy riches, has been more repressive than any other in Central Asia and more effective in dealing with its opponents.

Finally, Uzbekistan could be potentially the biggest tinderbox in the region. There is an issue of power transfer after the departure of the first president; there is militant Islamist activity, which led—in 1999, 2000, and 2005—to uprisings and terrorist attacks; there is the overpopulated Fergana Valley, where socioeconomic tensions can result in a major upheaval and spread to neighboring Kyrgyzstan and Tajikistan.

From 2003, Moscow has been hoping to make a comeback in Central Asia, as a self-interested great power this time, rather than an all-caring empire. It revamped the 1992 Tashkent Treaty and used it as a foundation for a security alliance, the Collective Security Treaty Organization (CSTO). Moscow exploited the fear among the Central Asian rulers of a color revolution in their countries, using Kyrgyzstan as an object lesson.

In particular, after the 2005 Andijan uprising, the Kremlin counted on Uzbekistan not only to distance itself from the United States but also to return to the Russian sphere of influence. However, this did not happen. By 2010, Uzbekistan had formally withdrawn from EurAsEC and de facto left the CSTO. According to Kuchma, Karimov told him that while he had "a survival problem," in view of the Islamist threat, he "could not receive serious aid from Russia, and probably did not seek it too much."[53]

Domestic instability is only part of Russia's security concerns in Central Asia. Tensions among Central Asian states, especially between Uzbekistan and each of its four former Soviet neighbors, are another worry. Tashkent is very unhappy with even a small Russian military presence in Kyrgyzstan and has protested any plans to expand it. Russian planners find it difficult to predict Tashkent's moves in a serious contingency in the region or its reaction to Moscow's moves. The scenario, popular in the 1990s, of the Taliban's offensive going all the way to the Volga is virtually discounted. Central Asian forces would stop them if they ventured across the border. It would be far more difficult to stop Islamist insurgents who would merge with like-minded indigenous groups from Uzbekistan, Tajikistan, and Kyrgyzstan. In 1999 and 2000, their attacks revealed the impotence of Tashkent and Bishkek vis-à-vis such threats. The Russian defense minister at the time could offer only missile attacks against insurgent training camps in Afghanistan. Today, his successor can send in paratroopers.[54]

The Russian element of KSOR, composed of paratroopers of the Thirty-First Air Assault Brigade (Ulyanovsk) and Ninety-Eighth Airborne Division (Ivanovo), can engage and defeat relatively small groups of insurgents. However, Russians and their Kazakh allies would be unable to deal with a mass uprising in the Fergana Valley. The most Russia and Kazakhstan would be able to do in that worst-case scenario is to stop the wave of unrest on the southern borders of Kazakhstan. This border is the southern strategic barrier of the Russian Federation.*

Meanwhile, Moscow is increasingly worried that the region has turned into a transit area for Afghanistan-produced drugs, which reach Russia in ever greater quantities and kill ever bigger numbers of young Russian people. As for Central Asia, the 1990s were only an introduction to the world of international politics. As Afghanistan was targeted by the United States in October 2001 because al-Qaeda enjoyed the hospitality and support of the extremist Taliban regime, Central Asia ceased to be a backwater and became a frontline region in the global war on terrorism. Drugs and terror: This is the shorthand for how Afghanistan is viewed from the north.[55]

Drugs, indeed, have become Moscow's principal concern with regard to Afghanistan. Immediately after 9/11, Russia closely cooperated with the United States and gave political, logistical, and intelligence support to Operation Enduring Freedom. Moscow supported the Bonn accords and, once Hamid Karzai was installed as Afghanistan's president, took a low profile in Kabul, not attempting to undercut Karzai in favor of its own allies.

---

* As chapter 3 will argue, this same border is also the realistic limit of economic integration between Russia and its neighbors.

After the "reset" in U.S.-Russian relations in 2009, Russia's support for the U.S./NATO operation has increased. Russia has become an important transit country for overland supplies that run from Riga, Latvia, to Termez, Uzbekistan, on the Afghan border. Russia also opened its airspace for U.S. troop transports. With the situation in Pakistan growing more precarious, the importance of the northern supply route has increased. In 2010, Russian and U.S. special services conducted a joint operation in Afghanistan to destroy four drug laboratories in the vicinity of the Pakistan border.[56]

In a major departure from its military doctrine, which viewed permanent foreign troop presence in the ex-Soviet republics as a potential danger, Putin, in the wake of 9/11, accepted U.S. military deployments in Central Asia, in the territory of Moscow's CSTO allies, Uzbekistan and Kyrgyzstan. As the U.S.-Russian relationship worsened in the mid-2000s—and the war in Afghanistan evolved into a prolonged conflict—the Kremlin's attitude to U.S. presence, often on Soviet-built airfields, turned negative. Moscow supported Uzbek President Karimov's suspicions that the United States had been behind the 2005 Andijan uprising, and, weeks before, encouraged the Tulip Revolution in Kyrgyzstan that toppled President Akayev. Russia welcomed Islam Karimov's decision to close the U.S. air base at Karshi-Khanabad. Later that year, Russia, China, and their Central Asian partners in the Shanghai Cooperation Organization (SCO) called for terminating the remaining U.S. military presence in the region.

By that time, only Kyrgyzstan still hosted a U.S. base, at Manas. The new Kyrgyz president, Kurmanbek Bakiyev, started a game with both Russia and the United States, with the aim of squeezing both for cash. By 2009, he had succeeded in raising the cost of the lease from the United States and in getting grant aid and an investment package from Russia, in return for the base closure. To be able to get away with both, Bakiyev officially closed the base—then immediately resurrected it as an antiterrorist center. That forever ruined his reputation in Moscow's eyes. Ironically, by that time, Russia no longer minded a U.S. base in Kyrgyzstan; it wanted only to be the de facto contractor. When Bakiyev faltered in the spring of 2010, Moscow did not lift a finger to save him or even give him refuge, as it had done for Akayev.

Watching the U.S.-led operation in Afghanistan from the vantage point of their own bitter experience, Russians saw that the Americans were making some of the same mistakes they themselves had committed. U.S. pursuit of modernization and democratization—despite the obvious importance of both—was at cross-purposes with the more immediate objectives:

a modicum of stability inside the country and, in any event, an absence of threats to the outside world originating in Afghanistan.

Instead of focusing on defeating the Taliban—or turning defeatist oneself and trying to rebuild a new Northern Alliance—a better strategy is to reach out to the Pashtuns. This largest ethnic group should be the mainstay of any stable Afghan government. Today, most Taliban fighters are Pashtuns, but the Taliban is a very broad movement whose members need not be lumped together. By 2010, this approach started to guide U.S. policy on Afghanistan.

As the U.S./NATO forces prepare to leave Afghanistan, the role of the countries in the region, including Russia, will rise. So will the burden they will have to carry. Yet one can refuse to assume that responsibility only at one's own peril. In the regional context, the SCO can play an important role.

The SCO emerged from the border talks between China and the Soviet Union, and later Soviet successor states that shared a border with China. In 1996, after the border agreement was reached, the parties to it—China, Russia, Kazakhstan, Kyrgyzstan, and Tajikistan—formed a Shanghai Five group to oversee its implementation.

By 2000, when the loose grouping was institutionalized as an organization, it had grown into a platform for regional dialogue on security and development issues. Its membership expanded to include Uzbekistan as a member, and India, Pakistan, Iran, and Mongolia as observers. SCO annual summits usually deal with the situation in Afghanistan, and the Russian president has formed a habit of meeting with the leaders of Afghanistan and Pakistan, sometimes in the company of the Tajik leader.

This also brings up the issue of the relationship between NATO and the Russia-led CSTO. Moscow has been calling for formal ties for a long time, to no avail. NATO's semiofficial explanation was the undemocratic nature of some of CSTO member-states—Belarus was usually mentioned—but the true reason was probably the unwillingness of the West to legitimize Russian politico-military dominance in the former Soviet space. Having established useful bilateral relations with several CSTO countries, including Russia, the allies saw no need to deal with the Moscow-led organization, which would probably reduce the freedom of its members in dealing with NATO or the United States. However, reevaluating Russia's international role, as well as looking beyond NATO's own engagement in Afghanistan, can change that. In 2009, Zbigniew Brzezinski was the first major Western voice suggesting a NATO-CSTO link.[57]

Since the disappearance of the Soviet Union, many observers have been regarding Central Asia as a venue for a new edition of the Great Game. In the minds of Russians, it was now being waged by Moscow and Washington. The United States moved in quickly, immediately recognizing all new countries and establishing embassies in all five capitals. Initially guided by the need to prevent nuclear proliferation, the United States later developed an interest in the Caspian energy resources. In Moscow, this activism was met with both jealousy and resentment. There were the issues of pipelines, military bases, degrees of political influence, and the like.

In reality, the former Soviet backyard saw multi-corner competition. The Chinese emphasized security, trade, and energy. Beijing initiated the process of border fixation and demilitarization, while making sure the neighboring states will not become safe havens for Uighur separatists. It later expanded its presence, looking for energy sources and markets for Chinese products. As a trading partner of Central Asian countries, China is second only to Russia. The balance is shifting in China's favor, and Russia is paying attention, though it does not express any anxiety publicly.

Interestingly, Moscow took a much more accepting attitude toward China's insertion into the region than its attitude toward the U.S. role. There seems to be an understanding for the needs of regional great powers—China or Turkey, for example—to project a modicum of influence to their neighborhood and a flat rejection of any "global role"—for the United States or for NATO. But there is also a reluctance to test a relationship with a mighty neighbor, which Russia can no longer balance on its own. China helped, too. Whatever Beijing's long-term strategic goals, its tactics were cautious, respected Moscow's sensitivities, and highlighted cooperation. As each country seeks to strengthen its position in Central Asia, in the short and medium term Russia and China can manage their differences of interest and find ways to cooperate.

Russia found the SCO formula much to its liking. Under the arrangement, Moscow and Beijing shared leadership in an increasingly prestigious Asian group. During the 2000s, the SCO also was a useful counterweight to U.S./Western presence in Central Asia. This does not diminish the fact that, above all else, the SCO stands for China in Central Asia.

At the outset, Turkey tried to raise its profile among the Turkic-speaking states. But it soon became clear that Ankara lacked the resources to emerge as the principal patron of the region. Also, during the 1990s Turkey was very focused on acceding to the European Union. Iran, too, reached out to its linguistic brethren in Tajikistan, helping broker a peace accord and establishing close relations with Dushanbe. Tehran also built a rail link to the neighboring Turkmenistan, thus establishing direct contact with its northern neighbor.

There is competition, but the Great Game is a false analogy. The future of Central Asia will not be decided by a match between Moscow and Washington, or a three-corner tournament with Beijing's participation. The deciders sit in Astana and Tashkent, as well as the other capitals of the region. Not one of those capitals imagines itself as a Moscow satellite. This is the most adequate interpretation of their refusal to back the Russian recognition of Abkhazia's and South Ossetia's independence. As will be detailed in chapter 3, not a single oil or gas producer in the region wants to depend on Russia as its sole market or sole transit route.

By the same token, however, no Central Asian leaders would think of fully entrusting their security to the United States. The color revolutions— in which U.S.-friendly regimes in Georgia, Ukraine, and Kyrgyzstan were toppled by revolutionaries proposing even friendlier policies toward the United States—were a vivid demonstration of the precariousness of the U.S. connection. China is welcome throughout the region as a trading partner, investor, and lender, but it is nonetheless feared as a potentially powerful regional hegemon.

As a result, Central Asians have developed "multi-vector" foreign policies, which elevate maneuvering among the major power centers—such as the European Union, Turkey, Iran, Pakistan, India, Japan, and others—to the level of strategy. The two leading countries of the region, Uzbekistan and Kazakhstan, also vie for regional leadership. Their three smaller neighbors cannot afford to ignore those ambitions.

In this environment, Russia needs to pursue a differentiated policy in support of its specific interests. A nostalgic approach aimed at keeping the region in the Moscow sphere of influence is bound to fail. Russia also needs to develop its soft power potential to work as a power of attraction for Central Asians. Russia's enlightened self-interest calls for stability and prosperity in the region that directly adjoins its territory. Central Asia is also one area where Russian and Chinese interests converge and intersect.

THE EASTERN FLANK

The evolution of Moscow's relations with Beijing over the past twenty-five years is a rare case in world history. It seldom happens that a long and bitter cold war between two big neighbors would transform, without a pause and apparently seamlessly, into a genuine partnership. And yet this is what happened after Mikhail Gorbachev's visit to Beijing in May 1989 and his talks with Deng Xiaoping and other Chinese leaders. Soon after that, the first major agreement on the disputed border was signed, and Russia started selling weapons to China. In the following two decades, those sales averaged $1 billion a year, which helped keep the Russian defense industry afloat and modernize China's military.

It also seldom happens that relations between two major neighboring states would continue to grow deeper and friendlier against the background of a dramatic reversal of fortune. In 1990, Russia's GDP was roughly the size of China's. Two decades later, China's was four times as large as Russia's. For all Russia's high growth rates during 2000–2008 as a result of rising oil prices, China's growth, over thirty years and enduring today, has been superior. When, as a result of the crisis, the Russian economy took the deepest dip among all major economies in 2009, China's growth continued almost unabated. China curbed its population growth, but Russia entered a demographic crisis, with a fast population decline in the sparsely populated regions along the Chinese border. Shining modern Chinese cities, such as Heihe or Suifenhe, where villages had once stood, opposite decaying towns like Blagoveshchensk or Ussuriysk—this is a picture postcard story of two great powers.

For the first time in some 300 years, Russia can no longer look down on China as the more backward, sleepy, isolated, technologically inferior—or militarily weak. The change of this scale happened within a mere decade, and in peace. The remarkable thing is that this change has not led to either new hostility or a hegemony of the stronger party. It has not even led to resentment on Russia's part, or jubilation on China's. Instead, China and Russia managed to establish reasonably good and, for the time being at least, mutually comfortable relations that they call a strategic partnership.

This relationship rests on several pillars. One is politics. Both Moscow and Beijing had supported a multipolar world order since well before this concept became generally acceptable in the United States and Europe. Both are fiercely protective of their strategic independence, national sovereignty, and territorial integrity. Yet each pragmatically pursues its own national interest and strives to achieve a higher status in global politics. The striking thing is that both countries are careful to avoid even serious friction, let alone conflict, between them. Central Asia is an interesting example. Moscow did not try to block Beijing's entry into the region it regards as its zone of privileged interests, and Beijing, in turn, has behaved in such a way as to avoid hurting Russian sensitivities.

Another pillar is economics. The tables have turned abruptly, and Russia, with a few exceptions such as nuclear weapons, has become a supplier of mainly raw materials—from oil to timber—to China, which exports manufactured goods, including, increasingly, machinery. China is also a major lender to Russian oil majors, such as Rosneft.

Chinese traders and workers have established themselves in a number of Russian cities. Of course, present-day Khabarovsk does not look like Harbin of a century ago, in reverse, but the shoe is definitely on the other foot. Yet there is comparatively little resentment in Russia over the influx of Chinese migrants, only quiet limits on Chinese investment in Russia's energy sector and on the military technology transfers.

Finally, there are human contacts. In the halcyon days of the Sino-Soviet alliance in the 1950s, relations between the two countries were entirely controlled by the ruling communist parties. From the 1960s through the 1980s, there was only the barest minimum of state-to-state relations.

Since the early 1990s, however, the two peoples have met again—now as individuals. Russian and Chinese "tourists" organized border trade that rivaled the official commercial turnover. Russian scientists shared their hard-won knowledge with Chinese colleagues. Chinese peasants grew watermelons on the Russian soil that Russians themselves had abandoned. Gradually, this changed. Genuine Russian tourists come by planeloads on chartered flights from Siberian cities to places like Hainan Island or Beidaihe. The Chinese, once avid Russian learners, have mostly given up, but ordinary Russians take up studying Chinese to be able to do business in China.

This does not mean that the Sino-Russian relations are problem-free or on autopilot. This is a relationship of unequals turned upside down. The two big unequals are also culturally and mentally farther apart than most nations. The Chinese were bewildered in 2003 by the sudden scuttling of their contract with Yukos on crude oil deliveries.* The Russians, for their part, were incensed by the Chinese practice of cloning weapons, such as the S-300 air defense system or the X-55 cruise missiles, which they had purchased from Moscow.[58] The sudden closure in 2008 of the Cherkizovsky market in Moscow—which used to employ hundreds of Chinese—became a subject for urgent government-to-government consultations: When the

---

* The contract was eventually inherited, and the shipments were carried out, much later, by Rosneft.

Russian authorities were making the decision, no one thought of the China connection. And so on.

The salient feature of the relationship is the keen sense of where its limits lie. A partnership, but not an alliance. Weapons sales, but no strategic dialogue. Together for something, but not against anyone. Full freedom to disagree—politely. Economic exchanges, but not integration. Immigration, but without Chinatowns. Human contacts, but across a clear and irremovable civilizational divide.

This is a good, even unique relationship—as long as it lasts. It suits China and Russia, their leaders, businesspeople, and ordinary citizens. An "axis of convenience," Bobo Lo, an astute Australian diplomat-turned-analyst, appropriately called it.[59] Russia and China have shown that this kind of relationship can deepen and develop. It can also withstand moderate complications and mild shocks.

The near- and even medium-term future of the relationship looks assured. For the Russians, there is no alternative, as they used to say in Gorbachev's time, to good-neighborliness and friendship with China. To have China as an adversary is a recipe for catastrophe, no less. Despite some suspicions in Russia, there is no reason to expect an adverse change in China's attitude.[60] All the recent assertiveness notwithstanding, the current leadership in Beijing and the one that will take over in 2012 are most likely to continue the present course. China is asking the West, not Russia, to make room for it, and its outstanding territorial disputes are with its neighbors to the east and south—Japan, Vietnam, and India—not the ones to the north.

The longer term is less clear. Russian attitudes will not change. No amount of realistic rapprochement with the United States and NATO will make Russia forget about the 4,355 km (2,707 miles) of common border with China. No one in Moscow, or anywhere in the world for that matter, can imagine that this border can be guaranteed by a third party or alliance. The question is over the direction of China's foreign policy, should more nationalistic trends prevail in Beijing, either as a result of a hardening of the stance of the subsequent Communist Party leadership or as a result of the fall of the communist dynasty and the emergence of a more democratic, nationalistic, and warlike China. This may be the horizon of 2025–2030.

Other risks to the Sino-Russian relationship are inherent in the dynamic of China's relations with the United States and other major Asian powers, India and Japan. A Korean crisis—resulting from the country's reunification, under Seoul's auspices, but with U.S. troops on the peninsula, and possibly also with nuclear weapons—can pit China against the

United States. Taiwan is another, though a less likely military contingency. Developments over the Senkaku/Diaoyutai Islands and the rocks in the South China Sea will have a marginal effect: Russia will keep out of the fray. Moscow will probably resist Beijing's insistence on backing China's territorial claims. It is time Moscow returned the compliment for China's nonrecognition of Abkhazia and South Ossetia.[61]

Russia's relations with Japan exhibit a number of paradoxes. In the late 1980s, it was arguably easier for Tokyo than, say, for Bonn or Beijing to reach an all-round accommodation with Moscow, including on the territorial issue. Yet the Japanese were among the strongest skeptics, west or east, as far as Gorbachev's perestroika was concerned. In the end, they did not invite him to visit until May 1991, when he was already unable to make major decisions. Soon they had another chance, under Yeltsin. Russia at that time desperately needed money and was open to various options.

Yet very little progress was achieved between Russia and Japan in those years. Japan held back on economics and stood firm on its territorial demands. Russia was initially accommodating, but the rise of nationalism in the country prevented a wholesale cession of the South Kuril Islands, which the Japanese demanded. A third chance came with Putin, who sought a compromise and offered the formula of the 1956 Moscow Declaration, admittedly tilted very much in favor of Russia. The Japanese not only rejected the offer, but prohibited their leaders from seeking a compromise formula: it was all or nothing.

Twenty years later, Moscow feels under no pressure to do deals. In 2009, it thanked Japan for the assistance it had been sending to the Kuril Islanders, and asked Tokyo to send no more aid. Moscow feels much stronger, has substantial foreign reserves, and is visibly irritated when Tokyo politicians or officials raise the issue of "Russian occupation of the four islands." In November 2010, despite vehement Japanese protests, Medvedev visited the South Kurils—something no Kremlin leader had ever done. This was probably done with an eye to the 2012 elections: More than 80 percent of Russians consistently support full Russian sovereignty over the Kurils, but it was also a sign of frustration over the inflexible position adopted by Tokyo, which refused any compromise on the issue. Moscow must have calculated that Tokyo would continue to withhold official development assistance anyway but that it cannot prevent Japanese companies from doing business with Russia. The volume and depth of Russo-Japanese economic interaction is constrained not so much by the politics in Japan as by the investment climate in Russia.

For Japan, again paradoxically, Russia is perhaps the friendliest country on Asia's Pacific coast. While the Japanese still brood over Russia's 1945 entry into the war, in its final weeks, and the fate of the lost islands and their expellees, Russians feel satisfied—they had fully avenged the defeat in the 1904–1905 war, started by the Japanese, and are ready for eternal peace. They actually like the Japanese: peaceful, industrious, sophisticated, technologically advanced, and culture-loving. The image of Russians in Japanese eyes is far less positive.

Of course, Moscow should be very interested in expanding its links with Japan, for the sake of the general policy of modernization, and, more specifically, to accelerate the development of the Russian Far East and Siberia. The idea of Japan as a Germany of the East should be compelling. To feel more confident and comfortable, Russia needs more international partners in the Asia-Pacific region. It should be ready, at some point, to consider the same approach it has allowed Moscow, to use recently to resolve other territorial issues, notably with China and Norway. However, without diplomatic flexibility and strategic thinking on the Japanese side, this will be impossible.

Demand for modernization pushes Russia toward Japan, although the country was conspicuously absent from the short list of Moscow's modernization allies announced by Medvedev. The needs of regional development of the Far East are another pressing issue. As for Japan, there is one strategic factor that might make it compromise with Russia: China. Japan's principal ally is across the Pacific, and it does not need—and cannot have—another. That said, Japan would be much better off with a genuinely friendly Russia.[62]

Recognizing the current limitations of the Japan relationship, Moscow has been trying to expand economic relations with South Korea. Of course, Korea is also important for geopolitical and strategic reasons. While South Korea is an economic powerhouse, North Korea is a nuclear power with missiles. The Russians have little leverage in the North, but—being even a somewhat passive member of the six-party talks on North Korea—they are part of a united international front and leave Pyongyang no option to play on its differences with Washington.

South Korea is a rising power that at one point will achieve reunification. For all the financial burden, sociopolitical complexities, and the needs of psychological adjustment, reunification is likely to increase the vitality of the Korean people, whose ambition will be to speak with a strong and influential voice in Asia and globally. Historically, Koreans resented Chinese mentors and Japanese occupiers. The Russian empire and the Soviet Union also meddled there, but, luckily, only briefly. There is a chance to build a strong relationship between Moscow and Seoul that would work for peace and stability in Northeast Asia. Mongolia is often missing from discussions on Northeast Asia, along with Russia. This shorthand is wrong if one talks geopolitics and security. For the vast, strategically positioned, and sparsely populated country, the changes brought about by Gorbachev's perestroika and its aftermath were tremendous. The Mongolians did a good job building on that: They transited to a functioning democracy; they established a market economy; they diversified their external relations way beyond their two great neighbors and, in doing so, achieved a co-equal relationship with Moscow, without becoming Beijing's satellite; and they transported themselves, mentally, from Eastern Europe to Northeast Asia.

Of course, Mongolia benefited from the political changes in Russia, which promptly withdrew the 75,000 troops stationed in the country and allowed it to freely choose its course. Essentially, Moscow summarily abandoned Mongolia and did not think of it at all throughout the 1990s. The economic changes meant the loss of the Soviet/COMECON market, and subsidies, but this was also stimulating. The Mongols benefited from the great Chinese market next door and from the strategic interest in it demonstrated by two other countries, Japan and the United States. When Moscow finally rediscovered Mongolia in the mid-2000s, mostly for business reasons, it saw a self-confident and mature partner.

In fact, Russia's easternmost neighbor is the United States. Until 1867, the Russian empire extended beyond the Bering Strait and included Alaska. Fort Ross, the farthest Russian settlers ever reached into North America, is a mere 100 miles north of San Francisco. In the Pacific, U.S.-Russian relations have been very different than they have been in Europe, and somewhat friendlier.

In 1945, the Soviet Union entered the war against Japan at the insistence of the U.S. government. In 1950, at the height of the Cold War, Stalin gave the go-ahead to Kim Il Sung to start a war in Korea, but he preferred to operate through proxies: Kim and Mao Zedong. Nikita Khrushchev despised the nuclear adventurism of Mao, which was one of the reasons for the Sino-Soviet split in 1960. After that, it was China, not the United States, that was the Soviet Union's biggest strategic worry in the Asia-Pacific. The famous strategic triangle established the framework for complex big-power relations, in which Moscow's relations with Washington were incomparably better than those with Beijing.

Since the end of the Cold War, U.S. military presence in Asia—Washington's alliances with Tokyo, Seoul, and others, or even ballistic missile defense sites in Alaska and California, or U.S.-Japan missile defense cooperation—do not evoke any protests in Moscow. The comparison to Moscow's attitude to NATO enlargement is striking. The explanation: in the Asia-Pacific, the United States—in Russian strategists' view—is needed to balance China. Also, except for Mongolia, there are no countries in the region that Russia considers strategic buffers. Unlike Beijing, Moscow does not particularly worry if, as a result of Korean reunification, the North Korean state disappears: Pyongyang is Beijing's, not Moscow's, buffer.

For any modernization/development of the Far East and Siberia, Americans, Canadians, Australians, and other Pacific nations should be most welcome. Economic, technological, and educational partnerships across the Pacific are a massive resource for a more open and proactive Russian foreign policy. The maritime focus also leads directly to exploring Russia's "last shore," its Arctic coastline.

THE NORTHERN FLANK

Goodwill for cooperation will also be needed to organize international relations in the High North. The Arctic is Russia's fourth geopolitical façade. Russians established their presence in the Arctic a very long time ago. The first border treaty between Norway and Novgorod dates back to 1323, and the border now is roughly where it was then. Archangel used to be Russia's main port for Western European trade through the end of the seventeenth century.

During World War II, Murmansk was the destination for allied polar convoys that delivered war matériel and other supplies to the Soviet Union. During the Cold War, the Arctic was heavily militarized, with Severomorsk—the headquarters of the Soviet Northern Fleet—the home for ballistic missile submarines, and the island of Novaya Zemlya, a nuclear testing ground. The Arctic airspace was regularly patrolled by strategic bombers and, in wartime, U.S. and Soviet ballistic missiles would have flown above it toward their targets in enemy countries.

The Arctic's rise to prominence two decades after the end of the Cold War is the result of several factors: changing climate; rising demand for energy resources; and the quest for new transportation routes—all against the background of an unregulated legal regime of the world's last frontier.

The rapid melting of the Arctic ice has made exploration of undersea resources technologically feasible. The growing demand for energy resources can make this commercially possible. The same climate change that has turned vast swaths of the Arctic, previously icebound, into navigable waters, revives interest in the Northern Sea Route—or Northeast Passage between Europe and Asia—and the Northwest Passage between the Pacific and the Atlantic.

Russia hopes to profit massively from all these changes. It has made a claim, to be formally supported by scientific data, to an exclusive economic zone of some 1.2 million square kilometers. This area is believed to contain most of the natural resources outside of the currently recognized exclusive economic zones. It has reactivated the Northern Sea Route, which passes exclusively in Russian territorial waters or in its economic zone.

The issue of the Arctic caught global attention in 2007 when a Russian undersea capsule placed a small Russian metallic flag on the seabed at the North Pole. A period of commotion and confusion followed, with a few strongly worded statements in a number of capitals and several military exercises.[63] The tensions started to subside when Russia and other members of the Arctic Council agreed in 2008 to decide matters peacefully, through negotiations and in court. To make its own position clear, Russia and Norway agreed in 2010 to a compromise solution of their forty-year dispute over maritime boundaries in the Barents Sea. This was truly a landmark decision, hopefully setting the right course and tone for the future. In 2011, Russia's Rosneft signed a deal with BP to jointly develop the energy resources of the Kara Sea, east of Novaya Zemlya.

Other mitigating factors include the fact that most resources in the area like the Shtokman gas field, Russia's biggest, lie within the currently undisputed exclusive economic zones of the littoral states and that commercial development of those resources is a long way off.

One major unresolved issue is who has a say in how decisions are made concerning the Arctic. Moscow's strong preference is to keep this within a narrow circle of five littoral states—Canada, Denmark, Norway, the United States, and Russia itself. This is a principled stance, which Russia has adopted toward the Caspian. Russians want to see no involvement of the European Union (through EU member Denmark) and certainly no role for NATO (to which all four other countries belong). Russians reject the argument, advanced by the Chinese, among others, that the part of the Arctic currently outside of the littoral states' exclusive economic zone is some kind of a "global commons." The Russians feel they have few comparative advantages and want to exploit those that they possess to the fullest extent.[64] Thus, a clear "no" to internationalization.

CONCLUSION

This brief *tour d'horizon* of Russian geopolitical and security thinking and practice leads to important conclusions.

Russia has abandoned the age-old pattern of territorial growth. A merger with Belarus was not pursued as a priority. Abkhazia and South Ossetia were turned into military buffers, but only in extremis. The only purpose of fanning Crimean separatism was to deter Ukraine from joining NATO. There is a basic recognition of all new neighboring states as geopolitical realities.

Moscow stopped thinking of the former Soviet Union as a unit. Not only is there no policy at the level of the CIS but even within regions— whether the New Eastern Europe, or the South Caucasus, or Central Asia, or indeed the Baltics, Moscow is consciously dealing with individual states, using very different approaches toward each of them.

From the Russian government's perspective, the former Soviet clients in Eastern (now Central) Europe, including the Balkans, are part of the EU and NATO, either already or in some not-so-distant future. Thus, Russia is, for the first time in 300 years, out of Europe politically and strategically, while engaging the Europeans at different levels, in different formats, on a broad range of issues, and with an emphasis on economics.

At the Kremlin, traditional and somewhat ideological imperial thinking has been replaced by a pragmatic great-power mentality. Putin's postimperialism is different from Yeltsin's, but it continues the march away from the empire. Moscow is no longer shy about using its advantages when dealing with the smaller countries, but seeking advantages is not the same thing as seeking annexation.

The Russian leadership has defined its interests in the new regions of Eastern Europe, the Caucasus, and Central Asia. These interests fall short of dominance, but they include respect for Russian security sensitivities—as the Kremlin defines them—and point to Moscow's ambition to play a leading role in economic and cultural fields.

Culturally, only Ukraine and Belarus are considered part of the same "family," and thus not exactly "foreign," while many others—starting with the Central Asians and including the countries of the South Caucasus, such as Christian Georgia and Armenia—fall into the "foreign" category. Moldova and the Baltic states are in the same group.

Russia is awakening to the reality of powerful and dynamic centers rising all around its borders: the EU, China, Turkey, Iran, and India. It can no longer hope to play a major geopolitical role in Europe—which is unified—or in Asia, where the two heavyweights are China and India. It is certainly not eyeing any major role in the Greater Middle East. Focused mainly on itself, and trying to escape being dominated by any other countries, Russia believes that in the globalized world it has enough resources to play an important role of a makeweight, affecting the global balance. Whether these hopes have any foundation depends on how successful Russia's recent modernization bid is. And this, in turn, depends on the dynamics and diversity of the Russian economy.

Yet as a relic of the past, the Russian establishment inherited a fear of an attack from the United States. Insecurity about the ends of U.S. power—especially since American power has grown so much since the end of the Cold War, even as Russia's has markedly declined—is a major problem in terms of Euro-Atlantic security, even though it may not even be recognized as such across the Atlantic. NATO enlargement; ballistic missile defense system deployments; support for Georgia and Ukraine—all are more reflections of that Moscow insecurity vis-à-vis Washington than evidence of some neo-imperialist urge to restore control over the former provinces and satellites. Even in the heyday of the reset, at the close of 2010, Medvedev and Putin said, darkly, that either the United States builds joint missile defenses with Russia, or Russia builds its own system—to protect itself from the United States.[65]

3

ECONOMICS AND ENERGY

The Soviet empire was essentially a politico-military construct. In the immediate post–World War II period, the Soviet Union profited from having the more developed economies of East Germany and Czechoslovakia in the communist bloc. From 1945 on, reparations from Germany took the form of relocating whole enterprises to the USSR. In 1947, Moscow objected to Prague's joining the Marshall Plan, thus keeping Czechoslovakia off-limits to the West.

These advantages, however, were spotty and short-lived. Not all Eastern European countries, which in 1949 formed the Council for Mutual Economic Assistance (COMECON), had advanced economies. But even where they were initially advanced, as in East Germany or Czechoslovakia, they were quickly degraded as a result of command economy practices. COMECON outliers—such as Cuba, Mongolia, Vietnam, and Laos—were huge and often ineffective development projects from the start, consuming millions of dollars of Soviet aid daily.

The "socialist-leaning" countries of the Third World, mostly poor, were essentially recipients of Soviet arms and assistance. There was no question of the Soviet Union's securing special rights to exploit precious natural resources in the few client states that possessed them. Angola's oil and diamonds remained in the hands of U.S. and other Western companies. Algeria's oil and gas were jealously guarded by its government, just as the oil in Libya and Iraq was shielded by the respective governments. The best Moscow could hope for was that Algiers, Tripoli, and Baghdad would pay cash for the Soviet arms that less well-endowed countries, such as Ethiopia or South Yemen, were getting de facto free. In economic terms, the Soviet "overseas empire" was definitely a losing proposition.

Its value, in Moscow's eyes, was its politico-ideological and strategic significance.

When the Soviets, toward the late 1980s, got tired of the Cold War and vowed to end it, they treated the off-loading of their Third World clientele as a peace dividend. The new Russian government proceeded to immediately cut off aid to the countries that were still receiving it—such as Afghanistan and Cuba—thinking little of the economic, sociopolitical, or military implications of their move. There was only a little more regret in seeing the countries of the COMECON sail off.

What killed it was the decision in 1991 to replace the transferable ruble, a fictitious common currency, with the "real" hard currency in intra-COMECON trade. There had been long-standing resentment in Moscow of the practice of exchanging Soviet energy and raw materials supplies—all easily tradable for convertible currency—for shoddy East European products. After that, COMECON was done. And it took a decade for the Russian economic interest in Central Europe to start reemerging.

The historical empire was a different matter. In Moscow, the entire Soviet Union was treated as an economic whole; there was no division between the "metropolitan area" and the "colonies." Even though Uzbekistan, for example, could be seen as a traditional source of raw materials—from natural gas to cotton—for the industrialized regions of the Union, Tashkent, its capital, was a major industrial hub in its own right. The Russian republic, after all, was the principal source of raw materials for the other fourteen republics.

The Soviet economy was highly integrated, on purpose; indeed, political decisions were consistently made to tie enterprises in faraway parts of the country into a single complex. It was guided by the similar idea to send conscripts to serve as far away from home as possible: the Soviet, the national, had to reach above the local. When the Soviet Union itself disintegrated, there was a widespread belief in Moscow that economic unity would survive political divisions and lead to reintegration on a new level, even more advantageous to Russia. The reality turned out to be different. Already in 1993, Russia had to stop using the Soviet ruble and thus dissolved the "ruble zone."

As soon as the Soviet Union was formally dissolved, the Russian Federation acted as its sole heir in terms of the former Union's rights and liabilities. Moscow assumed responsibility for $103 billion of Soviet (mostly short-term) foreign debt and simultaneously claimed $140 billion of Soviet assets abroad. This act relieved all newly formed states of any foreign obligations, which allowed them to start free from preexisting liabilities. It also left them without embassy buildings abroad, a "zero option" as much resented for the latter as unappreciated for the former.

Throughout the 1990s, Russia's economic relations with other CIS countries were plagued by constant penury. This led to barter deals, delays in payment, and inevitable political tensions. Isolated and premature integrationist steps—such as the abolition of customs barriers or the practice of value added tax collection—led to mutual recrimination among the CIS states.

By the mid-1990s, the first post-Soviet shock having subsided, there was some stabilization in the CIS. Russia's successful macroeconomic policy and the strong ruble gave the CIS countries, briefly, an opportunity to export to Russia. The 1998 Russian default, however, sharply reduced Russia's role in CIS regional trade. Early hopes of economic integration were finally buried. Ukraine, whose currency immediately devalued 2.7 times after Russia's, and other new states started to look to the EU as their main economic partner.

In the early 2000s, Russia's energy-powered growth began to draw CIS labor and goods back to Russia. The rise in Russian living standards—Russia's per capita national income in 2008 was 3 times that of Ukraine, 6.5 times that of Moldova's, and 11–16 times that of Uzbekistan, Kyrgyzstan, or Tajikistan[1]—made it more attractive. However, the gas shock of 2006, with Gazprom raising prices for its deliveries to CIS neighbors to "international levels" essentially struck a coup de grâce to the *former* Soviet Union. Freed from Russian subsidies, CIS countries were at last politically free from the former metropolitan power. But now they had to pay the full price for gas.

Two decades on, integration is still going slowly among the former republics. Russia is clearly dominant in the CIS, accounting for 72 percent of the gross regional product. However, Russia's economic role in the CIS is essentially reduced to energy and raw materials supplies and a relatively open market for its neighbors' goods and labor. In principle, Russia should be interested in political stability and economic growth in the CIS. That would certainly be good for its own development, and good for capital expansion.

In the short term, however, Russia draws benefits from its neighbors being less developed, and from the unresolved conflicts. It realizes that the opacity of post-Soviet practices gives Russian companies certain competitive advantages over Western competitors that they can lose if there is more transparency and a more level playing field. For political reasons, Russia was quick to ignore Georgia's post-2003 growth and Ukraine's successes during the "Orange era."

RUSSIAN ECONOMIC INTERESTS IN THE CIS

Even though Russia is focused on EU members as its biggest trading partners, and on China, it still has important interests in the CIS. At some metaphysical level, Moscow sees the post-Soviet Commonwealth as a necessary pedestal for its great-power status, but in practice the emphasis is strongly on economics. Considering large economic regions—such as the EU, NAFTA, ASEAN, South America's MERCOSUR, and the emerging community in East Asia as the principal units of the global economy—Russian leaders hope to lead such a bloc in the CIS. They want to dominate the economic space between the European Union and East Asia.

More specifically, Russians are interested in getting access to the mineral resources of the former borderlands. Even though non-Russian CIS countries account for a puny 1.3 percent of the global GDP (in terms of purchasing power parity), Kazakhstan and Azerbaijan produced about 5 percent of the world oil output in 2008, and Turkmenistan produced 6 percent of the global natural gas output. Insisting on channeling these exports through Russian territory, Moscow seeks to reduce competition from the Caspian producers and enhance its own position as a "guarantor of global energy security."[2] Russia seeks assets in strategic industries, such as defense, nuclear, and aerospace. Between the two of them, Kazakhstan and Uzbekistan account for 25 percent of the world's uranium production.

These interests, in essence, were also the rationale for a "liberal empire," the idea put forth in September 2003 by Anatoly Chubais, the architect of Russia's privatization.[3] Chubais called on the Russian energy companies, from oil and gas to nuclear to electricity, to use their comparative advantages to turn the new countries into their area of domination. Russia could also use its transportation companies and networks to turn the ex-Soviet space into an "empire of a new type."

Except for the word "empire," most of Chubais's ideas made sense. Stretching things a little bit, one could also talk about Gazprom's empire, or that of UES, the electricity company Chubais headed at the time. UES, for example, owned electricity companies in Georgia and Moldova.

However, organizing Russian companies' diverse interests under the overarching concept of an empire—directed from Moscow and closely tied to, if not led by, the Russian government—was a sure project-killer. Chubais, himself much more of a liberal than an imperialist, sought to marry liberal capitalism and imperial tradition in Russia. He wound up placating no one at home and putting quite a few people abroad on alert: Russian business began to look like an arm of the Kremlin.

In the end, this may not have mattered much. Within weeks of the publication of the liberal imperial manifesto, Mikhail Khodorkovsky was arrested; within a year, his company Yukos was disbanded and nationalized, and big Russian business, from oil to gas to metals, came under direct or indirect control of the Kremlin. Liberal empire was dead before it was born, and illiberal empire stood no chance. Apart from outside expansion in the former borderlands, Russian business wants to attract some resources from the new countries for the benefit of the Russian national economy. Thus, suffering from an acute and worsening labor shortage, Russia wants to tap into the CIS countries' burgeoning labor surplus. Alongside qualified and unqualified workers, Russia would like to attract intellectuals and technical specialists from the former republics, to partially compensate for the brain drain to the West. Other interests besides immigration include trade, investment, and integration.

TRADE

Russia and the other CIS states account for a tiny portion of world trade: 3.5 percent in goods and 2.5 percent in services. More than half of their total trade turnover is with EU countries, 20 percent is within the CIS, and about 10 percent is with Asia. When the Soviet Union collapsed, there was a hope that close economic relations would keep the common economic space together. That hope evaporated within a couple of years. Trade patterns diversified at an astounding speed, and old links—created within the command economy, which elevated autarky to a high principle—often made no sense in the market environment. Intra-CIS trade plummeted immediately.

Over the past two decades, Russia's trading links with the CIS countries have dramatically weakened. The collapse of manufacturing everywhere and the domination of extractive industries in a number of countries left very little complementarity and enhanced competition in raw materials exports. Trade patterns in the former Soviet space have greatly diversified. The 20 percent of intra-CIS trade compares weakly to 40 percent of intra-bloc trade among NAFTA members, and about 65 percent within the European Union.[4]

Russia's share of trade with CIS countries has decreased from 24 percent in 1994 to less than 15 percent in 2009. This compares with 52 percent for the EU. Only three countries—Belarus, Ukraine, and Kazakhstan—are among Russia's top fifteen trading partners. (In 2009, Belarus was fifth; Ukraine, sixth; and Kazakhstan, thirteenth.)[5] EU countries, led by Germany, and China top the list.

Yet CIS countries now absorb a greater share of Russia's non-mineral exports (25 percent versus 15 percent): 55 percent of Russian manufactured exports head for CIS countries. The Russian market, in turn, absorbs 60 percent of machinery and 50 percent of consumer goods produced in the CIS countries.[6]

The CIS countries' exports to Russia dropped from 42 percent in 1995 to 15 percent in 2008, although their imports—due to the high share of energy—decreased from 48 percent to 32.5 percent.[8] No longer dominant, Russia is a major trading partner across the CIS. It is the most important export market for Armenia, Belarus, Kyrgyzstan, Turkmenistan, and Ukraine, and the most important source of imports everywhere, except Moldova and Georgia, which has withdrawn from the CIS. In particular, agricultural produce and machines and equipment from CIS countries vitally depend on the Russian market.

Medium- and long-term projections suggest that trading links between Russia and its CIS partners are likely to continue to weaken.[9] Russian and CIS manufactured goods remain woefully noncompetitive in each other's markets, their quality products are not in sight anywhere, transport tariffs are high, corruption rife, and protectionism rampant.

TABLE 3.1

RUSSIA'S TRADE WITH CIS COUNTRIES, 2009[7] (percent)	
Belarus	34.2
Ukraine	33.4
Kazakhstan	18.7
Uzbekistan	3.7
Azerbaijan	2.6
Kyrgyzstan	1.9
Moldova	1.5
Turkmenistan	1.5
Armenia	1.1
Tajikistan	1.1
Georgia	0.3
TOTAL	100, or $68.5 billion

In principle, bilateral trade among CIS states is governed by free trade agreements concluded in the 1990s. These agreements, however, are famous for their exemptions, which are reviewed on an annual basis. Conflicts are frequent, especially between Russia and Ukraine, which seek to protect their domestic markets from their neighbor. Trade wars are also frequent between Russia and Belarus. In addition, tariffs in CIS countries, which are relatively low compared with Russia's, devalue the effect of free trade for Russian exporters who have to compete hard on CIS countries' markets. There are noneconomic obstacles, too.

Notoriously, Russia, being outside of the World Trade Organization, has used trade for political purposes. Leonid Kuchma, as Ukraine's prime minister, remarked in 1992 that "anti-Russian political actions, as a rule, led to anti-Ukrainian economic consequences."[10] In the 1990s, imports from the Baltic states were singled out for boycotts to put pressure on Estonia and Latvia to improve their naturalization practices. To put pressure on Moldova after the failure of the Russian-brokered conflict settlement deal and Chisinau's embrace of the West, Moscow in 2004 imposed sanctions on Moldovan wine and agricultural produce. The sanctions are still partially in effect to this day.

It was Georgia, however, whose economy bore the brunt of Russian anger. From 2006, Russia stopped importing Georgian wines and mineral water, cut air travel, and severed postal links, making it impossible for Georgian workers in Russia to transfer money back home. (The workers soon found an indirect route, via Ukraine.) Moscow also ordered police raids against Georgian illegal immigrants, deporting some of them. The Russian sanitary control authority has become notorious for raising barriers to trade with selected countries, thus making itself a mere tool in the hands of the Kremlin.

In general, beyond the big three of Belarus, Ukraine, and Kazakhstan, Russia's trade with the new states is of marginal importance to it. Russia's hugely positive trade balance comes from selling energy resources to developed and emerging countries. Some of these proceeds are used for investment. How does the CIS area look from that angle?

INVESTMENT

Russian investments in CIS countries, generally speaking, are small. They stood at $1.5 billion in 2001, before the great oil price boom, and reached almost $13 billion by the end of it, in 2009. These figures represent a puny 6 percent and 8 percent, respectively, of Russia's investment abroad.[11] Energy-rich neighbors see almost none of Russia's investors. In Azerbaijan, two-thirds of foreign investments come from the United States and the UK; about a fourth, from Japan, Turkey, and Norway. Russia is ninth.[12] In Kazakhstan, Russia, with its 1.6 percent of that country's foreign direct investment (FDI), does not make it onto the list of the top ten investors. In Ukraine, Russia is sixth, with just 5.6 percent of FDI. Seen from the opposite angle, CIS countries have invested only $880 million in Russia, 0.4 percent of all FDI in Russia.[13]

Russian investors usually complain about protectionist policies of other CIS states, their authorities' reluctance to give up valuable assets, and the ubiquitous rent-seeking practices. Ukraine, under Prime Minister Tymoshenko's leadership, took steps to roll back Russian ownership in favor of domestic interests. However, the government formed by the Party of Regions, for all its Moscow-friendly rhetoric, views Russian business as a competitor.

Western and other non-Russian investors are often deemed safer than the Russian ones, and politically more apropos. Liberalization of the CIS business climate and the introduction of elements of the rule of law in some countries favor Western and Asian companies and deny the Russians their former advantage.

Since the denouement of the Yukos affair in the mid-2000s, phobias have arisen regarding Russian economic activities abroad. Baltic states and even some CIS countries, such as Ukraine, fear not only the proverbial aggressiveness of Russian companies, but, even more so, the Kremlin, which stands behind them or at least can be imagined behind them. Thus, Russian businesses have to pay for their association with the Russian government, real or imagined.

Still, Russian investors have a key role to play in a number of areas and geographical regions across the CIS. "If money, mainly Russian money,[14] does not arrive in the Crimea, it will remain underdeveloped," admits Leonid Kuchma. The arrival or non-arrival of Russian money can also make the difference between the continued existence and quiet demise of whole branches of industry, such as aircraft manufacturing, nuclear power, and shipbuilding in Ukraine. Even absent political obstacles after 2010, there is no clear answer to the question.

Similarly to investments, Russian financial assistance to the CIS countries has not played a significant role, except for the large amounts of energy-related debt accumulated by Ukraine and Moldova. For geopolitical and strategic reasons, Russia has given financial support to Belarus and Armenia. However, Russian financial assistance to fellow CIS countries was largely ineffective because of the lack of reform conditionality. Russian state credits helped maintain macroeconomic stability, deal with emergencies, or launch individual major projects. Money was given, accepted, and often misused, contributing little to the modernization of the recipient countries' economies.

It was fashionable, on the eve of the economic crisis, to speculate about Russia's chances to become a global financial center and of the ruble as a world reserve currency, dominant in the vast space between the eurozone and the sovereign territory of China's RMB. President Medvedev, then newly inaugurated, led the chorus. These dreams were dispelled within a few months, alongside the notion of Russia as a safe haven in a time of global economic woes.

Ordinary Russians, unaware of most of this rhetoric, trusted traditional convertible currencies more. In late 2008 and early 2009, the Russian government devalued the ruble by 40 percent against the basket of currencies. In Kazakhstan, the dollar and the euro were twice as popular as the Russian ruble.[15] The pattern held across the CIS. After the crisis, the idea of an international financial center in Moscow did not die, but it was scaled down in 2010 to focus on the countries of the Customs Union, which is to say, Belarus and Kazakhstan.[16]

The economic crisis has revealed disparity between Russia's financial resources and those of the international financial institutions, and even some countries. By late 2009, the total value of International Monetary Fund anticrisis packages for countries in the former Soviet Union reached $23 billion, including $16.5 billion for Ukraine, $3.5 billion for Belarus, $1.2 billion for Georgia, $800 million for Armenia, and $600 million for Moldova.

At the same time, Russia, for its part, announced aid packages worth $5 billion: $2 billion each for Belarus and Kyrgyzstan and $500 million each for Armenia and Moldova.[17] China allocated $1 billion to faraway and seemingly unimportant Moldova, twice the amount promised by Russia. Moscow, however, went beyond the CIS and offered $300 million in credits to Mongolia.

MIGRATION

Russia's biggest assistance to its neighbors lies in the capacity of its labor market to accept large numbers of guest workers. In 2008, the Russian Migration Service counted 1.8 million legal workers from CIS countries. Even though that number had grown sharply over the previous eight years, from a mere 106,000 workers in 2000, the true number of migrants is variously estimated to lie between 10 million and 20 million.

Remittances from people working in Russia are a major source of income for many CIS countries. According to the World Bank, in 2008 they accounted for half of the GDP of Tajikistan, almost a third of Moldova's, over a quarter of Kyrgyzstan's, and under 10 percent of Armenia's. The Russian Central Bank put gross payments to migrants from 2000 through the first half of 2009 at $68 billion, or $8 billion per annum, on average. On the other side of the ledger, the migrants' contribution to the Russian economy, however, is estimated to be 3–5 percent of the GDP, or about $37.5 billion–$62.5 billion per annum (2007 figures).

Since the reform of migration legislation in 2007, Russia has been establishing quotas on labor migrants, seeking to stem and control the process. Immigration—especially when it's illegal and the migrants are from culturally distant societies—has become a political issue in Russia, fanning nationalism and xenophobia. However, the vast majority of migrant workers in Russia continue to work there illegally. Their integration, or lack of it, will be discussed in chapter 4. In this chapter, integration will be analyzed in terms of international economic interaction.

INTEGRATION

Unlike the countries of Central and Eastern Europe and the Baltic states, the CIS area as a whole has not followed the transition paradigm. This is usually taken to be a pretty straightforward passage from communism to EU-style liberal democracy and social market economy, embedded for good measure within a NATO framework. The evolution in all CIS states is away from communism, and, broadly, toward capitalism. But it got stuck at the point where the early winners can capitalize most on the position they have secured, and let no other groups, or society at large, share in their profits.

At the level of government rhetoric, Russia has consistently favored integration among all CIS states. In reality, it soon discovered that it had more leverage with the new states in one-on-one relationships. Thus, post-Soviet integration was reinterpreted as their integration with Russia, on an *à la carte* basis.

After it had become clear that some countries, such as Ukraine, would strongly resist anything that hinted at subordination to Russia, Moscow opted for scaled-down versions of integration, involving one, two, or five of its CIS partners, hoping that the "nucleus" this formed could later expand to include the outliers. Russia-led integration revealed itself as a predominantly political project, serving, above all, the interests of Russia as a great power. Politically, that was a nonstarter for most countries whose elites prioritized consolidating their recently won independence from Russia.

From an economic angle, CIS countries lack the central requirement for economic integration: a high level of manufacturing and concomitant diversification of export and import operations.[18] Russia's trade with them, as we have seen, is overwhelmingly in commodities. Russia, which was a leader in economic reform in the early 1990s, has lost that advantage and with it its attractiveness to the new states. The WTO accession process, which Russia began in 1993, is still incomplete.

Meanwhile, besides the three Baltic republics, four post-Soviet states—Georgia, Kyrgyzstan, Moldova, and Ukraine—have joined the world trade body. Also, while some CIS countries—such as Azerbaijan, Kazakhstan, Russia, and Turkmenistan are energy producers, most others are consumers, leading to conflicting interests. The fact that the consumers, like Ukraine and Belarus, were also transit countries exacerbated the situation.

Just before the 2008 crisis struck, Russia and its key economic partners, Kazakhstan and Belarus, had reached their pre-1990s levels of GDP. With economic rehabilitation achieved, cooperation became more feasible. The Russian government talked about adopting—and adapting—the integration paradigm of the European Union.

In the EU practice, there have been three stages of economic integration: A free trade area led to a customs union, which helped create a single economic space, eventually topped by an economic and currency union. Two decades after the breakup of the USSR, there was a free trade area of the CIS—mostly on paper; a Customs Union of Belarus, Kazakhstan, and Russia; a Eurasian Economic Community (EurAsEC); and a Russo-Belarusian union state.

A CIS-wide agreement on a Free Trade Area, signed in 1994, was never implemented, and trade has been regulated on a bilateral basis. It was not until a decade later that Moscow reenergized the process, and a full-fledged treaty on free trade among eight countries—Armenia, Belarus, Kazakhstan, Kyrgyzstan, Moldova, Russia, Tajikistan, and Ukraine—is expected in 2011.

This is the broadest group of countries to take part in common economic projects in the post-imperial space. Other groups are smaller. The six-member EurAsEC, an essentially political project launched in 2000, saw its mission as creating an area for the free movement of goods and capital; a common transportation system; and a common energy market, all of which would lead to a common currency. It even created a Eurasian Development Bank with capital of $1.5 billion, two-thirds of which was provided by Russia, and an Anti-Crisis Fund with $10 billion, three-quarters of which again came from Russia. These instruments, however, largely remain on paper. In reality, EurAsEC serves as a political platform for economic integration.

One project that failed but may be revived is a Single Economic Space. When Russia in 2003 first promoted the idea, it was done with the express purpose of drawing Ukraine into a common integration project with Russia and its close partners, Kazakhstan and Belarus. This was abandoned in 2005 after the Orange Revolution, and a new, softer attempt failed in 2010 after Yanukovych's presidential victory. Clearly, no matter what leadership is in power, Kiev is not interested in economic integration with Russia. This attitude, however, does not apply to several other countries, which may indeed form a single economic space without Ukraine.

This smaller group has been formed around a Customs Union of Russia, Kazakhstan, and Belarus, which came into being in 2010. This was actually its second coming: A treaty on such a union involving also Kyrgyzstan and Tajikistan had been launched in 1999 and was embedded within EurAsEC a year later. That original treaty, however, was a dead letter; a common customs zone between Russia and Belarus, created in 1995, was equally underperforming.[19] Now, the idea is to use the Customs Union to create the foundation for a future common market of some 170 million people.

The creation of the Customs Union was linked to a sudden and abrupt reversal in mid-2009 of Moscow's stance on WTO accession. The announcement of the union was accompanied by another bout of economic conflict between Moscow and Minsk—hardly an auspicious start. Russia was unhappy that the Customs Union would turn it into a "junior partner" of Belarus and Kazakhstan, which seek to take full advantage of their transit situation.[20] Ironically, among the Customs Union members, Russia's customs procedures are the most cumbersome. What takes two hours at a Belarusian customs post takes ten working days—which may mean, in practice, a month—at the Russian one.[21]

Russia first applied for membership in the World Trade Organization in 1993. President Putin initially was enthusiastic about joining. There were repeated promises—from both the United States and the European Union—

of an imminent admission. Yet Putin failed to achieve his goal during his eight-year presidency. This led to an agonizing rethinking and course correction. The global financial and economic crisis created a new situation and pressure in favor of protectionism. Sergei Glazyev and some other economists considered economic integration with Russia's neighbors as salvation.

The Russo-Belarusian union state emerged as a purely political, even personal, project. Toward the end of Boris Yeltsin's presidency, Alexandr Lukashenka sought to succeed him. When this failed, Lukashenka made use of the union state to receive economic benefits and concessions from Moscow, amounting to some 60 percent of Belarusian GDP,[22] which he successfully traded for anti-NATO rhetoric. Putin eventually trimmed, but did not terminate, the special preferences to Belarus, which basically put the "union state" on hold. By the start of the Medvedev presidency, the "union" was more dead than alive. It will be officially superseded by the Customs Union.

So far, post-Soviet integration has been marked by optimistic pronouncements and little action. Government bureaucracies are fully, if often inefficiently, involved; businesses are largely ignored or staying aloof. The Russian government has been doing very little to make the CIS safe for Russian business interests.

Another salient feature is the continuing center-periphery pattern of economic relations within the CIS. For example, while Belarus and Kazakhstan are important trading partners for Russia, and vice versa, imports from Belarus account for only 1 percent of Kazakhstan's import trade.[23] At the popular level, there is equally strong support in Kazakhstan for integration with Russia and the European Union.[24]

Russia's economic weakness enhanced centrifugal trends in the CIS. The crisis became a moment of truth for the CIS.[25] One major reason for the failure of so many Russian-led attempts at economic integration within the CIS is Moscow's unwillingness to pay for such integration. Russian policy makers, almost invariably, look at the CIS as their own economic resource. Through integration, they seek to add to Russia's GDP. They reject the notion that unless Russia pays for post-Soviet economic integration, unless it offers serious concessions to its would-be partners, there will be no integration. Moscow, however, is now in an acquisition mood, not a spending mood. In 2003, it proclaimed a policy of market pragmatism vis-à-vis the new independent states.

This is a reaction to the role of a donor, which Russia played within the Soviet Union. In Soviet times, the Russian republic exported energy and raw materials to the borderland republics and received consumer goods and agricultural products from them. Compared with world prices, the energy category was underpriced, while the consumer goods category was overpriced. These indirect Russian subsidies amounted in 1989 to an equivalent of \$41 billion yearly.[26] The desire to end this situation was behind the decision by the Russian republic Supreme Soviet to proclaim Russia's "sovereignty" within the Soviet Union in June 1990. This set in motion the "sovereignty parade" that led to the breakup of the USSR within eighteen months.

Little thought is given in Russia to correlation among the various integrationist projects. It is not clear how the union state of Russia and Belarus relates to the Customs Union—which also includes Kazakhstan—and how the Customs Union in turn relates to EurAsEC, which adds Armenia, Kyrgyzstan, and Tajikistan. When Russia signed in 2005 a "road map" of common action with the EU, the goal of a common economic space of Russia and the EU bore no mention of Russia's integration partners, in particular Belarus, which lies between Russia and the European Union.

When Moscow tries to factor its CIS interests into its global position, things do not necessarily become easier. A lot of confusion was produced in mid-2009 by Prime Minister Putin's surprise announcement that Russia—after sixteen years of still-incomplete negotiations to join the WTO—would seek membership in the world body as part of the Customs Union troika. There had been no precedent for WTO accession by a group of countries, and Kazakhstan and particularly Belarus were far behind Russia in their talks with the WTO. At the time, it was interpreted as Moscow's conviction that the crisis put a premium on regional, rather than global, groupings, and that building a Russia-led economic bloc in the CIS was more important to Moscow than gaining membership in a world body. Russian decision makers saw the WTO accession as an agreement on the terms of trade, rather than a vehicle for economic modernization.

Regardless of whether integration processes in the CIS area are productive, Moscow seeks to lead and control them. Russia has been very suspicious of the attempt by several new states to create their own organization without Russia. Georgia, Ukraine, Azerbaijan, and Moldova (and, between 1999 and 2002, also Uzbekistan) formed an Organization for Democracy and Economic Development, better known as GUAM (also referred to as GUUAM during Uzbekistan's membership). Even though GUAM has been utterly ineffective, with its only real project being a transit corridor for Caspian hydrocarbons to Europe,[27] Moscow was suspicious of this "anti-Russian tool in the hands of U.S. promoters of geopolitical pluralism in the CIS."

ENERGY

The Soviet Union was a major energy producer of oil and gas. Toward the end of its existence, the Soviet economy depended so much on the proceeds from energy exports that a sharp drop in the oil price in 1986 pushed it to the brink of a financial abyss. However, when the USSR broke up, oil production plummeted. In 1999, it was only half of the 1987 peak of 11.5 million barrels per day.

When the Soviet Union disintegrated, some of its energy-rich regions became independent states. Gazprom alone lost a third of its Soviet-era pipelines, a third of its gas deposits, and a quarter of its compressor stations.[28] Relying on their natural wealth, Azerbaijan, Kazakhstan, Uzbekistan, and Turkmenistan immediately started to pursue outwardly independent policies on the world stage.

Already in 1994, Azerbaijan signed a "contract of the century" with Western oil companies and has received much investment and favorable attention from both the United States and Europe. With the launch of the U.S.-supported Baku-Tbilisi-Ceyhan (BTC) oil pipeline, in 2006, it broke the Russian transport monopoly from the Caspian. With the production from the Shah Deniz gas field, it stopped buying gas from Russia and started selling its own, to Georgia and Turkey, via BTE, the Baku-Tbilisi-Erzurum gas pipeline.

Similarly, Kazakhstan—with its giant oil fields of Tengiz, Kashagan, and Karachaganak—has attracted major Western energy interests and won a measure of respect from the Western governments. Putting its "multi-vector" policy into practice, it exports part of its oil via BTC, which irritates Russia; another part via the Caspian Pipeline Consortium (CPC), where Russia is present; and yet another part to China. Uzbekistan has followed a tortuous international road, being in and out of GUAM, EurAsEC, and the CSTO. Turkmenistan, starting with the maverick Turkmenbashi, opted for semi-isolation, self-styled UN-registered neutrality, and a legally nonexistent "observer" status in the CIS. It, too, has vowed to export its gas in all directions.

Energy is hugely important to Russia's post-Soviet economy. Never before have oil and gas been so critical than at the close of the twentieth century and the beginning of the twenty-first. In 2000, energy production accounted for 25 percent of Russia's GDP, and it was still 15 percent before the crisis.[29] After the crisis, the process of reduction of energy dependency has reversed. However, since a surge in 2002–2004, energy production has stagnated. With domestic consumption rising, and the domestic prices eventually aligning with those prevailing in the world market, Russian exports will increase only insignificantly.

It needs to be borne in mind that gas supply and transit agreements among CIS countries are essentially agreements between the respective governments. Gazprom stands for Russia; Naftogaz, for Ukraine. During the 1990s, Russia continued to be a de facto donor for CIS countries, above all Ukraine and Belarus. Moscow continued to sell them oil and gas at subsidized prices. However, the subsidies were accompanied by low transit tariffs and non-transparent schemes for profit-sharing. Gazprom's deals with Ukraine were especially opaque.[30] Ukraine did not pay, but Gazprom (and Itera) acquiesced. Putin himself referred to "swindling" dominating in the gas sales sphere between 1991 and 2006.[31] Very important also, energy prices throughout the 1990s were relatively low, and they slumped in 1997–1999. Even in those days, however, Russia sought—unsuccessfully—to convert Ukrainian gas debts into strategic assets in Ukraine.[32]

The situation changed in the early 2000s, as oil prices started a long surge. The indirect subsidies shot up. Between 2000 and the first half of 2009, Belarus and Ukraine received a de facto discount for oil and gas amounting to $52 billion.[33] Both countries used this situation as a comparative advantage in setting up export-oriented enterprises, whether metallurgy or petrochemicals.

Within Russia, the new situation resulted in a steep rise of power and influence of the private oil companies—above all, Yukos, and its confrontation with the Kremlin. The defeat and subsequent dismantlement of Yukos opened the era of resource nationalism, with energy becoming the preferred tool of the Russian state. Russia's power as a top energy producer was likened to the power of nuclear weapons in its impact on Moscow's foreign partners. Unlike nuclear weapons, however, nuclear energy was deemed usable. It was also definitely profitable—for those who controlled the state.

UKRAINIAN GAS CRISES OF 2006 AND 2009

In Ukraine's open economy, for a long time, market prices on oil existed alongside politically or administratively regulated prices on domestic coal and nuclear energy, and on Russian gas. One of the world's most energy-intensive economies, Ukraine has long been used to cheap Turkmen and Russian gas for its industry. (Ukraine's population received domestically produced gas.) Ukraine has developed the same habits of profligacy in energy consumption as Russia. In a situation where Gazprom paid Ukraine for transit in kind (15 percent of export-bound gas), the Russians feared that Ukraine would simply resell the gas at a huge profit.

In 2005, Russia decided to start phasing out the subsidies. The timing suggested that the decision was a reaction to Ukraine's Orange Revolution and the new government's refusal to pursue the Single Economic Space project. Evidently, the color revolutions in Georgia, Kyrgyzstan, and especially Ukraine itself played a major role, but only as a final argument that subsidies be withdrawn. Apart from any political calculations, Gazprom needed money for acquisitions; its owners were interested in raising the company's capitalization, for which they needed a liberalized shares market and the right price for the company's principal product. The Ukrainian gas crisis of January 2006 was a result of several factors: Gazprom's abrupt change of policy and its unwillingness to compromise on Ukraine's need to adapt to a new regime; Ukraine's extreme penury and lack of policy cohesion; and a sharp increase in the price of gas in the EU, among others.

Ironically, the first shot in what became the gas crisis was fired by President Yushchenko, who suggested in April 2005 that barter agreements with Gazprom be replaced by a money relationship. This played directly into Gazprom's hands. Most realistically, Prime Minister Tymoshenko at the same time was trying to find alternative sources of energy in Turkmenistan, Libya, and elsewhere. As Ukrainian negotiators were talking their way into an impasse, Putin—who became de facto the principal negotiator on the Russian side—was subjecting them to ever harder pressure, starting from $100 (doubling the 2005 price) and finally quoting the same price for gas ($230) that Germany was paying.

Faced with the Kremlin's ultimatum, the Ukrainians did not really know what to do. They did not have the money: Indeed, even when prices had been much lower, they accumulated enormous debts. They refused Putin's offer of credit as a trap. What they could do was to appeal to the West: The Orange Revolution is in danger! This was a conflict between the corporate interests of Gazprom and the rent-oriented leadership in Kiev.[34]

Led by commercial interests, Gazprom did not heed enough the political side of its dispute with Ukraine. One can certainly be cynical and naïve at the same time. The Kremlin believed that—by cutting off supplies to Ukraine, in the absence of a new gas contract, but continuing to pump gas across Ukraine to the EU—they would isolate Ukraine. Moreover, if the Ukrainians would start siphoning off gas for their domestic needs, they would bring upon themselves the wrath of the Europeans. In the end, Russia and the EU would have Ukraine in their pincers!

Things turned out completely differently. Instead of ganging up with the Russians on Ukraine, the Europeans sided with the Western-leaning, seemingly democratic Ukrainian government against authoritarian and neo-imperialist Russia. Moscow had utterly failed to win the EU over to its side before issuing the ultimatum to Kiev. By contrast, Kiev managed to extract the maximum from its new democratic credentials and its underdog position. Gazprom's strong-arm tactics had evoked all the old phobias among the European publics, and it was Russia, not Ukraine, that was made responsible for the crisis.

Under the 2006 agreement, Gazprom received better terms of transit—cash payments instead of barter—which allowed it to increase its exports to the EU. However, this was only a marginal increase in the proceeds from Ukraine itself, which opted for cheaper Central Asian gas over the more expensive Russian gas. Altogether Gazprom received an extra $2 billion.

The political ramifications from the gas dispute were many. True, as a result of the 2006 parliamentary elections, Yanukovych replaced Tymoshenko as prime minister, which the Kremlin saw as its big victory. The underside, however, was considerable. The EU was jolted into thinking about energy security, energy strategy, and diversification of energy supplies.

Russia, which heretofore had been regarded as an absolutely reliable supplier, lost that status. Few cared now that Russia continued to pump gas to Europe in 1991, even as the Soviet Union was disintegrating. Few appreciated the fact that Russia had been subsidizing Ukraine for a decade and a half after that. Russia, a major source of energy for Europe, was transformed—almost overnight—into the greatest threat to Europe's energy security. The latter was now defined as security from Russia! When U.S. Senator Richard Lugar called for an "energy NATO" on the margins of the Alliance's summit in Riga in November 2006, the idea found many followers.

The Central Asians, wooed by the United States, the EU, and Ukraine—all in the name of diversifying energy deliveries—now received better deals from Gazprom, which bought their gas for Russian domestic needs, and also for re-export to Ukraine. Essentially, Turkmenistan and Kazakhstan became Ukraine's suppliers, with Russia acting as a transit country.

In principle, Ukraine won a large measure of independence from Russia. As the more sophisticated people in Kiev opined, independence truly starts when others stop paying for you. Profiting from this new situation, however, required taking conscious steps toward reducing the inefficiency of energy use and going ahead with serious industry restructuring. This was not in the cards while the Orange coalition remained in power.

The crisis of 2009 was, in many ways, a very different story. All the usual public posturing on TV screens notwithstanding, Prime Ministers Putin and Tymoshenko had basically agreed, in their private meetings, on the new price for gas for Ukraine. The solution to the dispute, on the eve of the usual New Year's deadline, was to have bolstered the chances of Tymoshenko in the Ukrainian presidential race. However, President Yushchenko, Tymoshenko's rival, scuttled the agreement by withdrawing the Ukrainian delegation from Moscow even as Tymoshenko was about to take off to fly there.

It turned out that Putin, overconfident, did not have a Plan B. When Yushchenko, who saw the new crisis with Russia as a boon for himself, refused to make any concessions to Moscow, Putin and Gazprom lost their nerve. They stopped supplies to Ukraine, but the Ukrainians started using the gas transiting Ukraine from Russia en route to the EU countries. Against better judgment, Moscow cut off the flow of gas to Europe across Ukraine. This produced the worst crisis in Russian-EU energy relations. The Europeans did not spare Ukraine again—as they did in 2006 so soon after the Orange Revolution—but they were angry with the Russians. In the middle of the winter, several European countries—mainly in Southeastern Europe, totally dependent on Russian gas—physically suffered. The reputation of Russia and Gazprom as reliable suppliers was in tatters. The losses incurred by the Russian gas monopoly as a result of the crisis amounted to no less than $1.5 billion. Ukraine, however, was not the only problem transit country for Russian energy exports to Europe.

BELARUSIAN CRISES OF 2007 AND 2010

Gazprom decided in 1994 to build a gas pipeline from the Yamal Peninsula to Europe across Belarus, and construction began in 1996. By that time, Ukraine's gas debt to Russia had reached $900 million. Ironically, at the same time, Gazprom forgave Minsk $700 million of its debt.[35] Belarus's standing in Moscow was better than Ukraine's, and the Belarusian transit pipeline was seen as a way to diversify Russian exports to Europe away from Ukraine.

Soon, however, Russia contributed to the Belarusian economy on a scale unimaginable in Ukraine. Estimates suggest that as much as 20 percent of the Belarusian income came in the form of Russian gas subsidies. Add cheap oil to the gas, and the figure was even more impressive. In return, Gazprom sought ownership of the gas transportation company Beltransgaz. Lukashenka, however, balked at ceding his crown jewel, and this angered Gazprom and, eventually, the Kremlin.

Lukashenka, as the Belarusian economist and opposition politician Yaroslav Romanchuk has observed, was "playing on the Russian politicians' imperial inferiority complex, and was able to get away with unprecedented benefits and super-favorable contracts, while not giving in return a single drop of Belarusian sovereignty, land or assets."[36] Gas prices in Belarus were 1.5 to 3 times lower than elsewhere in Europe.

Moscow also supplied Belarus with three times as much cheap oil as it could consume, so that Minsk could sell the balance on the market and pocket the difference. However, in 2007 Gazprom made Minsk agree on a gradual transition to market prices, and from 2010 it cut Minsk's cheap oil quota down to its actual needs. This still amounted to a subsidy worth some $2 billion. In the next move, Russia will probably demand a Belarusian refinery in exchange for its largesse.

Belarus was cut off by Gazprom in 1997 and again in 2007, and—like Ukraine—also in a price dispute, but it received little attention in Europe outside Poland, which was immediately affected, due to the lack of sympathy in the West for the Belarusian regime and its leader. Moscow's decision to withdraw subsidies from Minsk, however, was serious evidence supporting the basically commercial reasoning behind the ending of Russia's de facto subsidies to CIS countries. At times, Gazprom would decrease pressure in the gas pipeline to make sure that Belarus received only as much gas as it was paying for.

From 2008, Gazprom has linked gas prices for Belarus to the oil price. It also threatened to take Minsk to court when it failed to pay.[37] The difference was in the process. Abrupt termination of subsidies for Ukraine contrasted with their painstaking phase-out for Belarus. Gazprom, however, was hoping to get the assets in Belarus (Beltransgaz) that were denied it in Ukraine.

GAZPROM AND THE REST OF THE CIS

After Ukraine had switched to Turkmen gas and adjusted its transit fees, Russian subsidies to it became a thing of the past. Russia, however, still remains a donor country vis-à-vis Belarus. Russia also used to subsidize Moldova and Armenia. In a quid pro quo, Moldova conceded to Gazprom gas distribution networks and its section of the main export gas pipeline, and Armenia allowed Gazprom into its gas distribution network. A peculiarity of the Moldovan situation is the large debt—more than $2 billion and growing—accumulated by Transnistria. In conformity with Chisinau's claims to full sovereignty within the 1991 borders, this huge debt is attributed to Moldova's obligations toward Gazprom.

As energy prices within the CIS increasingly align with those on the world market—which are going down as well as up—and diversification of sources of energy proceeds, Russia's leverage in the energy field will continue to wane. While Ukraine has minimized its gas purchases from Russia, it still pumps large quantities of Russian oil and gas across its territory.

Russia has been often accused of using energy as a weapon. Besides the Ukrainian and Belarusian cases described above, there is a record of explosions in the pipelines that can be interpreted as politically motivated. In January 2006, as Gazprom was engaged in a conflict with Ukraine's Naftogaz, pipelines leading to Georgia were blown up in the North Caucasus. With Moscow's relations with Tbilisi strained since the summer of 2004, this incident was perceived in Georgia as a pressure tactic on the part of Moscow.

Even more explicitly, an abrupt decision by Gazprom to drop the pressure in the main pipeline leading from Turkmenistan to Russia resulted in an explosion in April 2009, which left the pipeline from Central Asia inoperable. It occurred at a time when Gazprom was no longer interested in purchasing Turkmen gas, which had become too expensive. However, during the five days of Russo-Georgian hostilities in August 2008, Georgia continued to receive Russian-provided electricity and gas.

PIPELINE GEOPOLITICS

Russia's broader energy relations with the European Union are marked by a fundamental disagreement over the 1994 Energy Charter Treaty, which Moscow signed but has refused to ratify. In 2009, Moscow declared that the treaty was dead, as far as Russia was concerned. In essence, Russia opposes any internationalizing of its pipeline operations. It wants to keep control over the existing pipelines in Eurasia. This, however, puts Russia at odds not only with the EU, but also with other CIS countries.

In the Soviet Union, export pipelines, such as Urengoy-Pomary-Uzhgorod, the main route for gas deliveries to Europe, also served the borderland republics. Decades after the pipelines were built, all need repair and modernization. In Ukraine's case, upgrading the pipeline system is probably beyond the country's means.

Gazprom's strategy of business expansion calls for taking over the neighboring states' pipeline transport. This is also essential for securing uninterrupted transit to the West. It has long been eyeing the Ukrainian pipeline system; the Russians are ready to partner with the Europeans. In 2002, Putin and then–German Chancellor Gerhard Schroeder proposed a trilateral gas consortium to Ukraine. Kiev declined, fearing putting itself between the hammer and the anvil. So Russia went for the North Stream, just as Putin had warned in advance.

While Russia does not mind an equitable arrangement with the EU, it resents being cut out of any deal over Ukraine's pipelines. Already in mid-2008, the Russian National Security Council stated that Russian interests as an energy power would be met only if the Ukrainian pipeline system were taken over by an international consortium with Gazprom's participation.[38] Some in Europe, meanwhile, sought to take over the pipelines right up to the Russian border. In March 2009, Moscow was engaged in a *bras de fer* with the EU over this issue. Reacting to the EU-Ukraine "separate" agreement on the Ukrainian gas transport network modernization, Prime Minister Putin branded it as a major attack on Russian interests. Putin threatened Europe with a revision, across the board, of all European energy—including nuclear and electricity—and transport contracts in Russia. Companies such as TNK-BP, BASF, E.ON, ENI, Enel, Total, and Fortum all stood to be affected. Russia's business in Ukraine was not *only* business, after all.

The bilateral EU-Ukraine deal went nowhere. After Yanukovych's victory in the 2010 Ukrainian presidential elections, the idea of a trilateral consortium was revived.

The 2009 gas conflict pushed the EU's efforts to diversify gas supplies. A number of steps were taken. They included building facilities to receive liquefied natural gas from such producers as Qatar, and Trinidad and Tobago. They also included building connector pipelines among the EU countries themselves. The idea of a pipeline alternative, the Nabucco project, gained new currency.

Nabucco was originally scheduled to be built between 2011 and 2014, at the cost of 8 billion euros ($10.9 billion) and with a capacity of 31 billion cubic meters (bcm). Nabucco critically depends on gas deliveries from Central Asia and Iraq. To diversify Europe's gas imports in a truly big way, however, it needs to access Iranian gas. This is possible only through the resolution of the Iranian nuclear crisis, a very big obstacle.

For its part, Moscow acted decisively to leave as little gas as possible for Nabucco. It contracted for Central Asian deliveries and even bought some quantities of gas from Azerbaijan, a Nabucco stalwart. Most important, the continuing crisis over the Iranian nuclear program prevented any serious discussion of securing Iranian gas for the project. Russia—which does not object to Iran (potentially), or Turkmenistan (since 2009), for that matter, selling their gas to Asian customers, such as China, India, and Pakistan—is resolved not to allow them to compete with Gazprom in the lucrative EU market.

Moscow's strategy has been to influence the gas flows from Turkmenistan and Kazakhstan, as long as all pipelines from those countries lead across Russia. The Kremlin's Caspian policy rests on two key demands: no new pipelines going around Russia or across the Caspian, and no military presence in the Caspian by a non-littoral state.[39] Moscow vowed to block any Caspian pipeline project on legal grounds: the lake's legal regime remains undefined, due to the differences among the five countries over the principles of its division. In Moscow's view, only the floor of the lake is subject to division, and the water is commonly shared.

After the breakup of the Soviet Union, Gazprom refused to share its hard currency proceeds with Turkmenistan, arguing that Turkmen gas going through Russia was reaching only Ukraine, Georgia, and Armenia. This pushed Ashgabat, as early as the mid-1990s, to look for alternative routes. The options included going over land to Turkey, across Iran; building a pipeline across the Caspian to Azerbaijan, Georgia, and Turkey; and finally to Pakistan and India, across Afghanistan or Iran or both.

Russia objected to the first two options, helped by the United States on Iran and by the Azeri-Turkmen sea border dispute on the Trans-Caspian line. As far as Gazprom was concerned, the Turkmens were free to pump east if they wished. Rem Vyakhirev, who led Gazprom in 1992–2001, was essentially free from imperial ambitions.[40] However, the Taliban, which had just emerged at the time, looked to the more geopolitics-conscious Russians as an armed guard to provide security along the first pipeline from a post-Soviet country that was not controlled by Moscow. Some went so far as to claim that the Taliban had been invented by the Unocol company (with the United States behind it) simply to siphon off gas from the ex-USSR. In any event, the idea fell through.

In 2003, Putin and Turkmen President Niyazov signed a deal under which Russia said it would buy all Turkmen gas for the next twenty-five years. Moscow saw the deal as a great success: The idea was to get its hands on as many resources as possible. With energy prices at their peak, Gazprom committed itself to buying 80–90 bcm at $375 per 1,000 cubic meters.

In 2009, prices plummeted, and Gazprom balked. It broke the contract and demanded that the price of Turkmen gas and the volume Russia was taking be reduced. Crisis ensued. No deliveries took place from April to December 2009, and when deliveries resumed, they were only minimal (10 bcm). In the future, Russia can hardly buy much more. In 2015, it estimates gas imports from all of Central Asia at 57–82 bcm: a very wide spread. Currently, there is a gas glut on the market, but the medium-term prospects are uncertain. And Russia, in order to preserve Gazprom's monopoly, is unlikely to allow the Turkmens access to the Russian pipeline system.

Gurbanguly Berdymukhamedov, Turkmenistan's current leader, believes, rightly, that he has a range of options. First, China. In 2009, the country bought the gas that Russia had refused to take. The Chinese plan is to expand the capacity of the pipeline they built in 2009—to pump up to 60 bcm from Turkmenistan, Uzbekistan, and Kazakhstan. This will be ten times the original capacity of the Turkmenistan-China pipeline. Second, Iran. Tehran is prepared to build an extra line and expand its take from 8 bcm to 20.[41] Third, South Asia. Turkmenistan has not given up the idea of a TAPI (Turkmenistan-Afghanistan-Pakistan-India) pipeline with a capacity of 30 bcm. Iran is considering an IPI route (Iran-Pakistan-India), with a similar capacity (33 bcm), in which Gazprom has also expressed interest.[42]

Another idea is to lay a pipeline across the Persian Gulf and the Arabian Sea to India. Finally, despite Russian pressure, Turkmenistan has not turned its back on Nabucco. It is building a pipeline to the Caspian coast and, even if a pipe across the Caspian may not be built, the Turkmens would be able to ship their gas in liquefied form to Azerbaijan.

Russia's own alternative to Nabucco—the South Stream, announced in June 2007—is a much more expensive project than its rival. Its projected capacity is 63 bcm, and the cost is put at 20 billion euros ($27.2 billion). Gazprom has struck a strategic alliance with Italy's ENI, with the two companies having equal stakes in it. The Russian government has reached a deal with Turkey, a Nabucco partner, which thus hopes to become a major energy hub. Relying on Italy and Turkey as the two pillars of the project, Russia has proceeded to persuade the countries of Southeastern Europe—many of them Moscow's former satellites—to join the project. Building on the existing Blue Stream gas pipeline to Turkey, Gazprom is also aiming south, to get to Israel.

While the South Stream is still a project with unclear prospects, like Nabucco, Gazprom's other venture, the North Stream, announced in September 2005, has made significant progress. The pipeline—linking Russia and Germany across the Baltic Sea with a capacity of 55 bcm and costing in excess of 7 billion euros ($9.5 billion)—is scheduled to be built between 2011 and 2013. Originally a Russo-German joint venture with Gazprom having a 51 percent stake and BASF and E.ON sharing the rest, it has broadened to include the Dutch Gasunie and the French Gaz de France, all without threatening Gazprom's majority position.

The North and South streams are part of a general pattern that Russia has been following since the late 1990s, when it decided to stop using the Baltic ports—Latvia's Ventspils and Estonia's Tallinn—for oil exports. This appeared as punishment of the Baltic states for their unwillingness to extend citizenship rights to all their ethnic Russian residents, but it had a more fundamental strategic rationale. Finland was cut off from Russian oil re-exports at about the same time. The Russian Federation wanted to have as few intermediaries as possible, and ideally none, between itself and its major customers in Western Europe. The Baltics were simply the first ones to go around; Ukraine and Belarus were next.

Even before the EU countries started diversifying away from overdependence on Russian gas, Russia began diversifying its oil and exports away from the increasingly stagnant European market. The Russian companies and the Russian state eyed the United States and Asia as the next promising markets. In the early 2000s, two major oil pipeline projects were proposed in Russia—both by Mikhail Khodorkovsky, the CEO of Yukos at the time. One was to link the oil fields of the Russian Far North to the Arctic port city of Murmansk in the Kola Peninsula. From Murmansk, oil tankers were to deliver oil to the East Coast of the United States. The other pipeline was to link Siberian oil fields with northeastern China.

The first project was to embody the budding Russo-American energy partnership. It failed when it was revealed that the Russian and American views of that partnership were very different. While the Russians sought to gain a foothold in the U.S. domestic energy market—and thus not only earn money, but also acquire the hitherto nonexistent "economic basis" for the bilateral political relationship—Americans eyed a piece of the Russian energy industry. Khodorkovsky, eager to enter politics, had been in talks with U.S. oil majors (ExxonMobil, Shell) about selling his company. When President Putin got the news, Khodorkovsky's fate was probably sealed.

His other project has survived, though. The state-owned Rosneft, which had acquired the main assets of the dismantled Yukos, started building a pipeline to the Chinese border, and then on to the Sea of Japan. In terms of bolstering Russian positions in Asia, this project is likened to the building of the Trans-Siberian Railway in the late nineteenth century.[43] The VSTO (East Siberia-Pacific Ocean) pipeline, with a capacity of 30–80 million tons per annum, is aimed at entering the Asian energy market and thus diversifying Russia's exports and reducing its dependence on European customers, as called for in the Russian energy strategy to 2030. Initially, there was some competition in terms of the pipeline's destination between China and Japan, but in the end Moscow decided to aim for both markets, with China getting its oil first. In 2009, China signed a contract with Russia under which it is to receive 300 million tons over twenty years[44] though Gazprom has not been able to agree on the price for its gas deliveries to China.

Japan's enthusiasm for the VSTO subsequently cooled somewhat, but its interest remained. The Japanese government set the maximum quota of 10 percent for oil and gas imports from Russia, so as not to become too dependent on its neighbor. Russia, for its part, sees the Pacific countries—including Japan, but also South Korea and the United States—as markets for oil and liquefied natural gas exports from Sakhalin Island. If the Russians manage to secure a share of those markets, they will diversify their energy exports, still very much directed at Europe. The Europeans, meanwhile, are looking for ways to reduce their dependence on Russian energy.

In the Far North, the biggest energy project in the area is development of the Shtokman gas field in the Barents Sea. The original idea was to aim for the same goal as the ill-fated Murmansk project: enter the U.S. domestic market, but with gas, rather than oil, and with the state-owned Gazprom, rather than the privately owned Yukos, in charge. When this was deemed unlikely, the destination was changed toward Europe. Norway's Statoil and France's Total were chosen as the first partners. Due to its complexity and location, Shtokman is likely to become a major area of energy cooperation between Russia and its neighbors in Europe.

Although the Arctic is believed to contain large deposits of hydrocarbons, and Russia seeks to expand the area of its exclusive economic zone still further, any serious exploration—not to mention exploitation—of those resources is a long way off. When the time comes, however, the premium will probably be on international collaboration in the very severe and demanding environment. This, actually, is the general trend, which has already integrated the formerly autarkic Soviet economic space into the global economy.

OPENING OF THE CIS MARKETS TO THE WORLD

Russia's share of CIS countries' manufactured goods imports has been going down dramatically. During the boom years preceding the 2008 crisis, it almost halved. Better quality, technologically advanced, and often cheaper products from the EU, China, the United States, Japan, Turkey, and other countries have come to dominate the former Soviet markets. Not everyone was happy about that. President Kuchma related a conversation with Russia's premier Viktor Chernomyrdin in which both complained about the West's selfish cynicism toward the former Soviet states.[45]

The European Union has become the leading trading partner for most CIS countries. Its exports to the CIS (excluding Russia) increased six times between 2000 and 2008, to reach $65 billion.[46] Over half (53.3 percent in 2009) of Russia's own exports go to the EU, from where Russia also receives 45 percent of its imports, the highest proportion of trade of any former Soviet republic.[47] Moldova, Kazakhstan, Azerbaijan, Belarus, and Armenia send 40 to 50 percent of their exports to the EU; in terms of imports, Moldova, Ukraine, Georgia, Kazakhstan, Armenia, and Azerbaijan are in the lead.

Since 2003, the EU has been promoting a European Neighborhood Policy (ENP) designed to adapt to EU standards the neighboring countries of New Eastern Europe (Belarus, Ukraine, and Moldova) and the South Caucasus (Armenia, Azerbaijan, and Georgia). Since 2009, the ENP has been enhanced by an Eastern Partnership program that addresses the same six countries. Since the mid-2000s, the EU has been paying attention to Central Asia, particularly Kazakhstan, mainly as an energy exporter.

Between 2000 and 2008, China's exports to the non-Russian CIS countries soared from $1 billion to $31.5 billion. Russia's exports to China are about a tenth (5.5 percent in 2009) of its exports to the EU, but China's share in Russian imports is more substantial (13.8 percent). Around a third of China's exports are light industry products, about 30 percent are machines and equipment, and 20 percent various consumer goods.[48] China's massive entry into the CIS market has further reduced intra-CIS trade to energy and raw materials. China's exports have undermined EurAsEC, whose members increasingly shop in China,* thus rendering their own economic community a sham. China's economic clout is particularly strong in Central Asia, which Beijing sees as a source of energy, an export market for Chinese goods, and an overland transit corridor linking China with the Middle East. The October 2009 economic cooperation program between Moscow and Beijing confirmed the Russian Far East and Siberia as a raw materials resource for China, and China as an exporter of manufactured goods to Russia.

In 2009, China became the first country to break Russia's near-monopoly on gas supplies from Central Asia. Turkmenistan started pumping natural gas (40 bcm) via a pipeline to Khorog, on the Tajik-Chinese border. By 2012, Kazakhstan plans to expand its gas pipeline to China to reach 30 bcm.

To promote its economic interests in Central Asia and the Caspian, China has been generous with credits and development aid to the new countries of the region. It has been investing heavily in such sectors as oil and gas, electricity, and infrastructure. China has also been seeking to prioritize the economic dimension of the Shanghai Cooperation Organization. Thus, while the EU through its sheer existence—but also by means of its programs—hampers Russia-led integration efforts in New Eastern Europe and the Caucasus, China does the same in Central Asia.

As an economic partner of CIS countries, the United States has been far behind both Europe and China. American companies are heavily present in the energy sector, particularly in Azerbaijan and Kazakhstan. In the latter country, U.S. investments reached $47 billion by 2010. The U.S. government has consistently promoted diversification of energy routes out of the Caspian region. In 2006, the Baku-Tbilisi-Ceyhan pipeline ended Russia's monopoly on oil transit from the Caspian. That project enjoyed full political support from the White House. The United States also supports the Nabucco project, which it sees as a guarantee of decreased EU dependence on Russian energy supplies.

Of the regional players, Turkey has established itself as a major trading partner for Georgia (about 20 percent of its foreign trade), Tajikistan

---

* Which accounts for 11.8 percent of imports in Tajikistan, 12.6 percent in Kazakhstan, 16.6 percent in Uzbekistan, and 20 percent in Kyrgyzstan.

(27 percent of exports in 2008), Azerbaijan (15 percent of imports), Turk-menistan, and Uzbekistan. Yet Russia has become Turkey's biggest trading partner. Iran has won markets in Armenia, Tajikistan, and Turkmenistan.

CONCLUSION

The Soviet Union used to boast that it accounted for a fifth of the world's output; with its COMECON allies, Moscow could rely on a third of the global production. These figures had a propaganda value but could not be verified, because of the non-market nature of the Soviet economy. Yet even though the USSR was only partially present on the world market, it was credited with abundant resources and impressive industrial (espe-cially defense industrial) capacity.

This situation has dramatically changed: The Russian Federation, by any definition, is not a major economic "pole" on the global scale. Its share of the global GDP is around 2 percent, the same as its share of the world's population, and it is unlikely to grow significantly. It is an energy and raw materials producer par excellence. But lacking industrial, technological, and financial potential, it is noncompetitive in virtually all other areas.

As a would-be magnet to its immediate neighbors, Russia lacks par-ticular attractiveness. It is not a source of major investment, financial assis-tance, or technical aid. CIS countries' trade with Russia has been decreas-ing. Moreover, Russia still treats the new states as less than equals. The gas wars with Ukraine and Belarus have greatly damaged Russia's reputation in the two countries that are economically and culturally closest to it. They also destroyed Russia's image in Europe and the wider world as a reliable energy supplier. Still, some forms of economic integration—such as the Customs Union with Kazakhstan and, depending on the political developments, also Belarus—can lead to the creation of a "Eurasian" market, which would in-crease the present market of the Russian Federation by about one-fifth.

In the 2000s, other international economic centers have assumed the role of magnets for the former Soviet states. The European Union attracts its immediate neighbors, Belarus, Moldova, and Ukraine and, increasingly, the countries of the South Caucasus: Georgia, Azerbaijan, and Armenia. China is ascendant in Central Asia.

Other countries, from the United States in the energy field, to regional powers Turkey and Iran in their neighborhood, to East Asian countries Japan and South Korea, are all active in the former Soviet Union. The more the new countries liberalize their economies, the harder it is for Russian companies to compete with stronger international rivals. The post-Soviet space has opened up to all, and Russia is no longer the dominant economic force there.

Russia's role as an energy power does not give Moscow the dominance that many suggest. In the years since the 2006 Ukrainian gas crisis, European countries have taken steps to reduce their dependence on Gazprom. Liquefied natural gas has recently become more readily available and is beginning to compete with piped gas. Shale gas is changing the market even further. Making a switch from Europe to Asia is not easy and may not bring similar profits. Since the global economic crisis, the Russian budget depends on proceeds from oil and gas even more than before the crisis. And gas transit cannot be fully phased out.

Despite its deficiencies, Russia continues to be a major factor in its neighbors' economic development. It is a source of energy supplies; it is a sizable market for their goods, from agricultural products to manufactured goods; its labor market absorbs surplus populations of the former Soviet south; and it is a transit country. It also still has some technological and intellectual capacity, which could become the basis for a Russian economic rebirth, should one come. Whether or not that happens depends on the Russian people themselves.

4

DEMOGRAPHICS AND IMMIGRATION

This chapter of the book should, in principle, contain all the answers to the most important questions raised before. In reality, it raises a number of hard questions of its own: Does Russia face a demographic catastrophe, in which the largest country on earth will gradually, but rather quickly, die out, leaving the world's biggest plot of land with its immense natural riches up for grabs? Are Russians really a "divided nation," and how serious is "the Russian Question"? How should Moscow's pledge to protect Russian citizens abroad be read?

In addition, how is mass immigration changing the complexion of the Russian population? Can xenophobia and an anti-immigrant backlash pave the way to a Russian version of fascism? Is China engaged in "creeping demographic aggression" against Russia, and how should Russia deal with the huge demographic imbalance along the two countries' border? With Russians leaving the North Caucasus in droves, is the region fast becoming Russia's "inner abroad"? If so, what are the consequences?

With its close to 150 million subjects, the Russian empire was, in 1913, the third most populous country in the world, behind China and India, and it was fast growing. (India, of course, was part of the British empire, but *that* empire's population did not exactly mix with the metropolitan one.) Seventy-eight years later, the Soviet Union, with about 286 million inhabitants at last count, occupied precisely the same place in the world, in terms of its population weight. Throughout the entire twentieth century, except for its last decade, the top troika remained the same, and Russia's position in it was stable and comfortable. It was far superior to any place in Europe and was clearly ahead of the United States.

This comfortable stability prevailed despite the horrendous demographic losses sustained by Russia in the twentieth century. The First World War left 6 million of its subjects dead; the Civil War that closely followed left 3 million dead and a similar number of refugees; political repression between 1921 and 1985 took the lives of 5 million to 5.5 million; in addition, between 3 million and 4.5 million peasants were driven off their land and banished to Siberia and elsewhere;[1] the Second World War topped that grim record with 26 million victims. But for these man-made disasters, the country's population might have achieved the 400 million mark by the end of the 1990s. Still, the Soviet Union managed to stay well ahead of any other countries save the two Asian giants, China and India, which barely mattered in the power games of the last century.

The fall of Russia's "people power" had most to do with the end of the empire—that is, the breakup of the Soviet Union, peaceful and orderly as it was. To begin with, the Russian Federation inherited two-thirds of the Soviet territory but just over half of its inhabitants. So population-wise, the new Russian state was only half the country the Soviet Union had been. Two decades later, with only 141.9 million people in 2010,[2] the Russian Federation is the world's ninth largest in population, well behind China and India, but also the United States, Indonesia, Brazil, Pakistan, Bangladesh, and Nigeria. If the current trends continue, Russia is likely to slip to the seventeenth position four decades from now. Except for the United States, all fifteen countries with populations above that of Russia will be in Asia, Africa, or Latin America.

Physical halving of the population was one thing. Today's population of all post-Soviet states is a mere 5 percent of the world's total. From exactly the same moment when the breakup of the USSR occurred, the Russian population stopped growing and went into decline. The decreasing trend had been there for years, but the growth actually turned negative in 1992. From 147 million

TABLE 4.1

POPULATION OF THE RUSSIAN EMPIRE & THE SOVIET UNION (the present territory of the Russian Federation, in millions)

1897	128.2	67.5
1926	147.0	92.7
1939	170.5	108.4
1959	208.8	117.2
1970	241.7	129.9
1979	262.1	137.4
1989	285.7	147
2002		145.2

people at the time of the Soviet breakup, the population slipped by more than 5 million in twenty years. The net loss would have been far bigger but for immigration.

Russia's demographic future looks bleak, but it is probably not as bleak as some projections suggest. The U.S. National Intelligence Council, in its 2025 forecast, projected Russia's decline to hit as low as 130 million by 2015.[3] This looks unlikely. The United Nations medium variant has Russia with just 116 million people by 2050.[4] These projections, too, may be overly pessimistic, but the trend is there, and it is worrisome to Russian leaders, to say the least.

Negative population growth is among the strongest and most obvious arguments in support of the post-imperialist thesis of this book. Russia is no longer expanding, but shrinking, and shrinking fast. Its people's post-1991 motto was starkly simple: to survive. It has survived, but in a very different shape and form than before.

Russia now has problems where, in the past, it used to have seemingly unbeatable advantages: It finds it difficult, for example, to draft enough conscripts for its much scaled-down armed forces. Ironically, but not atypically, the demographic crisis came to the surface in the absence of wars and repression, at a time when Russians, at long last, began to enjoy and learn to manage the freedoms previously denied to them. Present-day Russian communists, true to form, blame the crisis on the dismantlement of the Soviet Union; Russian conservatives place the onus on the liberal policies of the 1990s. In reality, the roots of the present crisis are both deeper—going back to the late Soviet period, and wider—involving much of the developed world.

Demographic Crisis

In terms of negative population growth, Russia is clearly not walking alone. Actually, it is in the same league as nearly all its neighbors to the west and southwest: the Baltic states, Belarus, and Ukraine, as well as much of the European Union. Most European countries—east and west, north and south—are experiencing marked population decline because of low birthrates. True, Russia's decline of the birthrate has been most dramatic. In the fifteen years from 1976 to 1991, 36 million babies were born, while the following fifteen years registered only 22.3 million new births, a fall of almost 40 percent. The current Russian birthrate is 60 percent less than what is needed for simple reproduction.

What makes Russia's case so much more serious than other countries is its very high mortality. Since the early 1990s, about 2 million people have been dying annually. Russia's death rate is higher than anywhere in Europe; twice as high, proportionally, as in the United States; and 50 percent above the world's average.[5] Much of it is due to alcoholism, smoking, widespread neglect of health, reckless behavior, and, more recently, spreading drug abuse.

After the collapse of the Soviet welfare state, such as it was, the availability, affordability, and quality of medical services in Russia took a deep dip. Social controls weakened, and many norms were no longer observed. As a result, life expectancy for men in Russia has dropped to 58.9 years, a decline of 13.5 years; for women, life expectancy is now 72, a decline of 7.4 years. This puts Russia, in terms of life expectancy, in one-hundredth place among all countries of the world: ninety-first for women and one hundred and thirty-fourth for men. Though both the birthrate and men's life expectancy have improved somewhat in the late 2000s, a combination of low births and high deaths is popularly known as "the Russian cross." To a pessimist—and there are many—"Russia is dying out."

Such a dramatic fall in demographic numbers means a stunning erosion of the foundation of national power. It also implies new vulnerabilities; the world's biggest piece of real estate will be populated by a relatively small and dwindling population. True, Russia will remain, for the foreseeable future, the most populous country in geographical Europe, even if only the population west of the Urals is taken into account. While the UN 2050 forecast has Russia with 116.1 million residents, the United Kingdom is credited with 72.4 million, Germany with 70.5 million, and France with 67.7 million.[6] Such countries as Nigeria (which has already overtaken Russia) and Egypt (which might, by 2050) are physically far away and of little direct consequence to Russia. However, Turkey and Iran, with 75 million people each in 2010, already surpass, between them, Russia's demographic weight. By 2050, running neck and neck, they can come close to it, with a projected 97 million in each country.

Still closer to home, things are not what they used to be. The countries of Middle Asia, as well as Azerbaijan, have been demonstrating very high rates of population growth. This changes the equation between them and Russia. When the Soviet Union collapsed, their population amounted to just over a quarter (27.7 percent) of Russia's. Now it is about two-fifths (39.4 percent); by 2030, it can be well over half (53.4 percent), almost twice the original proportion. This leads, in different cases, to a growth in power, or in poverty; to internal conflicts over land or water rights or cross-border migration; and to international disputes or foreign involvement. In all cases, however, it leads to the former borderlands requiring much more attention, if only on demographic grounds, from Moscow.

Beyond the former Soviet border, the demographic realities have also changed in the past two decades. The loose community of the European Community evolved into a union of nearly 500 million people. This union has expanded way beyond Western and Southern Europe to include nearly all former Soviet neighbors: Finland and Sweden; Poland and Hungary; Romania and Bulgaria. In the past, the USSR could easily dwarf any one of the bigger European nations, and was a Gulliver, or a Godzilla, to the smaller ones. Now, its population is just over a quarter of that of United Europe.

That China's population (1.3 billion) is now nearly nine times as big as Russia's is a quantitative, but not a qualitative, change. The number of subjects of both the Soviet Union and the Russian empire was only a fraction of

TABLE 4.2

DEMOGRAPHIC FORECASTS, 1990–2030
(UN Population Forecast, 2004, in millions)

Country	1990	2000	2005	2010	2020	2030	2030 / 1990 %	2030 / 2005 %
ARM	3.5	3.1	3.0	3.0	3.0	2.8	80	94
AZB	7.2	8.1	8.4	8.7	9.4	9.7	135	115
BEL	10.3	10.0	9.8	9.5	8.9	8.3	81	85
EST	1.6	1.4	1.3	1.3	1.3	1.2	77	92
GEO	5.5	4.7	4.5	4.3	4.1	3.8	69	84
KAZ	16.5	15.0	14.8	14.8	14.9	14.6	88	98
KYR	4.4	5.0	5.3	5.6	6.1	6.4	146	122
LTV	2.7	2.4	2.3	2.2	2.1	2.0	73	86
LTH	3.7	3.5	3.4	3.4	3.2	3.0	82	88
MLD	4.4	4.3	4.2	4.2	4.1	3.9	88	92
TAJ	5.3	6.2	6.5	7.0	8.2	9.2	174	142
TRM	3.7	4.5	4.8	5.2	5.8	6.3	171	130
UKR	51.9	49.1	46.5	44.1	39.6	35.1	68	75
UZB	20.5	24.7	26.6	28.6	32.5	35.3	172	133
RUS	148.4	146.6	143.2	140.0	133.1	125.3	84	88

China's. It may not even be important that Russia's population east of the Urals, and especially in Pacific Russia, is very small—25 million, of whom fewer than 5 million live east of Lake Baikal—and is easily overshadowed by the population of each of the three provinces of Northeastern China*: collectively, their population equals that of the entire Russian Federation.

Static demographic numbers do not tell the whole story. The problem is the differing economic and social dynamics of the two countries. China is rapidly growing, rising in might and stature; Russia has been going through an excruciating transformation, still incomplete, even as it holds onto its age-old ways and painfully sifts through its legacy, while attempting to adjust, along the way, to a post-imperial condition.

This has strategic consequences. The conscript army, despite all the efforts of the traditionalists at the General Staff, is on the way out, if only by fits and starts. The pool of potential draftees is dwindling. Since 2008, young Russians have to complete only twelve months of compulsory military service, compared with 24 months at the time of the Soviet collapse and 36 months until the early 1970s. Since 2009, the Russian military doctrine has stopped preparing for a large-scale war, which in the 1970s–1980s meant wars against NATO or China, or both. Now, the emphasis is on smaller professional forces capable of dealing with various kinds of emergencies on the country's southern periphery. For truly big jobs, there is nuclear deterrence—and nothing else.

The Russian government is anything but unaware of this new situation. Vladimir Putin focused on demographic issues ever since he became president. Population decline was the major theme of his first annual address to the Federal Assembly in 2000. It might have appeared that the attention worked, but the effect of the government population growth incentive package was marginal. By 2006, the economically active population had increased by 3.2 percent, capitalizing on the surge in births in the mid- to late 1980s. That, however, was the last such rise for the foreseeable future.

Since then, things have started to deteriorate. In 2007, the working-age population declined for the first time. From 2007 to 2016, the economically active segment is expected to drop by 2.4 percent. The aging of Russia's population will lead to a reduction in the share of the working-age population (78 million at present), from 65 percent to 59 percent. The tightening of supply of new indigenous workers to the labor market, initially modest

---

* Heilongjiang, Jiling, and Liaoning.

(minus 1.8 percent by 2010 compared to 2006), will accelerate after 2011. By 2016, this will amount to minus 5 percent compared to 2006.

The reduction in the working-age population will constitute a major constraint on economic growth.[7] With labor productivity in 2008 only 25 percent of the U.S. level, Russia, one might think, has a major resource that it can tap. However, Russian economists are skeptical that a realistic increase in labor productivity would be able to compensate for the demographic shortfall.[8]

To offset the trend, Putin proposed an economic package designed to boost the birthrate as early as 2006. Still, acute labor shortages in textiles, metallurgy, woodworking, and other branches of industry can hardly be closed without importing labor from abroad. Experts estimate that, to cover the labor shortage, Russia will need 15 million guest workers, or more than 10 percent of its current population. Seen from a different angle, in order to modernize and innovate, Russia will need to facilitate issuance of work permits for Western specialists.[9] Either step represents a huge challenge to the established ways.

RETURNING RUSSIANS

Immediately after the collapse of the Soviet Union, Russia started to receive demographic aid from what it called its near abroad. More than 6 million people moved to the Russian Federation from the newly independent former borderlands. Of these, 1.6 million were officially registered as refugees or internally displaced persons. Seventy percent of them were ethnic Russians.[10]

The tide has turned. For centuries, ethnic Russians had been moving from what is called Central Russia—roughly the area of the medieval grand duchy of Muscovy—to the expanding borderlands. They established themselves on the plains and foothills north of the Caucasus; across Siberia all the way to the Pacific; in the urban enclaves of Central Asia and the Baltics; and elsewhere. The peak of ethnic Russians moving outward to what were then the Soviet republics was reached in the 1960s. From the 1970s on, the direction of internal Soviet migration reversed itself, resulting—within the USSR's final two decades—in a 2.5-million-person net gain for the Russian republic.[11]

This well-established trend was massively accelerated when the former "sister republics" became independent—some plunging into wars and conflicts, and others making it clear that local Russians were a legacy of the totalitarian or colonial past and thus were not welcome in the new states. Moldovan nationalists came up with a chant addressed to ethnic Russian residents: "suitcases—railway station—Russia!"

As a result of this attitude, the Russian population of Moldova, Uzbekistan, and Kyrgyzstan halved; it shrank by three times in Armenia and Azerbaijan, and by four times in Georgia; in war-torn Tajikistan, only one in seven local Russians remained. This exodus—Uzbekistan alone produced 900,000 ethnic Russian returnees in 1991–2008[12]—is similar in kind to the departure of European colonists once the colonies gained independence. However, it is different in degree, because of the geographical and cultural proximity of Russia's ex-borderlands; the widely practiced intermarriages; and the absence of last-ditch efforts to salvage the empire by colonial wars. The case of Chechnya will be discussed separately, but suffice it to mention here that ethnic Russian residents have almost completely vanished from this republic, which is formally part of the Russian Federation.

On the eve of and then in the immediate aftermath of the Soviet Union's breakup, ethnic consolidation was a common trend. In 1990 alone, 150,000 Ukrainians returned to their homeland, followed by 200,000 more before the end of the decade.[13] Between 1990 and 2007, 260,000 ethnic Belarusians returned to their home country.[14] In Armenia and Azerbaijan, national consolidation was driven by the war over Nagorno-Karabakh and pogroms in Baku and elsewhere.

Most of the 25 million to 26 million ethnic Russians who found themselves in December 1991 beyond the borders of the Russian Federation, chose, however, to stay put. In the countries of their highest concentration, Ukraine and Belarus, they not only received automatic citizenship rights—this was the practice everywhere in the former Soviet Union, except in Estonia and Latvia—but they also felt comfortable and at home. Very important, Belarus, in a 1995 referendum, put the Russian language on a par with Belarusian and thus sealed its de facto primacy. In eastern and southern Ukraine, where most Russians live, the Russian language remains dominant, despite occasional Ukrainization campaigns in Kiev; Kiev itself, although majority Ukrainian, is a mainly Russian-speaking city. True, some hemorrhage occurred there as well, but mostly as a result of new self-identification and the relative economic attractiveness of Russia, especially vis-à-vis Ukraine. By the same token, most ethnic Ukrainians (2.9 million, according to the 2002 census) and Belarusians (just over 800,000) living in Russia did not feel compelled to move; some of them may not have felt particularly attached to their "old country."

In Kazakhstan, many among the 3 million who left after independence were Russians or other Slavs. Most stayed, and a few returned, thanks to Kazakhstan's resource-driven economic dynamism, President Nursultan Nazarbayev's wise protection of minorities, and the continued wide use of the Russian language. From the perspective of the Russian residents of the two Baltic states, the relatively comfortable way of life and economic opportunities outweighed the lack of citizenship rights. Chaotic and less well-developed Russia did not look attractive enough.

Thus, the nationalist slogans of a divided Russian nation rang hollow. Russians are not generally among the most ethnically conscious people. Their imperial "half millennium" taught them to focus on the state, not the population, which continuously incorporated ever-new ethnic elements. The totalitarian nature of the communist state ensured that society became atomized, with no broad horizontal links tolerated. The collapse of that state in 1991 changed the situation dramatically: having survived the unexpected demise of the state, people started to focus on themselves, wherever they lived instead of building a nation, either across borders or within Russia.

It should be added that as the Soviet Union disintegrated, and the formerly tightly closed borders opened, about 3 million former Soviet citizens left to live abroad, including nearly a million to the United States alone, and an equal number to Israel. Of that group, 1 million people had probably come from the Russian Federation.[15] The global figure can be compared to the number of White Russian émigrés—about 3 million—who fled the country during and after the Civil War of 1918–1921. At both the beginning of the twentieth century and at its end, many of those who left for good were highly educated and well-qualified—people who were difficult to replace in qualitative terms. The Russian Federation was no exception among the former Soviet states, of course. Ukraine lost about 10 percent of its population to emigration, and Georgia as much as 20 percent, with many of the best and the brightest—although hardly exclusively—having gone to the West.

The hopes that ethnic Russian returnees from the newly independent states would compensate for those who had gone to the West remained largely in vain. Those who might have wanted to go "back" were also deterred by the insufficient amount of decent and affordable housing in Russia, the limited economic and social opportunities available, and the generally unwelcoming attitude of Russian authorities and even the wider public.

Twenty years after the end of the USSR, the remaining potential for ethnic Russian emigration from other CIS states to Russia is estimated at around 4 million.[16] For more than a decade after the end of the Soviet Union, the Russian government had no policy on immigration whatsoever. Now it seeks to tap into it.

The resettlement program, announced by the Russian authorities in late 2006, has so far been a failure. In 2007 and 2008, only 9,800 people decided to move to Russia, against the expected 30,000–50,000—not to mention the runaway hopes of attracting 300,000 in three years.[17] Managing that puny influx was even more of a disaster. The Russian Far East, one of the regions that was supposed to benefit most from resettlement, has been able to attract only 30 families during the two first years of the resettlement program's implementation (2007–2008).[18]

Even if all of the 4 million Russians decide to repatriate, it would not solve the problem of labor shortages in the Russian economy. That can be achieved only by means of a well-thought-through immigration policy. Immigration is already a reality; a thoughtful approach to guide and regulate it has yet to be developed.

IMMIGRATION AND INTEGRATION

Within a few years, the country that had known no immigration in Soviet times and very little in the imperial period has turned into a land of immigrants. Driven mainly by economic reasons—and attracted by the relative familiarity of the core part of the defunct empire—many former Soviet citizens headed for Russia. In 1994 alone, 1.2 million such persons came to Russia. Over time, this flow has greatly diminished, to 98,000 in 2003. It then went up, to 130,000 in 2006 and 240,000 in 2007.[19] The freedom of movement, including migration, has become a major shock absorber amid the post-Soviet crisis.[20]

The number of new permanent residents and citizens of the Russian Federation, however, is being dwarfed by the number of migrant workers, pulled in by the high demand of the Russian labor market. Estimates of the number of guest workers in Russia vary widely: just before the 2008–2009 economic crisis, some sources referred to 10 million or 8 million labor migrants, while others—including the Federal Migration Service—put the figure at about 5 million.[21] The 2010 World Bank report quoted the figure of 12.5 million guest workers, which put Russia between the United States (42 million) and Germany (10.8 million). About four-fifths of these are believed to be illegal migrants. As a group, they are as ethnically, culturally, and linguistically diverse as the Soviet Union used to be.

Among the donor countries, Ukraine (population: 45 million) took an early lead. In the mid-2000s, probably 1 million Ukrainians, mainly from the eastern regions, flocked to Russia. At the time, only 245,000 of them were officially registered. This apparently high figure has to be compared, however, with 3 million, mostly from the country's western and central regions, who work in the EU countries.[22]

According to other data, in 2008 about 40 percent of all Ukrainian migrant workers went to Russia, about as many as those who traveled to work in Poland and the Czech Republic combined (19 percent and 17 percent, respectively). Annual remittances from those workers amounted to $5 billion to $7 billion. According to the World Bank, in 2004 as many as 400,000 Belarusians (population: 10 million) worked abroad; other sources refer to 250,000 Belarusians working in Russia.[23]

The 2009 revolution that toppled the communist government of Moldova (population: 4 million) was said to have been the work of the younger generation whose parents worked abroad. In relative terms, this is the highest proportion—one-quarter—of the country's entire working-age population. Many Moldovans have an option to reach the EU countries, thanks to Romania—which liberally grants passports to those who lived in Bessarabia during Romanian rule (1918–1940) or their descendants. Still, about 350,000, or 60 percent of all Moldovan migrant workers, find work in Russia, compared with 20 percent in Italy and 5 percent in Portugal.[24] In 2003–2008, their remittances accounted for 23 to 38 percent of the country's GDP.[25]

Workers going to EU countries earn more than in Russia, but they have to be able to negotiate the language barrier. This is relatively easy for Moldovans in Italy or Portugal, for Ukrainians in Poland, or for Azeris in Turkey. Europe also attracts more educated immigrants than Russia and those who also strive to settle permanently in the EU. Russia, by contrast, is less demanding: it does not elevate its guest workers to new levels of technical expertise or social life, but it is much more accessible than the EU. It still keeps borders open to all CIS countries, having made an exception only for Georgia, before it left the CIS. Russia also offers familiar conditions of work and living. In the last two decades, it has become a source of income for its CIS neighbors just as the United States has been for Latin America, Germany for Turkey and the Balkans, or France for North Africa.[26]

While workers from the New Eastern Europe can choose between the EU and Russia, those from the South Caucasus are attracted mainly to Russia (up to 1.5 million) and Turkey.

The Azeris (population: 8 million), at least numerically, tend to favor Russia. Before the global economic crisis, there were perhaps up to 1.5 million to 2 million Azeris in Russia (25 percent of the country's entire population),[27] many of them in retail trade and medium-sized business. Even as these people kept sending home $1.5 billion to $2.5 billion annually in remittances in the mid- to late 1990s, they were becoming progressively integrated into the Russian middle class.

Of the 700,000 to 1 million Armenians who left their country (population: 3.5 million) at the end of the twentieth century, many came to Russia. Armenians have lived in Russia for centuries, many of them well-integrated into the Russian elite.* This, coupled with the formal alliance relationship between Moscow and Yerevan, gives the Armenian diaspora in Russia excellent access to promote the interests of the "old country." Yet most ordinary Russian chauvinists and racists not only fail to distinguish between Armenians and other "people from the Caucasus," but also specifically target Armenians for others' heinous acts.

The new immigrants from Armenia began to arrive in Russia from the late 1980s, fleeing the war in Karabakh, the pogroms in Baku, and the earthquake in Armenia itself. Many reached Moscow; many more went only a few hundred miles north, to southern Russia: Krasnodar, Stavropol, and Rostov. Despite historical animosities, the economic blockade, and the absence of formal diplomatic relations, many Armenians also work in Turkey. During a spat over the genocide issue in March 2010, Turkey's prime minister threatened to expel Armenian workers, who numbered around 100,000, from his country.

Russia actually did expel some of the Georgian migrant workers during an acute crisis in relations between Moscow and Tbilisi in 2006, but most found a way to stay. Many Georgians also found work in Turkey and Greece. Like the Moldovans, the Georgians receive more remittances from their relatives working abroad than their governments receive foreign aid.

Between 1992 and 2006, 3.1 million people left Kazakhstan (population: 16.5 million), a net loss of 2 million. Kazakhstan's peak of emigration came in 1994 when almost 500,000 left the country. A decade later, the

---

* Anastas Mikoyan, a long-serving Politburo member, was the nominal Soviet head of state in the mid-1960s; several World War II marshals and top generals were of Armenian descent.

outflow stabilized at 50,000 per annum. Most of those leaving were Russians and other Slavs, as well as Germans, Jews, and Tatars.[28] One-fifth of the population—mostly Russians—would like to leave, half of them to Russia.[29] Ethnic Kazakhs, meanwhile, have found that opportunities at home are indeed better for them than in Russia. In the next several decades, Kazakhstan is likely to lose its "Eurasian" complexion and become more Turkic in its ethnic composition, with some Han Chinese settling there, too.

Kazakhstan apart, immigration from Middle Asia—estimated at 1.5 million to 2 million, has been growing. More than 700,000 Uzbeks, some 500,000 Tajiks, and 500,000 Kyrgyz work in Russia. They usually come from poor and overpopulated regions in search of any paying job. In most cases, they stay in Russia illegally and are subjected to super-exploitation by those who hire them. Still, they manage to send some money back home: Tajiks alone transferred $2.5 billion in 2008, which accounted for half of their country's GDP. The crisis reduced that figure to $2 billion, which is still 35 percent of Tajikistan's GDP.[30] More than any other group of immigrants in Russia, Central Asian workers face administrative abuse and harassment, or worse, by vigilantes. More recently, the Turkmens—who until the death of Turkmenbashi in 2006 had been effectively banned from traveling abroad on their own—are joining the ranks of labor migrants.

Russia has a tremendous need of labor resources. For the time being, most of that need can be satisfied by means of immigration from the countries of New Eastern Europe, the South Caucasus, and Central Asia. However, over the past twenty years, the quality of labor migrants to Russia has deteriorated. They are less educated; most come from small towns and villages; they are also poorer; and they are culturally (religion, language) more distant from ordinary Russians.[31] Thus, in order for this resource to be fully used, the Russian state needs to adapt to something it has never practiced before: large-scale immigration.

The process is already under way. After the chaotic laxness in approach throughout the 1990s and the unnecessary toughness of the early 2000s, Moscow adopted in 2007 immigration legislation that is generally liberal. This is a good base in principle, but the implementation can be abominable. Russian bureaucrats and police do a lot to turn the immigrants away from Russia. State Duma members occasionally become agitated over the outflow of money in the form of remittances: $18.6 billion in 2009, which puts Russia in fourth place in the world, behind the United States, Switzerland, and Saudi Arabia. In reality, foreign workers do the work that Russians themselves do not care to do.

What Russians need to be worried about instead is the high fluidity of the immigrants in their country: of 12.5 million, 11 million, or 88 percent, return home, which contrasts with 32 percent in Germany, 25 percent in France, and only 6 percent in the United States.[32] Beyond immigration, Russia needs a policy of integration. And as for Russian society, it needs to overcome its brimming xenophobia and develop tolerance and understanding. At present, both are sorely lacking. Moreover, anti-immigrant sentiments are on the rise, raising yet again the specter of "Russian fascism."

ANTI-IMMIGRANT SENTIMENTS

Anti-immigrant sentiments are a clear sign of a post-imperium. To unhappy residents of a defunct empire, the waves of people coming to their city from the former dependencies look like an undeserved punishment. They think they got rid of the empire all right; now they want the former subjects to leave them alone. The change of attitude from attempting to rule the world to keeping one's country safe for its residents is the essence of the post-imperial transition.

Migrant workers from the mainly Orthodox Christian countries of the New Eastern Europe not only find Russia relatively familiar, but are generally accepted by local residents as being essentially of the same stock. Outwardly, they are not conspicuous; all are fully fluent in Russian; their ways and habits are essentially the same as those of the Russians themselves. Things are very different when one has to deal with immigrants from Central Asia, the South, and even from the Russian North Caucasus.

Russians generally expect members of other ethnic groups to conform to Russian ways of public behavior. This corresponds to Russians' own attitudes. When they mean to settle down in a foreign country, as opposed to just visiting, they consciously seek to assimilate—and thus de-Russify—themselves. Yet twenty years after the end of the Soviet Union, many of the immigrant workers from the poor rural areas of Tajikistan or Uzbekistan speak little or no Russian. Many Chechens, Dagestanis, and others from the North Caucasus, meanwhile, speak very good Russian but are also usually dynamic and daring. Even before the Chechen war, 70,000 Chechens left their republic; the war added 130,000 to that number. Along with 100,000 Dagestanis, Ossetians, and others, they settled down in Moscow, St. Petersburg, and southern Russia.

The idea of Chechens fleeing to Moscow during the war is itself remarkable. It is also remarkable that the level of interethnic violence is generally low. The 2006 clashes in Kondopoga, a small town in Karelia—where a few local Russians were killed by Chechen migrants—stand out as the most serious case of this kind outside of the North Caucasus in twenty years.

The xenophobic slogan "Russia for the Russians" has been gaining support. Within a decade, the idea's popularity grew from 43 percent to 54 percent.[33] Undoubtedly, xenophobia masks social resentment and frustration, especially among the urban youth in large Russian cities. Yet all the political formations that tried to draw on xenophobic attitudes have remained marginal. The Movement Against Illegal Immigration organized rallies but made little headway elsewhere. There is one category of immigrants that captures nearly everyone's imagination in Russia: the Chinese.

"THE CHINESE ARE COMING!"

The issue of Chinese immigration into Russia has been a matter of intense speculation. Almost since the breakup of the Soviet Union, various sources spoke of millions of Chinese nationals in the Russian Far East and Siberia.[34] These stories—sometimes spread by local and national politicians (such as Dmitri Rogozin and Yuri Boldyrev in 1999)—added ominously that Chinese immigrants were marrying Russian women, acquiring property: "buying up everything," in the words of then–Khabarovsk Governor Viktor Ishayev in 1999.[35] Some believed or would have others believe that "mass infiltration" by the Chinese was part of a secret plan by Beijing's leadership to annex eastern Russian provinces through a "creeping demographic aggression."

Protestations that Chinese migration is traditionally southward, and that the Chinese find the Russian climate—not to mention police practices and popular attitudes—inhospitable have been refuted. References have been made to the experience of the Han Chinese settlement of Manchuria, where the lifting of restrictions on settlement in 1878 led to an increase in population from 3 million to 13 million within a quarter-century. With China's total population at the time at 300 million, that meant that within one generation, around 3 percent of the population migrated north, to a region whose living conditions are rather similar to the Russian Far East and southern Siberia.[36] It may be added that 13 million people is a mere

1 percent of China's population today and that it represents more than double the number of Russian residents east of Lake Baikal.

The reality has been different. Twenty years after the end of the Sino-Soviet cold war, the total number of Chinese residents in Russia is estimated at 300,000, up from 200,000 at the turn of the century and 30 times as many as in the days of the Soviet Union—but close to the number of resident Chinese in the Russian empire before the revolution. The number of registered Chinese guest workers in Russia[37] rose from 94,000 in 2004 to 161,000 in 2005 to 230,000 in 2006. Most of them live far from the border area, or the Far East. When he was governor-general of Siberia, Leonid Drachevsky estimated the number of Chinese in the Siberian federal district (population: 21 million) at 75,000 maximum.

Moscow has the biggest Chinese diaspora in Russia. The early migrants came to sell their goods, but most Chinese in Russia now want to stay, or to use Russia as a way station en route to Central and Western Europe. In the words of Professor Vilya Gelbras, who has closely studied Chinese migration, this is not a resettlement project but "a form of labor movement which accompanies transnational trade flows."[38]

Trade with China and imported Chinese labor critically help sustain the economy of eastern Russia. To a Far Easterner, proximity to China improves one's opportunities. Should economic and trade relations be disrupted, a shock will follow almost immediately. The local Russian authorities—and not only those along the border—were quick to see the benefits of dealing privately with Chinese businessmen. Cooperation extended from poaching to illegal exports of timber to large-scale contraband. The Cherkizovsky market in the capital functioned as a hub for Chinese commerce in the capital and employed hundreds of Chinese nationals. When, in 2009, the Russian government closed the market—a move that had nothing to do with China—the Chinese government immediately sent a deputy prime minister to Moscow.

China's demographic overhang is obvious, as is Beijing's interest in the resources of Siberia—from energy to timber to clean water. Beijing hardly hatches secret plans of demographic aggression, but it openly urges its nationals to "march across the world" as agents of Chinese business—and national—interests. However, if Russia is to "lose" its eastern territories, this will not be due to any Chinese "aggression" but to the Russians' own inability to develop the region. Should this occur, the historical roles of the two countries might reverse themselves: A strong and dynamic China would start using a weak and stagnant Russia. Then, a twenty-first-century

Khabarovsk could turn into a version of what Harbin was at the turn of the twentieth century: an outpost of foreign economic expansion, backed by a measure of political influence. Borders in such a scenario would not have to change necessarily, but, economically, Pacific Russia and Siberia would become a resource base for China and its sphere of influence.

A post-imperial Russia needs to go beyond fears. It needs to find a formula not only for economic relations with its giant neighbor but also for a more productive relationship with those Chinese who come to work or do business in Russia. Better education can help diminish popular xenophobia, and better communication with leaders of local Chinese communities can reduce distrust. And dealing with police and official corruption can ensure more transparency and openness.[39]

REGIONAL DEMOGRAPHIC VULNERABILITIES

The Russian Far East is not the only region of the country that might be considered vulnerable, from a demographic perspective. But, in the Far East, the Chinese who are coming are not the only issue. A bigger one is the Russians who are departing, mostly to Central Russia.

Depopulation struck the Far East and Siberia at the same time that the Soviet Union disintegrated. Through the last Soviet decade, the population of those territories was growing faster than that of the Russian republic as a whole. This was stimulated by clear government policies. In the first post-Soviet decade, when those policies were no longer in place, it decreased six times as fast as in Russia at large. Some 2.5 million left the High North and the Far East. The latter lost about 850,000 people, or 10 percent of its population.

Among the areas officially referred to as the High North, oil-rich Tyumen *oblast* was the only exception to the general depopulation trend. The northern territories in the European part of Russia lost 1 million people between 1991 and 2002; on the Pacific coast, the already small populations of Magadan and Chukotka shrank by two-thirds between 1989 and 2003. Chita and the Maritime Province (Primorsky krai), which lie just across the Amur and the Ussuri from China, lost a quarter-million people in roughly the same period.[40]

This depopulation was inevitable in the absence of a command economy and a totalitarian imperial state. Given the freedom and opportunity, people left the imperial outposts, which no longer could be sustained by a shrunken state. The peak of that process, however, was passed in the 1990s. Those who stayed are determined to slog it out. Yet the population of the Russian High North is still very big, compared with the similar regions of the United States, Canada, Denmark/Greenland, or Norway. It stands at 10.6 million, and accounts for 7.5 percent of the total population of Russia. Murmansk (population: 307,000) and Norilsk (population: 105,000) are megacities compared with other countries' settlements in comparable climate zones. In the future, with the warming of the Arctic, an increase in economic activity along the Northern Sea Route may attract more settlers.

Compared with the Far East and the High North, Kaliningrad—the extreme western enclave of the Russian Federation—has been doing rather well, in demographic terms. The region's population stayed just under 1 million; it also stayed essentially Russian, with very few ethnic Germans willing to settle there instead of Germany itself. The "encirclement" of Kaliningrad after 2004 by the European Union did not so much further "detach" the enclave from mainland Russia as give its residents new opportunities in the European neighborhood.

In the Russian mainland, the ethnic balance has shifted in the past two decades, if only slightly. In 1991, the population of the Russian Federation was more than four-fifths ethnic Russian. Since then, the non-Russian ethnic groups have increased their share. This was the result of several factors working for those groups: higher birthrates, lower mortality, and immigration. Despite its tiny area (0.65 percent of Russia's), the North Caucasus has a relatively significant population (6.6 million, or 4.6 percent of the population of Russia, according to the 2002 census). The density of population in the mountainous region is 59.4 people per square kilometer, compared with Russia's average of 8.4. In Ingushetia, the smallest republic, it is as high as 130.

Between 1989 and 2002, the population of the North Caucasus grew by 25 percent, while the ethnic Russian component in the region decreased by 27 percent. Metropolitan cities—such as Moscow and St. Petersburg—but also regional centers such as Stavropol (500,000 illegal immigrants in 2000), Krasnodar (1 million in the 1990s), and Rostov accept migrants from both the North and South Caucasus. As Russia's cities become more multiethnic, the exodus of ethnic Russians from the republics of the Russian Federation increases.

Before the war, Chechnya numbered some 350,000 non-Chechens, between 220,000 and 240,000 of them ethnic Russian residents, both urban dwellers—the Chechen capital, Grozny, was 72 percent Russian in 1989—and rural descendants of Terek Cossacks. Of these residents, 320,000, including 230,000 Russians, left during the war. This was quite logical, of course. More tellingly, however, virtually none returned after the war ended. Postwar Chechnya is essentially all Chechen, with ethnic Russians numbering at most 18,000 in the two traditionally Cossack districts in Chechnya's north (plus 22,000 Russian troops who rarely leave their barracks).[41] Over time, these remaining Russians are likely to "go to Russia," as they themselves say. Even as the Russians departed, the indigenous Chechen population grew.

Chechnya has gone through a war, but similar processes have been going on across the entire North Caucasus region. As 1 million people of Caucasian descent migrated back to their homelands between 1989 and 2002, more than 300,000 ethnic Russians left.[42] As a result, the share of indigenous population increased from 66 percent to 80 percent (from 66 percent to over 95 percent in Chechnya), while the share of ethnic Russians dropped from 26 percent to 15 percent (in Chechnya, from 25 percent to 2 percent; in Ingushetia, from 13 percent to 1 percent; and in Dagestan, from 9 percent to 5 percent).

Even in purportedly Russian-friendly North Ossetia, the share of the Russian population decreased from 30 percent to 23 percent.[43] Though the situation in some regions is different,* the notion of a Russian exodus agrees with a long-term trend. In 1959, the ratio of Russians to non-Russians in the North Caucasus was 38.9 percent versus 50.7 percent; in 1979, 29.3 percent versus 60.4 percent; and in 1999, 19.0 percent versus 70.6 percent. If this trend continues—and so far it has been only accelerating—ethnic Russian presence in the North Caucasus will soon become very thin.

Russians there are generally older, less fertile people, compared with younger and very active Caucasians. They find it hard to compete successfully with the indigenous people in business; they are increasingly less represented in the local and regional governments and power structures; they have fewer prospects of social or professional advancement. Thus, de facto decolonization proceeds even within a de jure common state.

The Russians' lower profile also has other consequences. These include further fragmentation of the indigenous groups; the weakening of cultural and emotional links between the North Caucasus and the rest of the Rus-

---

* In Karachaevo-Cherkessia, the Russians still make up 34 percent (down from 42 percent) of the population; in Kabardino-Balkaria, 25 percent (down from 32 percent); and in Adygeya, 65 percent (down from 68 percent).

sian Federation;[44] and a backlash in Russia proper in the form of what is referred to as Caucasophobia.

Even today, as a function of the decade-long Chechen war, several series of terrorist attacks in Moscow and elsewhere, seemingly unstoppable violence in the North Caucasus, and massive immigration from the region into Moscow and other cities, many ethnic Russians have come to regard the "Caucasians," especially Caucasian Muslims, as "non-Russians," or de facto aliens. Chechnya is already practically off-limits to ordinary Russians, who in most cases would not even think of traveling there. As the North Caucasus becomes progressively de-Russified, much of the area—with the exception of the Black Sea coastline with the 2014 Winter Olympics capital, Sochi—will be regarded as Russia's "inner abroad."

By contrast, other Muslim enclaves within the Russian Federation have demonstrated stability of interethnic ratios. There has been no Russian exodus from Tatarstan and Bashkortostan, the two big republics on the Volga. The Tatars increased their share during the 1990s, but only marginally, from 48.5 percent to 50.2 percent, while the Bashkirs have grown from 22 percent of the republic's population to 24 percent, still well behind both the Russians and the Tatars.

"Compatriots Abroad"

Two decades ago, the Russian Question loomed large. Quite a few observers believed the new borders of the Russian Federation, which cut through the single body of the Russian nation, were unsustainable. Russians, however, have so far resisted the temptation of aggressive nationalism. Whether at home or abroad, there is no single "Russian people," only individual Russian citizens.

Even as some people in Moscow during the 1990s hoped that ethnic Russian immigrants would help compensate for Russian emigration out of Russia, others took exactly the opposite view. They urged Russian minorities across the CIS to stay put and form the foundation of Russian cultural, economic, and ultimately also political influence in the former borderlands. As we have seen, expectations of a "compensatory" influx of professionals and highly skilled workers have fallen short. Hopes for consolidating ethnic Russian communities in the neighborhood with strong links to Moscow have also failed to materialize.

TABLE 4.3

RUSSIAN MINORITIES IN THE FORMER SOVIET REPUBLICS TURNED INDEPENDENT STATES (percent)

Country	Percent of ethnic Russians, 1989	Current percent of ethnic Russians	Year of latest count
Russian Federation	81.5	79.8	2002
Armenia	1.6	0.5	2001
Azerbaijan	5.6	1.8	1999
Belarus	13.2	11.4	1999
Estonia	30.3	25.6	2000
Georgia	6.3	1.6	2002
Kazakhstan	37.4	30	1999
Kyrgyzstan	21.5	12.5	1999
Latvia	33.9	29.6	2002
Lithuania	9.4	6.3	2001
Moldova	13	5.9	2004
Tajikistan	7.6	1.1	2000
Turkmenistan	9.5	6.7	1995
Ukraine	22.1	17.3	2001
Uzbekistan	8.4	5	1996

Source: Leonid Grigoriev and Marsel Salikhov, *GUAM – Pyatnadzat Let Spustya* (GUAM – Fifteen years later) (Moscow: Regnum, 2007), http://common.regnum.ru/documents/guam.pdf.

One reason for this has been the dwindling of the Russian minorities in all countries that used to be part of the Soviet Union. Of the 25 million people in that group in 1989, only 17 million remained by 2000. The numbers have been going down ever since. The share of Russian minorities has dropped significantly everywhere across the former Soviet Union. Even in the relatively comfortable countries such as Ukraine, Belarus, and Kazakhstan—and in the more affluent Baltic states—the share of ethnic Russians has decreased by 11 to 21 percent. It matters little that those who previously had an option and an incentive to describe themselves as Russians now prefer to identify themselves with the titular ethnic group: The result is the same.

Another reason for the much lower weight that ethnic Russians are carrying in the new countries has been official ethnic nationalism of the governments in a number of countries. To all of them, independence is first and foremost independence from Russia. Ethnic Russians are holdovers from the imperial/colonial past that the new regimes deplore.

Ethnic Russians are also far less rooted in local societies. They rarely speak indigenous languages. Their culture and worldview remain Russocentric. After independence, ethnic Russians were ordered or eased out of important positions in government, administration, police, armed forces, education, and other key institutions.

There are wide distinctions, of course. In Belarus, there is barely a distinction between ethnic Russians and urbanized Belarusians, and Russians hardly feel like a minority. It is also a country where the current (and very peculiar) brand of nationalism emerged on a political rather than a cultural basis. In neighboring Ukraine, the four presidents who succeeded one another after independence—Kravchuk and Kuchma; Yushchenko and Yanukovych—represented very different official attitudes toward Russia and all things Russian (more on this in chapter 5). In Moldova, where a number of leaders and officials had Russian-sounding surnames, the national identity was clearly distinct, treating Russians as an ethnic minority from the very beginning. In the political, economic, and social life of the South Caucasus—with the exception of Abkhazia and South Ossetia—Russians have de facto vanished, in full agreement with their currently minuscule share in those countries' populations.

In Central Asia, Russians have essentially been barred from politics or big government-connected business, though liberal professions, science, and sports are open to them. There is no overt oppression against ethnic Russians, apart from the occasional local civil wars or conflicts, but no real prospects of rising particularly high. As a Moscow observer remarked, "Life just goes by, and they are not part of it."[45]

Actually, the Russians are partly responsible for this situation. They are notoriously unwilling to learn the local languages, immerse themselves in new cultures, delve into other people's histories, assume new identities—and assimilate. Or, conversely, to come together, self-organize, demand fair representation, appeal forcefully to Moscow for support, and so on. Caught in the middle, they are an ethnic group, not a political group; nor are they an element in the new civic nation-building exercise. They thrive on fading memories and appear to be a thing of the past.

In Kazakhstan, ethnic tensions—high until the mid-1990s—have calmed down amid bilingualism and the economic upturn. President Nursultan Nazarbayev has played the role of a personal guarantor of ethnic peace. In a deft move to consolidate the new state, he transferred the capital to the north of the country, close to the Russian border and the Russian-populated towns alongside it. The Kazakhs—whose proportion of the population has risen from just under 40 percent at the time of independence to a very comfortable 63 percent today—feel more self-confident. The Russians appear to have accepted their position as a minority and the restrictions that go along with it.

In Turkmenistan, where at least 100,000 ethnic Russians still reside, the situation is markedly different. In 1993, Ashgabat was the only CIS capital that signed an agreement with Moscow on dual citizenship. In reality, this was a sham, with Russian "dual citizens" not even being able to leave Turkmenistan freely. A decade later, this agreement was unilaterally abrogated by Turkmenistan. The Russian government did not even protest, more interested in a twenty-five-year gas deal that promised Gazprom all gas produced in Turkmenistan. The "gas for people" deal produced a brief public outcry by a few Russian politicians, such as Dmitri Rogozin, but no lasting consequences. In 2008, a new Turkmen constitution banned dual citizenship. Moscow, still focused on gas contracts, remained silent.[46]

ETHNIC RUSSIANS IN ESTONIA AND LATVIA

Lithuania was the only Baltic state that, at independence, granted citizenship to all its legal residents. This generosity had a lot to do with the relative security of the titular nation. In 1991, Russians accounted for 9.4 percent of Lithuania's population; in 2010, their share was 4.8 percent. The demographic situation was radically different in the two other countries, Latvia and Estonia, where the share of Russians was 34 percent and 30 percent, respectively, and the titular ethnics were barely in the majority at the time of independence. Two decades later, Russians make up only 19.7 percent of Latvia's population and 12.9 percent of Estonia's. The halving of the share of ethnic Russians in the Baltic states resulted from their emigration and lower life expectancy and also from the greater willingness of those with mixed parentage to identify themselves with the dominant ethnic group.

In the two decades since independence, the number of ethnic Russians who received citizenship has grown to 60 percent in Latvia and 40 percent in Estonia. Yet many (36 percent of ethnic Russians in Latvia and 38 percent in Estonia) are still non-citizens, even though, since 2004, they enjoy new freedoms provided by the Baltic states' EU membership. Their standard of living roughly compares with Moscow's and is thus higher than the Russian Federation's average.

Crucially, ethnic Russians formed no pro-Moscow "fifth column" inside Estonia and Latvia. In Latvia and Lithuania, though not in Estonia—where 21 percent of ethnic Russians are also citizens of the Russian Federation—they did not reclaim Russian citizenship en masse. Many of them do not feel any special attachment to the Russian Federation, or any animosity toward the indigenous majorities. In terms of ethnic consciousness, they are rather nihilistic. Their level of political participation inside the countries of residence was very low in Estonia, with its largely blue-collar Russian component, and only moderate in Latvia, where many Russians are in business or in professions such as law or medicine. Basically, the Russians who overwhelmingly supported Baltic independence in 1991 have stayed loyal to the Latvian and Estonian states, even though neither deemed it right to grant them all citizenship rights without proper procedure. Russian parties continue to sit in the Latvian parliament but have lost their representation in Lithuania and Estonia.

The original idea in the ruling circles of both Tallinn and Riga was, essentially, to allow ethnic Russians to leave and to gradually assimilate those who were unwilling to move back to their "old country." Citizenship was available upon a personal request and subsequent passage of tests, particularly in the official language and the constitution. To make the assimilation of the new generations easier, Latvian and Estonian authorities phased out university-level education in Russian and progressively reduced the number of Russian schools.

Yet what emerges in Latvia and Estonia are two-tier societies, with a very low rate of intermarriage (11 percent in Estonia), which points toward bi-communal polities in the future. Baltic Russians are certainly distinct, and progressively more so, from their cousins in the Russian Federation, but they are also different from their nominal ethnic Latvian and Estonian compatriots. The more successful business people and professionals and youth identify themselves neither as Latvian/Lithuanian/Estonian nor Russian, but increasingly as European. They are more willing to learn the local languages, but their language of choice is English.

For years, Moscow has been pressing Brussels to lean harder on Riga and Tallinn to end discrimination of ethnic Russians, especially on the issues of civil rights, public education, naturalization procedures, and the use of the Russian language. This, however, has had little effect, especially with the EU conditionality ended and both Latvia and Estonia safely within the Union. The OSCE also closed its missions in the Baltics, declaring the minority issue there essentially resolved. Moscow was disappointed and accused the West of duplicity and double standards, but did little.

The Russian Duma passed a number of resolutions condemning the treatment of ethnic Russians in Estonia and Latvia; the Foreign Ministry issued strongly worded statements; periodically, there were noisy campaigns in the Russian media and boycotts of the few Baltic goods, such as sprats, still sold in Russia. Estonia faced more serious economic sanctions and an Internet attack from unidentified sources in the wake of the relocation of a Red Army war memorial in Tallinn and the war dead buried next to it. But there was little in terms of political subversion that the two countries faced from their eastern neighbor.

It mattered that most ethnic Russians themselves were rather passive politically, not easily swayed to become agents of the Russian Federation. The more successful people among them preferred individualism to irredentism. Be that as it may, Moscow did not use the "minorities card" to destabilize the small Baltic countries in the critical period before they joined NATO and the EU, and has shown no inclination to do this more recently. Rather than challenging the unpleasant realities, the Kremlin chose to adjust to them.

Russian "Foreign" Passports

The official rationale for the Russian military action in South Ossetia—which led to a war with Georgia in August 2008—was the Georgian forces' shelling of Tskhinvali, which was called "genocide" against the Ossetian population. Of the 45,000 residents of South Ossetia, 40,000 were Russian passport holders. When, a few weeks later, President Medvedev announced a new foreign policy doctrine that elevated protection of Russian citizens abroad to one of the main principles of Moscow's foreign policy, many people became concerned.

Ostensibly for humanitarian reasons, but clearly not without some geopolitical considerations, Russia launched a policy of giving its passports to people living in the unrecognized states. This led to predictable results. Of some 200,000 people in Abkhazia, 150,000 became Russian citizens; so did 100,000 of 600,000 residents of Transnistria. After that, any serious conflict affecting those areas would involve large groups of Russian citizens and thus would necessitate Moscow's intervention, likely to include the use of force.

Russia also reached out beyond the conflict areas. In Ukraine, which does not recognize dual citizenship, Russian consulates distributed a number of passports. The number of people in Crimea (population: just under 2 million) who hold such passports is estimated to be 60,000. One needs to factor in some 19,000 Crimean residents who are employed by the Russian Black Sea Fleet, whose lease has been extended to 2042. Russia, of course, is not imposing its passports on reluctant foreigners. Many seek them for pragmatic reasons.[47]

Russia is not the only country offering passports to people beyond its borders. In 2009, Romania intensified its own "passportization drive" in Moldova. From the 1990s, Hungary has also pursued a "welcoming approach" to ethnic Hungarians beyond the country's borders. As some observers noted, if the United States Embassy in Moscow were instructed to offer U.S. passports to Russians, most local people would rush to seize the opportunity.

RUSSIAN COMMUNITIES IN THE FAR ABROAD

The post-1991 wave of immigration from Russia has been essentially about people seeking new opportunities. As a result, there is a new diaspora, which—unlike its predecessors in the 1920s, 1940s, and 1970s—is cosmopolitan and politically passive and seeks to assimilate.

After 1991, Russia almost completely lost a group that had affected its culture and society more than almost any other: the Jews. Their number has gone down to a mere 228,000 in 2002, from 5.2 million in the Russian empire at the turn of the twentieth century and 1.4 million in the Soviet Union at the time of its breakup. This, however, had the effect of endowing Israel with a strong Russian-speaking community, making up as much as 20 percent of the Jewish state's population and a major presence in the media, culture, and the arts as well as in business and politics. In 1996, Natan Sharansky, a former Soviet dissident, became the first Russian-speaking minister in the Israeli cabinet; Avigdor Lieberman, a Russian-speaking native of Moldova, took charge of foreign affairs in 2009. This new situation has led to intense human contacts between Russia and Israel, which in 2009 lifted mutual visa requirements. Russia's policy toward the Middle East is informed by this new factor.

Conclusion

If the preceding chapters have been lacking in persuasiveness, this one should leave no one in doubt: The days of the Russian empire are gone; Russia has entered a post-imperial world. A demographic crisis, though obviously serious and deep, may not yet be the catastrophe that some observers see. The Russian Federation can well sustain itself, even with a decreasing population on still the world's biggest chunk of real estate. What it will not be able to do, however, is expand outward. Also, the complexion of the Russian population is changing and will continue to change. It will be, especially in the bigger cities, less Slav and more Turkic and Asian.

Russia's demographic crisis, of course, needs to be put in a wider context: From Western Europe to Japan, populations of "northern" countries are declining, ceding their longtime domination to the global South. In 1950, ten of the twenty most populous nations were "northern"; by 2050, only three will be left: the United States, Russia, and Japan. The combined share of the North in the world's population—which stood at 34 percent in 1950 and 14 percent in 2007—may go under 10 percent by 2050.[48] If anything, demographics alone may call for closer integration between the EU and the rest of Europe, including Russia and Ukraine. This, however, is not how things are generally seen in the EU countries.

Even substantially smaller than today, Russia by 2030 and 2050 will still be the most populous country in Europe, much bigger than Germany—not to mention France, Britain, and Italy. Yet in proportion to its territory, Russia is among the least densely populated countries in the world. This raises a major challenge to Russia and potentially carries immense geopolitical consequences. The Russian Federation differs from Canada, or, for that matter, Australia, in that it has many neighbors.

Russia will feel demographic pressure mainly from the south: the North Caucasus, within its own borders; Middle Asia and Azerbaijan; and East Asia, in particular China. To a degree, immigration from the south can be salutary: The Russian economy badly needs labor resources. However, Russian polity and society are conservative and resistant. Birthrates are flat, but xenophobia is on the rise. Statecraft and leadership will be required for developing and putting to work a sensible policy of integration.

Twenty years after the fall of the Soviet Union, ethnic Russian repatriation is virtually complete. Most of the millions of ethnic Russians in the neighboring new states feel at home and will not move back. Those who come and will continue coming to Russia are not of Slav stock. However, integration prospects can be helped by the fact that two-thirds of labor migrants come to Russia from former Soviet states. Smart immigration policy can help significantly; a policy that is poor or nonexistent may spell disaster.

Within Russia itself, the ethnic balance will shift. This will have serious domestic political consequences in some regions. The North Caucasus will lose the remainder of its ethnic Russian component. Although this slow exodus, by itself, will not lead to outright independence of the string of tiny statelets, it will strengthen the perception of the region as an "inner abroad." Having seen Russian settlement in the Caucasus in the imperial days, Dagestanis, Chechens, and others are now streaming to "conquer" Moscow, St. Petersburg, Stavropol, Rostov, and other cities in Russia. Post-imperium is also a boomerang.

5

CULTURE, IDEOLOGY, AND RELIGION

This chapter will attempt to address the following questions: Is the old imperial idea dead, or is it making a comeback, yet again? Is a "great power" a new description for the "empire"? What are the values, if any, that drive Russian policies? Does Russia possess "soft power"? Is the "politics of history" pointing a way to the future? Why is the history of World War II so important? What is the role of religion in consolidating a *Russkiy Mir*? What will be the medium of communication between Russians and Georgians?

IDEAS AND IDEOLOGIES

For a long time, Russian foreign policy contained a messianic streak. Ever since the late fifteenth century, the Russian grand dukes, and then tsars, looked at themselves as heirs to the great Orthodox empire of Byzantium. With Constantinople overrun by the Ottomans in 1453, Moscow was deemed to be the "Third Rome." For more than four centuries, right up to the First World War, the guiding foreign policy idea of the Russian state was to reunite the territories that once formed Kievan Rus and to assume tutelage over Eastern Christendom under the banner of Pan-Slavism. During the first half of the nineteenth century, St. Petersburg staunchly defended the legitimacy of European monarchies against revolution. On the margins, Russia was engaged in a *mission civilizatrice* in places like Turkestan.

The founding idea of the Soviet empire was world communist revolution. This revealed itself as an illusion within three years and was succeeded by the mid-1920s by an idea of a besieged fortress—"a red commune in a capitalist encirclement." When the Soviet Union emerged victorious after World War II and built its own sphere of influence, the lonely fortress turned into a "socialist camp" that faced a still more powerful adversary. From the 1960s, the camp was renamed a "socialist community," and it started to compete with "U.S.-led world imperialism" on a global level. This competition was at the heart of Moscow's policies, both foreign and domestic. It led to overextension and distortions that eventually produced the terminal crisis of the USSR.

Dismissed as irrelevant after the Bolshevik Revolution, the ideas of Kievan legacy and pan-Slavism resurfaced at the end of World War II. Galicia-Volynia, the last bit of Kievan heritage, was finally wrested from foreign domination. The Orthodox countries of Southeastern Europe, Bulgaria and Romania, became part of the Soviet bloc. So did the Catholic Slav countries Poland and Czechoslovakia, and the religiously heterogeneous Yugoslavia. Except for Turkey, which stood up to Stalin's pressure on the Straits and received support from U.S. President Harry Truman, the ancient tsarist dream was realized.

Still, the Soviet Union's domination within its Eastern European empire was largely due to hard power: the stationing of Soviet military forces and the satellite countries' participation in the Warsaw Pact; ideological and political control through the national Communist parties and security services; economic dependence on Soviet energy and other raw materials; and the Soviet market. When the Soviet leadership saw its geopolitical and ideological interests in danger—as in Czechoslovakia in 1968—it used force, even though this exercise of hard power forever destroyed the soft power that Moscow could wield in that country. This was considered expendable. Within the Soviet empire, cultural affinity as such did not play much of a role, and religion was marginalized. Beyond Eastern Europe, the Soviet empire rested ostensibly on ideological—but in reality on "hard"—geopolitical, and military-strategic foundations.

Afghanistan was a turning point. Equally difficult to portray as "brotherly help" or "internationalist duty" to a neighbor in its quest for a more just society or as forward defense against U.S. imperialist plotting, the unpopular war pulled the rug from the already shaky ideological foundations of Moscow's foreign policy. The imperial *élan* was no more. Before long, the empire and the ideology found themselves in a common grave.

THE FAILURE OF INTEGRATION

The collapse of the Soviet Union ushered in a new cycle. The 1993 Russian Constitution prohibited state ideology, but the early post-Soviet Russian leadership was moved by liberal and democratic internationalism. President Boris Yeltsin and Foreign Minister Andrei Kozyrev raised the slogan of Russia joining the civilized world, which is to say, Western integration. The empire was a hindrance, not worth much regret. The Russian Federation minimized relations with the reprehensible regime in North Korea and with Castro's Cuba. It attempted to play the role of a democratic leader vis-à-vis the authoritarian governments in Central Asia: a new edition of the *mission civilizatrice*.

This new enthusiasm did not last long. Russia was not integrated into the West, let alone given one of the leading roles to which its leadership had aspired. Meanwhile, all other former Soviet states were busy constructing their founding myths based on the idea of national revival. Even though life was hard, populations—and particularly the elites—could celebrate independent statehood.

Of course, the exhilaration over national independence could last only so long. Ukrainian nationalists like Vyacheslav Chornovil thought that once power was in the hands of nationally conscious Ukrainians, and the Russian vector was discarded, the country would be different. Chornovil, however, failed to keep mass support. By the time he died in a car accident in 1999, Rukh—the national movement he founded ten years earlier—had become marginalized.

Russia was different. The idea of Russia's independence from the Soviet Union—useful in the intense power struggle between Gorbachev and Yeltsin—was openly derided as ludicrous once the struggle was over and the winner in full command. Russia was born neither in June 1990, when its Supreme Soviet passed a declaration of state sovereignty; nor in August 1991, when the collapse of the putsch gave the coup de grâce to the communist rule that began in 1917 and the tsarist tricolor again became Russia's national flag; nor in December 1991, when that tricolor finally replaced the red Soviet flag over the Kremlin.

Post-Soviet Russia was not founded on some myth but rather on a thoroughly rational idea of democracy. However, the idea of democracy experienced a difficult time in the 1990s. Most Russians did not so much want democracy with its rights balanced by responsibilities; its principles of accountability and participation; or freedom married to self-discipline.

Rather, most people wanted to get rid of the oppressive and corrupt Soviet communism and step—as soon as possible—into a free world of material abundance. What they got instead was formal democracy, but also almost instant inequality, and, for some, real impoverishment. The fittest, who survived and succeeded, were not always the best. No wonder democracy soon lost its attractiveness to many ordinary people.

The government sensed that. Yeltsin decreed development of a "national idea" for the new Russian Federation. Kozyrev abandoned talk of democratic solidarity and focused on the national interest. These attempts came to nothing. The founding phase of post-Soviet Russian capitalism was essentially nonideological. The only real values in that milieu were those that could be quoted in dollars and cents.

After a while, when the elite had become immensely rich incredibly fast, its members started to seek enhanced status abroad to match its political and economic domination at home. To these people, the real or perceived losses from the imperial dismantlement appeared more vivid. If Russia was neither first founded as a state, like Kazakhstan, nor had its statehood restored, as Estonia, but simply continued in a somewhat different shape and form, what was the big idea? Why did the Soviet Union have to go?

Instead of trying to construct a wholly new state on the flimsy foundation of Yeltsin's democracy, the Russian elite opted for the seemingly more solid ground of the traditional great-power politics. When he became foreign minister in 1996, Yevgeny Primakov famously proclaimed: "Russia has been, is, and will be a great power!"[1] This became a rallying point for the Russian elite. Virtually everyone chimed in. What was less clear was what it meant to be a "great power" in the new era.

The official thinking on that score has undergone an interesting evolution, which, at the turn of the 2010s, is still proceeding. Yeltsin and Kozyrev; Yegor Gaidar and Anatoly Chubais; Primakov and Chernomyrdin; Vladimir Putin and Dmitri Medvedev not only had differing—and at times confused—concepts of "great power," but their own thinking on the issue changed throughout their government careers. Distilling that thinking is not an easy task. Yet doing that is indispensable for understanding the prime source of Russia's international ambitions and orientation after the loss of its empire. For that, the meaning that its leadership attaches to the notion of "great power" is key.

One obvious quality of a great power is its strategic independence. During the brief liberal internationalist period—roughly, Yeltsin's first term and Kozyrev's stint as foreign minister—Russia considered itself to be part of the Western world. To be sure, it regarded itself as a great power, but it was ready to treat "common Western interests" as its own and was not quite sure what special national interests it now had.

In reality, while Russia at that time retained the freedom of action and was never "standing on its knees," as it was claimed later,[2] it depended heavily on the West and looked to it for guidance. In a revealing 1993 conversation with former U.S. President Richard Nixon, Kozyrev left the impression with his interlocutor that post-Soviet Russia would embrace general U.S.-Western interests as its own. Nixon, ever the geopolitician, was bewildered.[3]

It makes sense to compare Russia's post-1991 predicament with that of post–World War II Britain and France. Unlike Britain, Russia never succeeded in forming a special relationship with the United States. During his 1992 visit to Washington, Yeltsin made a plea for an alliance with the United States, only to be told by President George H. W. Bush that—now that the global confrontation was over—there was no need for such an alliance.

The NATO alliance, however, was left in place, and—while Moscow's former satellites were invited to join—Russia itself was told not to bother. This produced a lot of bad blood on the Russian side. In their eyes, NATO enlargement became a symbol of Western exploitation of Russia's weakness as well as a breach of faith vis-à-vis Moscow.[4]

Unlike France, Russia did not have a European option where its leadership in integration would replace the trauma of the imperial collapse. Prime Minister Chernomyrdin's public statements about Russia's wish to join the European Union[5] betrayed a profound lack of knowledge about the EU. The Russian government talked, of course, about re- or new integration among ex-Soviet republics, but post-Soviet "integration" throughout the 1990s and much of the 2000s was largely a sham. Moscow itself hardly believed its own formal assertion of the priority status it notionally was giving to ties with the former republics.

Unlike postwar West Germany, Russia adamantly rejected being considered a loser in the Cold War. It was also not placed under foreign military occupation, protected on the outside, or allowed to enjoy the *Wirtschaftswunder*, or economic miracle, inside. On the contrary: Its GDP contracted by about half and did not recover its 1990 level until 2007, after which it slumped again. If anything, Russia was akin to post–World War I Weimar Germany: reduced in both size and status, still big and potentially powerful, saddled with suspicion—if not guilt—for its Soviet-era behavior, unhappy and unanchored.

The West's disappointment with Russia—which culminated in its abandonment in despair after the 1998 financial default—was more than matched by Russia's disappointment in the West, which had refused to adopt its once formidable, and now malleable, adversary. Almost miraculously, however, the window of opportunity opened again, in the wake of the 9/11 terrorist attacks, when Putin sought strategic alignment with the West on the global scale. This moment lasted barely more than a year. It disappeared with the George W. Bush administration's cold-shoulder of Russia as Washington focused heavily on Iraq and the Greater Middle East.

RUSSIA'S *ALLEINGANG*

Thus, integration *into* the West—on a "French model," as some Russians viewed it,[6] in the 1990s, and then *with* the West—in the form of an "alliance with the Alliance,"[7] in the early 2000s, became lost opportunities. Spurned, as an unrequited lover, Russia in the mid-2000s turned to reasserting its great-powerdom as a default position.[8]

By definition, a great power did not take orders from anyone. Russia, Putin claimed, would no longer be under the thumb of the United States. According to the official Putin-era concept, Russia "rose from its knees." It had preserved its nuclear weapons and was gaining a new usable instrument: energy. Against the background of the rapidly soaring oil price, some even called it a weapon.[9]

From then on, the boosted great-power mentality blocked—or at least placed severe restrictions on—any further integrationist effort: great powers do not integrate themselves, though they could integrate others. In Russia's case, ironically, *neither* was actually possible. Since 2003, Moscow's resumed attempts at economic integration with other CIS states—such as the Single Economic Space*—were inconsistent, hampered by Russia's own weakness and constrained by its CIS partners' desire for more independence. As to occasional neo-imperialist talk among the Russian elites, it was still all "on the cheap."

Ostensibly a firebrand, but essentially a gifted steam-valve mechanic, Vladimir Zhirinovsky was a caricature of this better than anyone. Rather

---

* An idea broached in 2004 with the aim of integrating Ukraine economically with Russia, alongside Kazakhstan and Belarus. It lost whatever meaning it might have had after Ukraine's Orange Revolution in late 2004.

than fomenting irredentism, he reduced it to *sound and fury* and thus neutralized it. Words substituted for action. Emotions were put onto a treadmill. Troubled souls could vent their feelings and relieve themselves, but—apart from a few ruffled feathers—everything remained in place.

At the top, there was neither money nor strong will for irredentism; at the bottom, the popular slogan was "Russia for the (ethnic) Russians," an anti-immigrant but essentially defensive attitude. The basic meaning of great power in Russian minds, then, was its own independence, rather than others' dependence on it.

As great-power trappings go, it comes after independence in this enumeration, but it might as well come ahead of it: great powers are domestically sovereign. If they are democracies, these are sovereign nations. If they are autocracies, these are regimes impervious to outside pressure. Post-Soviet Russia—with its mild authoritarian regime, enjoying the consent of the governed—falls into the latter category, where domestic independence means full sovereignty for the ruling elite. They are truly above the law and moral conventions. The experience of the 1990s—when the Russian federal budget lived from one IMF handout to another, when Moscow audiences listened to foreign lecturers, and foreign advisers had easy access to top Russian bureaucrats—is not fondly remembered by the ruling groups of the 2000s.

Putin's objective was to make the ruling regime safe from foreign pressure—and free from outside support—and to place it firmly on continuing popular assent, procured by a combination of effective manipulative policies. The massive inflow of oil and gas revenue in the mid-2000s made this largely possible. Foreigners were told to mind their own business, and domestic critics were disqualified as a "fifth column" of the West "scavenging at foreign embassies," in Putin's words.[10] It is a combination of strategic and domestic independence that formed the substance of the much-quoted formula of sovereign democracy. Because democracy requires political participation, of which there is not much in today's Russia, the reality is more like sovereign bureaucracy.

The notion of a great power, however, also has a meaning beyond the country's national borders. Like the king on stage, a great power, Russian traditionalists think, is played by the crowd of clients and supplicants. In the Realpolitik-grounded view of the Russian leadership, the world is composed of a handful of truly sovereign great powers—America, in a class of its own; China; and now again (after the interlude of the 1990s), Russia—and their respective "spheres of influence." It is in the nature of global politics, the Russian leaders and their advisers believe, that great powers should compete over these spaces, so as to extend their sway and establish authority. From this perspective, regional primacy is both natural and stabilizing; universal primacy is both an illusion and a threat.

In this competition, Russia's post-Soviet posture was essentially revisionist: Moscow militated against the U.S. "unipolar moment" and the "new world order" the United States established in the wake of the Cold War's end. Russia itself considered its own policies wholly defensive. Besides advancing multipolarity, a form of global oligarchy that would bar anyone's global predominance (more on it later), Russia has been trying to regain soft dominance—but not ownership—in the former Soviet (imperial) space.

The Russian leaders did not aspire to full control of that space, à la Lenin, at the close of the Russian Civil War; or in the manner of Stalin, before, during, and after World War II. Where Stalin's foreign minister, Vyacheslav Molotov, congratulated himself with having helped restore the "just" borders of the state,[11] Russia's current foreign minister, Sergei Lavrov, speaks about "civilizational unity" that binds Russia and its near neighbors,[12] whose formal sovereignty Russia nevertheless does not formally dispute (with the important exception of Georgia's borders).

In the early 2000s, ideas of a special Russian civilization—which can be traced to the conservative nineteenth-century philosophers Nikolai Danilevsky and Konstantin Leontiev—became more fashionable. By the end of the decade, the Kremlin came up with the concept of a Russian-speaking world, *Russkiy Mir*, which includes all those who associate themselves with the Russian language and culture. As a politico-mental construct, *Russkiy Mir* competes against such rivals as the "English-speaking world" and "*Francophonie.*" This concept is actively supported by Patriarch Kirill, who even outlined the geographical borders of *Russkiy Mir*. In his thinking, the Russian-centered civilization embraces—besides the mainly Orthodox lands such as Ukraine, Belarus, and Moldova—two other countries with ancient independent Christian churches, Armenia and Georgia, and—even more strikingly—a number of Muslim countries where Russian is widely used, among them Kazakhstan and Kyrgyzstan.

From that perspective, it is the United States that is seen as a poacher and intruder that has crossed all imaginable borders, as Putin stated in his 2007 Munich speech.[13] What business, the Kremlin was heard asking at the close of the George W. Bush administration, does the United States have in Ukraine, Georgia, and Central Asia other than to expand its sphere of influence and pin down, constrain, and diminish Russia? Why does the U.S. Sixth Fleet frequent the waters of the Black Sea? Why, of all things, is there NATO enlargement in the absence of a threat to the West from Russia? To counter U.S. moves, and to irritate Washington, Moscow has recently been using Venezuela and the other "Bolivarian" states—Nicaragua, Bolivia, Ecuador—to send one message to Washington: Get off my back!

YEARNING FOR A GLOBAL ROLE

This countervailing tactic, as the last example shows, means going beyond the "natural" area of Russian activism and carries the risk of reentering global competition with a very powerful rival, which puts Moscow at a clear disadvantage. Russia, however, refuses to accept the rank of a middle power with merely a regional role. It sees itself as a global actor, playing in the big leagues.

This is a hugely important point: To be a great power means to be a co-ruler of the world. Both Mikhail Gorbachev, in his final years in power as the last Soviet leader, and Yeltsin, in his early years as Russia's first president, envisaged something like a benign U.S.-Russian co-hegemony. This was not to be. In the later thinking of the Kremlin, the global anarchy prevailing after the end of the bipolar era can best be structured as a global oligarchy, also known as multipolarity. This is not an analytical conclusion, but an active posture. Multipolarity is the antithesis of unipolarity, or U.S. global dominance. Moscow started its campaign against it in the mid-1990s, symbolized by Primakov's replacement of Kozyrev as foreign minister, and has been more vocal than any of its fellow travelers, including China and France. True, the official Russian rhetoric is less strident than that of Mahmoud Ahmadinejad or Hugo Chávez, but these presidents are occasionally seen in Moscow as tactical allies in resisting U.S. global hegemony—much as the late Saddam Hussein and Slobodan Milosevic were in the past. Meanwhile, the real post–Cold War G2 began forming between the United States and China.

Since the days of Peter the Great, Russia sought to be a great power in Europe, a status it finally achieved as a result of victory over Napoleon. It then was a key member of the Holy Alliance, which maintained order in Europe. From the Russian perspective, being one of a half-dozen mightiest powers to jointly manage the world is a natural aspiration. Moscow's preferred, if not ideal, model is still the United Nations Security Council, with its supreme authority in matters of war and peace and its all-important veto right enjoyed by the five permanent members, including Russia. When the Cold War ended, and the forty-year paralysis of the UN was over, Moscow hoped that a revitalized United Nations would be the heart of a new global order. In Europe, Moscow proposed that the Organization for Security and Cooperation in Europe (OSCE) be reformed into an organization with its own UN-style Security Council for Europe. These expectations turned out to be illusions. Instead, Russia had to live with, and fight, the "unipolar moment."

After the end of the Cold War, Russia sought membership in the exclusive group of industrialized democracies, which became the G8 when it joined in 1998. This was a hard-won badge of equality with the United States and the leading Western powers. This formal equality, however, did not lead to integration. Even though it appreciated the G8 membership as a status symbol, Russia could not fully associate itself with the West. The West, for its part, did not see Russia as being "one of us," and occasionally threatened it with excommunication.

It is important and symbolic to note that Russia was not invited to join the financial core of the club, which remained the G7 right up until the 2008 economic crisis. The crisis has produced a group much more germane to the economic and political realities of the early twenty-first-century world than either the G7 or G8: the G20! True to form, Russia embraced the new club and sought to demonstrate its active posture there.

Thus, Russia seeks multiple and partially overlapping memberships: in the "home" post-imperial clubs it naturally dominates (CIS); exclusive Western/global clubs (such as the G8 and the G20); exclusive non-Western global clubs (such as BRIC, for Brazil-Russia-India-China, the leading emerging economies), and non-Western regional clubs (like the Shanghai Cooperation Organization, where Russia is a de facto co-chair, alongside China). As a country straddling Europe and Asia, Russia seeks to register its presence in broad groupings like the OSCE, which it hoped, in the 1990s, would supplant NATO; and the Asia-Pacific Economic Cooperation (APEC), which Russia joined in 1999. It took pride in hosting global and regional summits—the G8 in 2006; BRIC in 2009—and equally looks forward to hosting APEC in 2012.

Russia, however, shows relatively less interest in rules-based organizations with dozens of members without veto rights, such as the OSCE, the Council of Europe, APEC, the World Trade Organization, the Organization for Economic Cooperation and Development, or the UN General

Assembly, for that matter. There, Russia wants to gain membership, where it does not already have it, to ensure that these organizations do not act against Russian interests. It seeks to retain freedom to maneuver by staying away from the Organization of the Petroleum Exporting Countries and is being cautious about its gas equivalent, where Russia would have a major role but whose discipline might constrain it.

What is striking about this analysis of Russian government views and practices is that it lays bare a fundamental distinction between an empire and a great power. Empires, for all the coercion they necessarily entail, do produce some public goods, in the name of a special mission. Great powers can be at least equally brutish and oppressive, but they are essentially selfish creatures. The great debate in Russia on the national interest—which, in 1992, signaled the transition to the post-imperial condition—eventually evolved into a concept of national egoism. This required an adjustment of the official view of history.

Politics of History

The great debate of the 2000s in Russia was over the past.[14] It is the kind of debate that reflects the present and helps define the future. What is known as the politics of history is above all dealing with the historical legacy of the empire. Present-day Russian elites do not view themselves as heirs to the Soviet Union; they see themselves as continuing the Russian empire, albeit with some distinctly Soviet features. Throughout the 1990s, Yeltsin tried—unsuccessfully—to win the communist-dominated Duma's approval of the tsarist double-headed eagle as the country's official emblem. Putin did this with ease in 2000, in a package with the Stalin-era anthem—although the new lyrics refer to God and country rather than extol Stalin and Lenin.

Since 1991, Lenin has left most people cold, and the whole mythology of the Bolshevik Revolution was debunked even in the late Soviet period. As in a time warp, the Lenin Mausoleum is strangely stranded in Red Square—with rock concerts, military tattoos, and, during winter, hundreds of ordinary skaters performing at its walls. By contrast, the popular attitudes toward Stalin and his treatment by the current Russian authorities are particularly interesting and revealing. While both were quintessential Bolsheviks, Lenin worked as an empire wrecker, and Stalin became an empire builder.

Post-Soviet Russians are deeply divided over Stalin's personality and role. In an August 2009 poll, 12 percent would convict him as a state criminal, with 26 percent leaning in that direction. However, a guilty verdict is strongly opposed by 12 percent of respondents, with 32 percent generally siding with that view.[15]

A companion poll—assessing Stalin's contribution to Russia's history—had 49 percent calling his contribution positive, against 42 percent convinced it was negative: a shift from the 53 percent versus 33 percent ratio in 2003.[16] Stalin's name is closely linked to the Great Patriotic War and the 1945 victory over Nazi Germany, which is the one surviving national myth shared by most Russians.

Indeed, if Russian television had not managed the tallying of viewers' votes, as some suspected, Stalin would have probably become the most popular Russian leader of all times. The "masses" turn to Stalin to restore order—"He knew how to successfully fight that scourge [terrorism]," in the words of a popular comic[17]—to end corruption; to rein in the bosses. Many ordinary people, for their part, view Stalin primarily as an empire builder and a wartime leader. To them, he also stands for a strong state, near-perfect order, but above all for an awe-inspiring empire.

Interestingly and tellingly, Lenin has not been prominent in the new elite debate over history, not to speak of Trotsky, who gets more attention for the way he died than for what he did while he was alive. This points more to the disdain of the elite and the leadership for communism and the revolution. Among the population as a whole, 29 percent see the Bolshevik Revolution as a driver of socioeconomic development, while 26 percent consider it an obstacle to development or even a catastrophe. (A similarly strong group, abstaining from judgment, talks about the revolution as ushering in a "new era.")[18] Unlike the destructive revolutionaries, Stalin, his ministers, scientists, and generals are viewed as state and empire builders. Stalin's crimes are not hidden, but, for many, they do not cancel out his presumed achievements. Over time, the latter tend to look more relevant, and the former are ascribed to the brutalities of his time.

As to the winner of the 2008 TV contest, this was Alexander Nevsky, a thirteenth-century prince, made a saint by the Orthodox Church and revered by Peter the Great, who had his remains transferred to St. Petersburg. Alexander was made famous—in particular by Stalin, who had him immortalized in a 1940 film by Sergei Eisenstein—for checking Swedish and German incursions into northwestern Russian lands.

At the same time, not depicted in the film, Alexander allied himself with the Mongols, who had just conquered most of the Russian principalities (minus the northwestern ones), and accepted being an underling of the Khan. The Mongols, for all their battlefield brutality, preferred to rule indirectly, through the princes like Alexander; they also kept the Orthodox Church in place, and even favored it. By contrast, Western Catholics, like the ones chased off by Alexander, saw Orthodox Russians as schismatics, and—with the pope's blessing—sought to reconvert them. That was seen— then and after—as the bigger challenge.

While the focus in Russia has been largely on its imperial glory, the new states were busy developing a victim complex. In Ukraine, many nationalists described the country's status within the Russian empire and the Soviet Union as that of a colony, or an occupied territory. The reality is more complex. While Ukraine was not exactly a Scotland to Russia's England, Ukrainians were fully integrated into the Russian and later Soviet polity—on condition, of course, that they accepted that polity's overriding goals and objectives. Many Ukrainians did, and became active and efficient empire builders—not unlike the Scots—and a number rose to lead the Soviet Union. Some refused, and resisted, or even fought the Soviets in the name of an independent Ukraine.

Things came to a head in November 2007 when Ukraine bid, at the United Nations, for a resolution condemning the great famine of 1932— *Holodomor*—as genocide against the Ukrainian people. It needs to be stressed that Kiev did not accuse present-day Russia of the crime, but laid the blame with the 1930s Soviet leadership; moreover, it included the Ukrainian communist leaders of the day among the principal culprits.

Yet official Russian reaction was vehement. It was angry at the Ukrainian campaign, which characterized *Holomodor* as the "genocide of the Ukrainians organized by Bolshevik Moscow."[19] Moscow refused to support the draft resolution on the grounds that the famine had also affected large areas of Russia and Kazakhstan, and thus could not be termed genocide of the Ukrainian people. It also accused President Viktor Yushchenko of fomenting anti-Russian sentiments.

The Russian reaction was also revealing. True, there is little evidence to support the claim of genocide. In 1932, Stalin was desperately seeking resources for industrialization and thus squeezing the peasantry very hard. Simultaneously, he was trying to "collectivize" the countryside to destroy the peasants' independence and consolidate the communist regime. The dictator was probably couching his needs in class terms, but he was hardly thinking in ethnic ones. Ukraine's nationalist intelligentsia was in the cities, and Stalin dealt with them later and by other means. However, the Russian reaction, such as it was, also meant that Moscow regarded itself as the custodian of the entire Soviet legacy. Whoever was attacking risked provoking Russia's anger. There was no room for universal values in Moscow's response, only for geopolitics and the national interest.

Having assumed the mantle of heir to the USSR, the Russian Federation had to fight to defend communism internationally, even as the Kremlin was keeping the Communist Party firmly in check domestically. Russia protested against equating communism and Nazism in the resolution passed by the Council of Europe. In his remarks to the Russian ambassadors in July 2008, President Medvedev claimed that the aim of equating Stalinism with Hitlerism was to make Russia morally, legally, and materially responsible for the crimes committed by the USSR. If one were to accept this premise, 1945 would have meant the replacement of the German occupation of Central and Eastern Europe with a Soviet one.[20]

THE CONTROVERSIES OVER WORLD WAR II

This issue is tied to the most crucial point in history—World War II. By the mid-1990s, the Russian leadership discovered one thing. Like its late Soviet predecessor, it had no legitimacy other than the victory over the German invaders in the 1940s. As Stalin died—and the last hurrah of communist enthusiasm died down with Nikita Khrushchev's departure—the only thing Brezhnev and his cohorts could rely upon, in terms of legitimacy, was victory over Nazi Germany.

The tradition of celebrating Victory Day dates back only to 1965. It was initially carried over by Gorbachev, but was downplayed later. Yeltsin, who stopped the practice of military parades in Red Square, used the fiftieth anniversary celebration in 1995 to demonstrate the Western leaders' solidarity with him. Putin restored the practice of military hardware displays and expanded it. He also used the parades to send warnings to the United States against ignoring Russia's interests. In 2007, Putin went as far as comparing U.S. policies to those of the Third Reich. Medvedev's 2010 parade—sixty-five years after the end of the war, with but a handful of survivors left—was the biggest show ever.

This undoubtedly strikes a chord with the ordinary Russian people. The memory of the immense sacrifice and suffering is still alive; so is the pride in having defeated—virtually single-handedly, many would add—the world's mightiest war machine. If Russians were asked about their country's most important contribution to world history, they would probably name victory over Nazism. Twice as important as the collapse of the Soviet Union, it is the only positive pillar in the national consciousness.[21]

May 9, Victory Day, has been the true national day in the USSR/Russia since the 1960s. It still is today, and for a good reason. The Soviet Union, as one knew it in its last decades, and the "Soviet community of people," to the extent it existed, were both products of World War II. Even though most people living today are too young to have experienced the war, the result of Soviet, and now Russian, state propaganda is there. For most ordinary Russians, the Great Patriotic War remains sacred. It is the one thing in their common history that they can all be proud of: The Soviet Union, their country, defeated Nazism, the twentieth-century embodiment of evil.

Thus, the Soviet World War II victory is "sacred"; whoever seeks to revise it is an enemy of Russia, or at least an ill-wisher. "Revisionism" of the Soviet-era historical narrative, however, has long become a point of departure as the new states set out to rediscover their own past. The Baltic states, Poland, and Moldova fault the Soviet Union for the 1939 pact with Hitler's Germany that assigned the Baltic states and Bessarabia to the Soviet sphere, and divided Poland, so that its Ukrainian and Belarusian territories could come under Soviet control. For the Russian leadership, the Molotov-Ribbentrop pact is—while deplorable on moral grounds—essentially of the same nature as the Munich agreement of 1938, under which Britain and France delivered Czechoslovakia to Hitler, with Italy acting as a facilitator. The prewar Polish leadership is also seen as having plotted with Hitler, and it joined with him as late as March 1939 to get a piece of Czechoslovakia (the Teschen district) as it was being dismembered: villains and victims enmeshed.

The 1940 Katyn massacre of 22,000 Polish officers and civilians was first condemned by Gorbachev, then by Yeltsin, and again by Putin. In November 2010, on the eve of Medvedev's visit to Warsaw, the Kremlin leaned on the Duma to issue a formal statement holding Stalin and the NKVD secret police responsible for the mass murder. Six months before that, a moving ceremony to mark its seventieth anniversary was led by Putin and Polish Prime Minister Donald Tusk.[22]

For a long time, Russian commentators equated this mass killing with the plight of Russian POWs, 32,000 of whom died in Polish captivity in 1920–1921. Putin suggested that the 1940 act may have been Stalin's revenge for what had happened two decades previously.[23] To most Russians, the Polish officers were among the many millions who perished during the era of political repression. The Poles and the Balts, most of whom had been born subjects of the Russian empire, shared the fate of so many Soviets. For all the hideousness of these "crimes, committed by Stalin and his henchmen," in the words of Medvedev, this was hardly genocide. In any event, Putin's kneeling at the Polish memorial is an important symbol of the coming reconciliation.

Putin at Katyn, however, was no Brandt in the former Warsaw Ghetto.* Essentially, the official Russian view remains: No one was a saint, and the Soviet Union was certainly no worse in its foreign policy than either the Western powers or the countries of Central and Eastern Europe. The Russian government's aim is to prevent Russia's being saddled with political and especially legal responsibility for Stalin's actions. Thus, Russia recognizes that the Baltic states were annexed by the USSR, but it denies that this was an "occupation," which is fraught with material consequences. It talks about crimes but rejects genocide. Putin and Medvedev do not want Russia to become another Germany and put itself into a permanently inferior position, the moral lower ground. No locking oneself in a dock. On the contrary, they want to see Russia at the top of the Victory column and seek to turn this victory into a source of national and international strength. Victory Day parades in Red Square—like the one in 2010 with U.S., UK, French, and Polish troops marching past the world leaders after the Russians—could help form the needed image.

So much for defense. Since Russia rejects the notion that communism and Nazism were equally evil, it denounces those who fought against the Soviet army during or after World War II as Nazi collaborators, or worse. In particular, Russians have been incensed by the regular events staged in Estonia and Latvia by *Waffen SS* veterans. A row over the moving of a Soviet war memorial, and the remains of the soldiers buried close to it, from the center of Tallinn to a military cemetery led to the intensification of hostility between the two countries. What to many Estonians is an unwelcome reminder of Soviet imperial control, and a focal point for rowdy rallies, is a symbol of national glory to the Russians. When the Georgian government in 2009 ordered demolition, for safety reasons, of a giant memorial to 300,000 Georgian World War II dead in Kutaisi, Putin vowed to restore

---

* When visiting Poland in 1970 as West German chancellor, Willy Brandt knelt before the memorial to the victims of the 1944 anti-Nazi uprising at the Ghetto.

the monument in the War Memorial Park in Moscow. That ordinary war memorials in Russia itself are often in bad shape and the war graves are not always given proper care is beside the point. Russians want to be respected abroad. Period.

In the Baltic countries, the historical optics mostly divide the titular groups and the resident Russians. In Ukraine, the country as a whole is divided on the issue of the war. The more nationalist forces and western Ukrainian politicians have been highlighting the role of the Ukrainian rebel army (UPA), which fought against the Nazis and the Soviets. The majority of the Ukrainians, however, fought in the Soviet army. They basically share the same view of World War II as most Russians. They, and the Russians, were much angered by the willingness of Ukraine's third president, Viktor Yushchenko, to honor the anti-Soviet fighters and put them on an equal footing with Soviet war veterans. Although on a much smaller scale, Russians did not profess understanding for the equal treatment in Moldova of those who in 1941 were drafted into the Soviet army and those who were inducted into the Romanian forces that occupied Odessa and reached as far as Stalingrad.[24] Such moral equivalence, even for the sake of healing the wounds of a nation, is unacceptable, from Moscow's perspective.*

The refusal to continuously apologize and ask for forgiveness is linked to Putin's early conviction that the Gorbachev and Yeltsin periods were too heavy on criticism and self-denial and not nearly strong enough on the positive side of history. Ever since, Putin has been trying to make the case for positive Russian patriotism. Although this may look like the *Geschichtspolitik* practiced by Chancellor Helmut Kohl and his adviser, historian Michael Stuermer, in the 1980s, the authoritarian nature of the Russian political regime makes a world of difference.

Since 2006, Russia has seen a number of school textbooks that, in the words of the historian Alexei Miller, seek to "nurture patriotism understood as loyalty not even to the state, but to the authorities."[25] Echoing not so much the German debate but the famous nineteenth-century formula by Count Sergei Uvarov—orthodoxy, autocracy, nationalism—the new "vertical of history" rested on the ideas of a strong state, sovereignty, military might, and repelling the West.[26] In 2009, a presidential commission was formed to "counter attempts at falsifying history to the detriment of Russia's interest."

---

* Interestingly, in the somewhat similar case of General Andrei Vlasov and his Russian Liberation Army, which was composed of Soviet POWs and used by the Germans for noncombat missions, the Russian public in the 1990s viewed Vlasov as anti-Stalinist but later saw him as a traitor to Russia.

Putin was not only speaking for himself. The bulk of the Russian people, including its political class, are not eager to address the hard issues of recent history. Sociologists note that from as early as 1992, Russian society did not want to hear anything from history unless it was positive and encouraging.[27] Most now believe that all the hard issues had been fully dealt with during the years of Gorbachev's glasnost and Yeltsin's freedom of speech. Society is both tired of and dismayed by what it learned. There is no interest in discussing the nature of totalitarianism and personal responsibility. Value-less amoralism has set in.

Many of the younger Russians who never knew the Soviet Union personally take a selective approach to Soviet history. They tend to put "greatness" above the price paid to achieve it. At the verbal level, the "first free generation" is more "patriotic" than the last Soviet one. The recurring charges of Stalinist crimes now provoke irritation and bitterness.[28] Repentance has become almost a dirty word.

National pride is cultivated to boost respect for the state, which takes the place usually given to the nation in democracies, or to the constitution, in the United States. From sports events to historical anniversaries to opposition to U.S. policies or to the West as "the Other"[29]—Russia has been trying to assert and reassert itself against the West. The Soviet national holiday, October Revolution Day—renamed the Day of Accord and Reconciliation under Yeltsin—was replaced in 2004 by the Day of People's Unity in memory of the liberation of Moscow from Polish occupation in 1612.** While Putin rejected the notion of a unique Russian way, Russia has been more recently portrayed as the non-West, and occasionally anti-West. The West, especially the United States/United Kingdom, and a retinue of "pathologically anti-Russian" Poles and Balts, was painted as inherently aggressive, imposing, and hostile to Russia.

** As Mikhail Morozov notes, this "holiday shift" represents an interesting combination of the Soviet legacy (November 4, the new holiday, is very close to the old one on November 7); the Orthodox faith (the new holiday falls on the day of Our Lady of Kazan, one of the most revered Russian icons); monarchism (the start of the Romanov dynasty); and even an element of civil society (the Poles were defeated by a *levée en masse*, jointly led by an aristocrat and a merchant). But the main thing is the expelling of the Poles and assertion of Russian independence from the Catholic West. See Mikhail Morozov, "Istoriya v stile 'pop'" (History in the Style of "Pop"), *Iskusstvo kino*, issue 1, 2009, http://kinoart.ru/2009/n1-article2.html.

REAPPROPRIATING HISTORY

Even before Russia started to rewrite its history yet again, new states had been rediscovering theirs. Almost everywhere in Central and Eastern Europe, martyrdom became the underlying theme. During the 1990s, the three Baltic countries formed government commissions devoted to the investigation of repression under the Soviet regime. Poland and later Ukraine formed Institutes of National Memory to unearth communist-era crimes. Georgia and Latvia opened museums of Soviet occupation.

The new state historians had their work cut out for them. During the Soviet period, history of the union republics was not taught as a special subject, only the incongruously named "history of the USSR since ancient times." The politician and later two-term Prime Minister Mart Laar spoke for many, and not just those in Estonia, when he intoned: "Give back the people their history!" As the USSR collapsed, histories became immediately nationalized. The 1990 "war of the monuments" in Ukraine was a sign of the times: As Lenin statues were toppled, Ukrainian Insurgent Army (UPA)/nationalist leaders had their statues and busts erected.

The new nationalist pattern included several elements:

- Developing a wide-ranging nineteenth-century style national narrative. For example, formation of the Ukrainian nation, its millennium-long struggle for survival and independence.

- Creating a state myth: such as Ukrainian statehood, especially the Cossack period and 1917–1920.

- Distancing from the Soviet Union: essentially, the USSR was Russia; hence, communism, Stalin, *Holodomor*,* and the Red Army were all associated with Russia, and the Russian Federation as its heir and continuation state.

---

* *Holodomor* stands for the 1932–1933 famine created by the Soviet communist authorities in an effort to expropriate grain from the peasants and to fully subjugate, and practically enslave, the peasantry by means of mass starvation. It hit wide grain-producing areas of the Soviet Union: Ukraine, southern and central regions of the Russian republic, and Kazakhstan. It bears similarity to another largely man-made famine, a decade earlier, in the Volga Region.

- Developing a separate national story of World War II: UPA, in Ukraine. It is clear that a substantial part of the population in Western Ukraine considers UPA fighters and their leaders, such as Roman Shukhevych, as heroes. As a Russian historian laments, no propaganda can change that.[30]

- Developing a victim story: In Ukraine, this was *Holodomor* as the worst humanitarian catastrophe of the twentieth century. *Holodomor* was the centerpiece of President Yushchenko's nation-building strategy.[31]

With regard to Ukraine, the title of Kuchma's 2003 book says it all: *Ukraina—ne Rossiia* (Ukraine is not Russia). In Ukrainian school text-books, Russia is often portrayed as the source of the historical tragedy of the Ukrainian people, its leaders usually evil and treacherous. There is permanent confrontation: Ukrainians fight for freedom, Russians want to keep them under control. In the end, Ukrainians are credited with having overcome everything, and survived. They managed to keep their culture in the darkest periods of what is termed Russian-Soviet occupation. The main theme of school textbooks is that Ukrainian history is not part of Russia's.[32] There were conflicts with others, not just Russia. During 1943–1944, Ukrainian rebels under Stepan Bandera killed a number of Poles in Volyn.

Meanwhile, two decades later, the Soviet legacy lives on. "We stand with both feet in the Soviet system, and our heads are also there," quipped Kuchma, with reference to the Orange Revolution and its aftermath.[33] Post-revolutionary correction came a few years later. President Yanukovych, who succeeded Yushchenko, downgraded the National Memory Institute and redefined *Holodomor* as a Stalinist crime, but not genocide. This allowed visiting President Medvedev of Russia to lay the wreath at the memorial. Even before that, a Ukrainian court stripped Bandera of his hero of Ukraine title on the perfectly legal grounds that Bandera—who was assassinated by the KGB in 1959—was never a citizen of Ukraine.

The notion of common history that the Russians are fond of does not result in a shared view of the past. When in 2009 Russia invited Ukraine to jointly celebrate the tricentennial of the Poltava battle, Kiev gave Moscow the cold shoulder. The victory by Peter I over Charles XII may have elevated Russia to a major power in Europe, as the Kremlin chief of staff remarked at the festivities, but to Ukrainians it was a foreign war that gave Ivan Mazepa—their hetman, nominally a subject of the tsar—an opening to seek independence, with Swedish help. Peter prevailed, and Mazepa lost his bid, reviled in Russia as a traitor but featured on a current Ukrainian banknote.

In Kazakhstan, the first local history book appeared only in 1945. After independence, President Nursultan Nazarbayev has taken an active part in creating a national myth. He authored several books on national history.[34] Their main thesis is that Kazakh identity has endured through the ages, despite all the trials: loss of early statehood to the Russian empire; Sovietization; the great famine of the 1930s (*Holodomor*); being an ethnic minority in their republic created very late, only in 1936.* Nazarbayev rejects the notion, popular among the Russians, that the Kazakhs were just nomads roaming around the Great Steppe. He claims his people's hereditary ownership of the huge territory that is today's Kazakhstan. Unlike most Russians, the Kazakhs, Nazarbayev points out, know their forefathers over several generations.

By comparison to Soviet times, when Kazakhstan's incorporation into Russia was seen as generally progressive, the Russian conquest is portrayed as a negative development. The Kazakh film *Mongol*, released in 2007, gives a wholly different, and sympathetic, view of Genghis Khan than the standard view in the Russian school textbooks. Yermak's Cossack expeditions, which resulted in the destruction of the Siberian khanate in 1598, is viewed as a disaster for indigenous development. The Kazakhs' decision in the eighteenth century to accede to the Russian empire was taken in extremis. The Cossacks were colonizers who drove the Kazakhs out of their steppe. The Kazakh-populated territory shrank, its economy suffered. Russian settlers—from those sent by Peter Stolypin (around half a million in the 1900s) to Stalin and Khrushchev (over 1.2 million in the 1940s through early 1960s)—further exacerbated the plight of the local people. In 1916, the Kazakhs rebelled against the Russians, and when the rebellion was put down, a million people fled to China. Early Soviet communist satraps were brutal, ignorant, and uncaring. The famine of the 1930s, the *Holodomor*, resulted in 1.5 million dead in Kazakhstan. An equal number of people crossed into neighboring Xinjiang. Between 1929 and 1933, Kazakhstan lost half its population.[35] Khrushchev's claims about Kazakhstan's virgin lands, where humans had never set foot, was "ignorant and cynical." Gorbachev's 1986 decision to appoint Gennady Kolbin, an ethnic Russian, to succeed longtime Kazakh communist leader Dinmukhamed Kunaev was a

---

* Before that, Kazakhstan was an autonomous part of the Soviet Russian republic.

slap in the face to the Kazakh nation, which produced the Soviet Union's first ethnic revolt. In a word: Kazakhstan was a tsarist and then Soviet colony, unlike Ukraine, which was part of the imperial core.

In Turkmenistan, to cite a wholly different example, the founding President Niyazov, or Turkmenbashi, wrote the ultimate handbook for the new nation: *Rukhnama* (the book of the soul). Although a few years after Niyazov's death his book has quietly been downplayed, as part of dismantling the dead leader's cult of personality, it remains a testament of national identity.

RELIGION

When the CIS was founded, its original format—Russia, Ukraine, and Belarus—was dubbed Slavic Union, and the common bond, more than ethnicity, was culture. There were even calls at the time[36] to form a "community of culturally close peoples"—in other words, an Orthodox Christian club.

One of the first steps taken by the new post-Soviet leadership of Russia was to officially celebrate religious holidays. One of the first unusual images on television was to see the top officials: the president, prime minister, Moscow mayor, all recent members of the Communist Party, in church, candle in hand. The end of the empire signified an officially blessed revival of religious confessions in Russia and the new states.

In 1989, about 75 percent of the population described themselves as atheist, and less than one-fifth claimed to be Orthodox. Twenty years later, the ratio was just the reverse.[37] Today, the Russian Orthodox Church claims some 125 million adherents, many of them outside Russia: in Ukraine, Belarus, Moldova, the Baltic states, and Central Asia. Yet despite a marked rise in church attendance in Russia, the actual number of churchgoers is perhaps only 2–4 percent of the claimed number.[38] The rest are essentially post-Orthodox: *potomki pravoslavnykh*, as someone quipped: "descendants of the Orthodox people."[39]

In the Russian empire, the Orthodox Church was formally subordinated to the state, with the emperor as its de facto leader. In the atheist Soviet Union, after 1943—when the church was again allowed to function—this was possible only under very tight control from the state. Islam was tolerated under the tsars and in the postwar USSR, but its followers were isolated from their co-religionists in the wider Muslim world. On a much smaller scale, this was also true of Buddhists. Jews and Catholics were treated with suspicion precisely because they were closely connected, respectively, to international Jewry—some confused them with the Zionists—and the Vatican.

The breakup of the USSR broke that dam. All religious confessions experienced a revival, and reestablished long-severed ties with the broader communities beyond its borders. The Russian Orthodox Church started to move out of late Soviet-era hibernation with the officially sanctioned celebration of the Millennium of the Baptism of Rus, in 1988. In 1990, with the election of Alexi II as the fifteenth patriarch (1990–2008), it gained an energetic and thoughtful leader. Almost immediately, he was faced with a plethora of new opportunities and a large number of serious problems.

The end of the atheist communist state and the new independence of the Russian Orthodox Church from the Russian authorities allowed the seventy-year split within the church to heal. The émigré Russian Orthodox Church Abroad, after a long negotiating process encouraged and facilitated by Putin personally, agreed in 2007 to formally unite with the Moscow Patriarchate, while retaining a measure of autonomy. As in the temporal world, the *Russia at home* and what had remained of *Russia abroad*, divided by the Bolshevik Revolution, finally came together.

The church, however, also experienced serious problems arising out of the breakup of the USSR. The "Russian" in the name of the Orthodox Church denotes the old concept of "All Russias"—that is, Russia, Ukraine, and Belarus as a single unit. When the state unit disintegrated, it became very difficult for the church to preserve its unity. In 1992, the Ukrainian church split. A smaller, but substantial (30 percent of parishes) part of it formed a fully independent Ukrainian Orthodox Church (Kiev Patriarchate), while the larger portion organized itself as an autonomous Ukrainian Orthodox Church (Moscow Patriarchate). To make matters more complicated, the Autocephalous Ukrainian Orthodox Church—which split from the church's main body in 1917, essentially for the same reasons as the pro-independence clergy did seventy-five years later—was no longer suppressed and could function openly, but it chose to stay separate from the other formations.

For the moderate nationalists in Ukraine, forming a national church was a fully logical step: They wanted independence from Russia in the religious field as well. Traditionally, most Orthodox churches are very closely linked to the temporal authorities. Nearly all the existing Orthodox churches—Greek, Serbian, Georgian—are very nationalistic. Most are also closely involved in politics, often acting as arbiters among competing political factions. To allow the patriarch of Moscow to continue to wield religious authority in Ukraine goes against the grain of Ukrainian nationalism and the Ukrainian state-building project.

President Yushchenko sought to achieve Orthodox unity *within* Ukraine. He strove for unification of the three Ukrainian Orthodox churches and formation of a Ukrainian National Orthodox Church. This clearly meant separating the Ukrainian church from the Russian one and achieving Ukraine's religious independence from Moscow, both de facto and de jure. Yushchenko hoped that Patriarch Bartholomew of Constantinople, by tradition the world's most senior Orthodox cleric, would be the key figure in legalizing the necessary church split between Ukraine and Russia and thus laying the groundwork for future church fusion within Ukraine. This was timed to coincide with the one-thousand twentieth anniversary of the baptism of Rus, a date chosen for strictly political reasons: 2008 was a truly fateful year in many respects.

This was not to be, however. The Russian leadership saw the coming separation of the Ukrainian church as a looming catastrophe, on a par with, if not worse than, NATO enlargement. Were this to happen, Ukraine would become an anti-Russia. Moscow propagandists claimed, unconvincingly, that this was a project peddled by the enemies of Christianity.[40] Only months before his death, Patriarch Alexi II went to Ukraine for his first and only time since the breakup of the Soviet Union. The Russian press[41] reported that the Russian government and church leaders worked behind the scenes to undermine Yushchenko's plan. Their aim was to keep Ukraine within the Russian civilizational orbit.

With Yushchenko out of power, succeeded by a friendlier President Yanukovych, Moscow has tried to consolidate its gains. The arrival in 2009 of a new Moscow patriarch, Kirill, marked the end of the church's policy of passive defense. Kirill refused to be merely the head of the Orthodox Church of the Russian Federation and proclaimed himself the spiritual leader of "Saint-Russia." He had his residence in Moscow adorned with the flags of all of the countries under the jurisdiction of the Moscow Patriarchate—the Russian Federation, Ukraine, Belarus, Moldova—where Orthodox Christians form a majority.

Informally, as the head of the strongest Orthodox Christian Church in the world, Kirill evidently sees himself as the leader of all Eastern Christians. During his 2009 visit to Ukraine, Kirill sometimes spoke Ukrainian and called Kiev the "southern capital of the Russian Orthodoxy." He mentioned the possibility of splitting his time between Moscow and Kiev. Kirill also made sure that Constantinople supports the unity of the Russian Orthodox Church—in exchange for Moscow's recognition of its importance as an arbiter.

A similar problem, though on a smaller scale, appeared in Moldova. The church in Moldova, too, has been organized within the Moscow Patriarchate. In an effort to break this link, those seeking separation from Russia formed a Bessarabian diocese. Yet rather than founding a Moldovan national church, they attempted to attach it to the Romanian Orthodox Church in a simple switch of allegiance from Moscow to Bucharest. This plan, too, has only been partially successful. The unity of Orthodox Christians in Moldova has been shattered, but the Moscow Patriarchate is still the majority church even on the right bank of the Dniester, and it is dominant in Transnistria.

During the period of high tension in Russo-Belarusian relations in the fall of 2010, rumors began to circulate of President Lukashenka's intention to found a separate Belarusian Orthodox Church.[42] Unlike in Ukraine, there is no church schism now in Belarus, but the basic idea is clear. The general principle of Orthodox Church organization is "one nation, one church," with no Orthodox pope, only a church elder—who sits, powerless, in Muslim Istanbul. What applies to Bulgaria, Georgia, Greece, Romania, and Serbia can hardly be denied to Belarus, Moldova, and Ukraine.

As in a caricature, there were minor issues of the same kind. With Russia's recognition of Abkhazia's and South Ossetia's independence from Georgia, the issue of the status of the Abkhaz and Ossetian Orthodox parishes came up. While Patriarch Alexi II had been a supporter of integrity of canonical territory and refused to encourage those who wished to switch from Tbilisi to Moscow, things have been different since his death. Yet, the importance of the patriarch of Georgia as the informal intermediary between the governments and societies of the two countries, which broke diplomatic relations in 2008, has deterred Moscow from approving the separatist demands.

On a smaller scale, there has been an Orthodox split in the predominantly Protestant Estonia, with some parishes switching allegiance from Moscow to Constantinople, and thus gaining de facto independence, while others remain with Moscow.

"Only the atheist Soviet Union could unite the West and the East of Ukraine into one republic," the historian Roy Medvedev wittily remarked.[43] The Soviet Union, however, did that, and more. In 1946, Stalin forced part of the Greek Catholic clergy in Western Ukraine to renounce the 1596 union with the Roman Catholic Church and join the Russian Orthodox

Church. Church buildings were taken away from the Uniates and given to the Russian Orthodox Church. This laid a bomb under the future of inter-church relations in Ukraine.

Stalin's forced marriage lasted only as long as the Soviet Union. From 1990, the status quo ante was being restored, with the Uniates getting back cathedrals, churches, and monasteries. This led sometimes to clashes among the believers belonging to competing confessions and to tension in western Ukraine itself and between the Russian Orthodox Church and the Vatican.

The Russian Orthodox Church was adamant that the integrity of its "canonical territory"—that is, some analogue of a state's territorial integrity—be preserved. It demanded that the Catholic Church stop its "proselytic activities" in Ukraine and Belarus and de facto recognize those countries, and Russia, as being the realm of the Russian Orthodox Church. Largely due to this conflict, the Russian patriarch did not visit Ukraine between 1990 and 2007, and the Russian Orthodox Church denounced Pope John Paul II's visits to Ukraine.

In post-communist Russia itself, Catholics (1 percent of the population) were denied the legal status of an indigenous religious confession, which was given to Orthodoxy, Islam, Buddhism, and Judaism. The Russian Orthodox Church treated the fellow Christians essentially as poachers or even foreign invaders in the largely Orthodox territory. The Orthodox hierarchy accused the Church of Rome of trying to reconvert actual or potential Orthodox followers and working in particular to annex the western regions of Ukraine and Belarus, tearing them away from the Russian Orthodox Church.

Relations with the Vatican were especially tense under John Paul II (1978–2005). Despite his frequently expressed desire to pay a visit to Russia, the well-traveled pontiff was not allowed there, even though he visited a number of neighboring countries: Ukraine, Belarus, Kazakhstan, and Azerbaijan. Many in the Russian church regarded the Polish pope with suspicion, and even with contempt, as a "stage performer." The inter-church situation has improved under John Paul's successor, Pope Benedict XVI, a German, but the historic meeting between the patriarch and the pope is yet to happen.

For all the incursions of the Roman Catholics into Orthodox territory, it was the revival of Islam that was the single most powerful change in the religious geography of the post-imperial space. Until the Iranian revolution and the Soviet Union's intervention in Afghanistan, Islam was lying dormant. The developments in Iran and Afghanistan first awakened the Soviet leadership to the Muslim factor.

The breakup of the USSR let that factor loose. Islamists became a major force and contenders for political power across the entire former Soviet south. Acting independently or in alliance with much more feeble democrats, they challenged the communist authorities in Tajikistan and Uzbekistan. The former was plunged into a bloody civil war, with Russian military participation, in which the Islamists were defeated but not annihilated.

The five Central Asian states and Azerbaijan identify themselves in terms of Islamist legacy. This ranges from the very moderate, as in Azerbaijan and Kazakhstan, to the more pronounced in Tajikistan. The Azeris are secular on the Turkish model; Kazakhstan's Nazarbayev, mindful of his country's religious diversity, visits the church for Easter, and the mosque at Ramadan. Elsewhere, Islamicization is palpable. As Irina Zvyagelskaya writes, "For the secular regimes [of Central Asia] Islam has played the role of a passport to the Muslim world."[44]

Islam also became the officially recognized dominant religion in many parts of the Russian Federation. Its revival was visible. The Kazan Kremlin, the official residence of the president of Tatarstan, received an impressive mosque that dominates the area. Grozny boasts the largest mosque in Europe. Hundreds of mosques have been built across the North Caucasus. None of this was controversial. Traditionally Muslim areas were reviving the core part of their culture and identity. What was more problematic was the appearance of mosques in historically non-Muslim areas.

The need to build mosques in ethnic Russian cities was dictated by the demographic changes. Even though only 6–7 percent of those polled claim to be Muslim,[45] the traditionally Muslim community is at least twice that size. Very important, massive immigration since the end of the Soviet Union changed the ethnic composition of large Russian cities. Moscow alone (population: 11 million) has between 1 million and 2 million Muslims but only four mosques. In September 2010, some 50,000 pious Muslims stunned the Muscovites, and the authorities, when they started praying in the streets around the city's main mosque, which could accommodate only a fraction of the faithful.

LANGUAGE

Nationalist stirrings in the Soviet Union initially took the form of movements in support of indigenous languages. In 1989, the Abkhaz staged mass rallies, and the Moldovans passed a law proclaiming Romanian the only state language. In 1990, even de facto Russophone Belarus passed a law establishing Belarusian as the only state language. In Estonia and Latvia, naturalization and citizenship prospects for local Russian residents were closely tied to their proficiency in the local languages. Two decades on, Russian has lost ground everywhere, mostly to the local languages, but also to English.

Belarus is the only country where Russian remains absolutely dominant, despite an early post-Soviet law, later repealed, making Belarusian the sole state language. In Ukraine, "the threat of Russification is a real one," said Kuchma, who, somewhat inconsistently, initially promised to reinstate Russian as a second official language in Ukraine but then dropped the idea.[46] Kiev, with its 80 percent ethnic Ukrainian dominance, remains a Russian-speaking city.

In the country at large, the language situation remains very complex. Basically, there are three groups: Ukrainian-speaking ethnic Ukrainians; Russian-speaking ethnic Ukrainians; and Russian-speaking ethnic Russians. In the mid- to late 1990s, Ukraine counted 23 percent ethnic Russians, but 36 percent Russian speakers, or, to put this differently, 73 percent ethnic Ukrainians, but only 64 percent Ukrainian speakers. At the national level, the situation at the family level was almost balanced: 36 percent Ukrainian-speaking families, 33 percent Russian-speaking families, and just under 30 percent bilingual ones.

However, regional differences were much more pronounced. In western Ukraine, there were only 3 percent Russian speakers; in the country's central regions, that share went up to 16 percent; while in the east and the south, Russian speakers held slight majorities, 55 percent and 56 percent, respectively.[47] Still, the ability to speak Ukrainian has had a huge impact on public life. Kuchma and Yanukovych, who had not spoken Ukrainian most of their lives, had to learn it as they prepared to run for president.

In the South Caucasus and Central Asia, Russian has ceased to be the language of everyday communication. Members of the elites still speak it, but not the ordinary people, and not the new generations. In the near future, young educated Russians and young educated Georgians will probably need to know English to communicate.

At independence, Kazakh was promoted to the position of the sole state language of multiethnic Kazakhstan. However, in 1991, only 30 percent of Kazakhs did not speak their language at all, and just about 1 percent of ethnic Russians did. The authorities relented. Russian was promoted as an official language, alongside Kazakh, the state language. Fifty percent of the country's population uses Russian in everyday life, and it is still the principal language of the government, culture and the arts, and science and technology. President Nazarbayev often uses Russian in his public addresses. However, since 2007 the Kazakh language has been promoted in government offices.

Faced with the gradual weakening of the Russian language and, more broadly, Russian cultural and political influence across the former empire, the Russian government has made a series of moves. In 2008, it formed a special federal agency for CIS affairs to focus on humanitarian issues and the diaspora. Modeled on the United States Agency for International Development, this autonomous agency reports to the foreign ministry. Its mission is to "help the CIS countries resolve their problems, under Russia's aegis," according to a Ministry of Foreign Affairs official.

While in the past Moscow relied on the force of arguments and the impact of threats, it now seeks to buy support. The new methods include support for Russia-friendly nongovernmental organizations (NGOs), including branches of Russian NGOs; targeted support for educational, humanitarian, and cultural projects; and stipends and libraries.[48] The government-funded *Russkiy Mir* foundation was specifically tasked with boosting the learning and use of the Russian language across the former USSR.

Even without government support, Russian mass and "high" culture has been relatively popular in the new states. From Riga to Yerevan and from Chisinau to Bishkek, taxi drivers turn on Russian pop music channels. In Kazakhstan, major Russian TV channels and FM radio stations are widely rebroadcast. In Georgia, Russian TV is treated as enemy propaganda; there is only one radio station and virtually no newspapers.

The new elites, however, prefer to send their children to study in the West, rather than in Russia. Many among Kazakhstan's young professionals have received their education in the United States or Britain. Georgia's young elite is almost universally English-speaking. English is becoming the language bridge between the local societies and the global community, assuming the role that Russian played in the nineteenth and twentieth centuries, within the empire. In this new environment, Russian becomes a regional language, still useful for communicating with the biggest neighbor, and to some extent with other former Soviet states.

Orientation toward Russia and psychological dependence on it are gradually becoming a thing of the past. Moscow, which used to be a mecca for the parents, is often just another point on the map for the children. The Kremlin is an Italian-built fortress with a few palaces and Orthodox churches, and no longer the center of the universe. Today, Red Square may be actually more fun—with its occasional open-air concerts in the summer and a skating rink in the winter, and even the reinstated parades on Victory Day—but the Lenin mausoleum, once its sanctum sanctorum, is definitely out of place there. Among the privileged in the new states, many know Western, Asian, or Middle Eastern capitals better than Russia's. Moscow is simply not cool; and Russia at large is even less attractive. True, it does have a higher per capita GDP than any other CIS country, but that attracts labor migrants, not the forward-looking members of the elites.

CONCLUSION

This may be the final act of the imperial unraveling. The waning role of Russian in the new states means the loss of popular identification with what is the most powerful about Russia: not its arms, but its culture. With Pushkin, Tolstoy, and Bulgakov viewed as foreign authors, Russia is finally becoming a foreign country to its former provinces. In terms of visual and audio culture, when Soviet-era films cease to be the sources of quotable quotes, and Soviet-time songs are no longer associated with one's own past, the Post-Imperium, at long last, will be over. New generations around the neighboring states will develop more relaxed, but also much cooler, attitudes toward Russia.

In Russia itself, this process is going even faster. Central Asia and the Caucasus—including its northern part—are already seen as foreign by most ordinary Russians. So is Moldova. So, it now seems, the Baltic states have always been. Ukrainians are—and will remain—"cousins," as will Belarusians. Closeness generates warmth, but it also sometimes leads to friction. The new community that all former subjects of the Russian and Soviet empires have entered is global. There, they will meet so many members of other former empires for whom history has limited practical relevance. Welcome to the new world.

In this new world, Russia will seek to project an image of a great power, but it will have to fit into a new structure, with an even greater power—the United States—at one extreme and really small neighbors at the other extreme. Establishing an acceptable relationship with the United States will not be easy and cannot be done single-handedly. New multipolarity notwithstanding, America will continue, for the foreseeable future, to be not only the most powerful, but also the leading, nation in the world.

Adjusting to this situation, as Britain, France, and the lesser post-imperial powers have done—essentially by accepting U.S. leadership—continues to be anathema in Moscow. Russian leaders crave equality, but they know that it exists in one area only: nuclear arsenals and missiles, which frames the relationship in a Cold War setup. In principle, this dilemma could be solved by a more imaginative and engaging U.S. strategy toward Russia, but the prevailing view in Washington about Russia is that it is a declining power, not worth a major dedicated effort.

Russia, by contrast, can do much more to promote reconciliation with its neighbors. It can start by acknowledging crimes committed by Stalin and, more broadly, the Bolsheviks, against all the peoples of the Soviet empire, starting with the Russian people. It can win many hearts through genuine signs of compassion. It can win some minds by opening up the Soviet-era archives. It can seek to build a better future through more exchanges, especially among the young. It can commit fewer mistakes by reaching out to the new nations in the neighborhood, and developing a better understanding of their cultures, histories, and aspirations.

Russia needs to go "soft" as far as its neighbors are concerned and share with them the riches it still possesses. Its objective needs to be the opposite of what it has been seeking recently: less Russia the Terrible, more Russia the Benign. Culture and the arts, which used to be Russia's secular religion, can play a salient role here.

Russia will never again be an empire. To be seen as a great power in the twenty-first century, however, it has to become a great country, above all for its own people. The final chapter will reflect on whether this is possible.

CONCLUSION

The Russian empire is over, never to return. The enterprise that had lasted for hundreds of years simply lost the drive. The élan is gone. In the two decades since the collapse, imperial restoration was never considered seriously by the leaders, nor demanded by the wider public. Rather, Russia has gone in reverse—expansion has yielded to introspection, and grandiose public schemes have made their way to myriad private agendas. This is a Russia the world has not known before the start of the twenty-first century.

Fascinating as Russia's post-imperial story may be, in its key features, it is hardly unique. Other countries, such as Germany and Japan in World War II, "lost everything," then revived themselves soon afterward. Still other countries, following the end of the Cold War, went through succession conflicts, as in the former Yugoslavia, before they moved toward new integration within the European Union. The USSR's split was not quite as graceful as Czechoslovakia's, and most of its constituent parts did not manage to integrate with more advanced neighbors. But in the last twenty years, the Russian Federation did not fare too badly. What makes Russia different is that, having closed the books on itself as an empire, it has managed to continue, without interruption, as a major power.

There was no new Marshall Plan in the 1990s, although much aid did flow Russia's way—but then, in the 2000s, Moscow earned hundreds of billions of dollars of oil money. True, Russia did not integrate into the European and Atlantic institutions, but it is a significant independent player on the international scene and has a chance of becoming a modern power. The belief, shared by so many in the West, that Russia is essentially finished as a serious country is still to be tested and might well be premature. What is important is that the future lies entirely in Russia's own hands, and there are enough resources to make it a happy one.

Here, it is useful to keep in mind that post-World War II Germany did not rise because it had great friends, who also doubled as its occupying powers, but largely because of its homemade *Wirtschaftswunder*, or economic miracle. It was the Deutsche Mark, it was Adenauer's *Westbindung* and Erhard's *Soziale Marktwirtschaft*—integration into the Western world and social market economy—that did the job. Until Russia itself rises to the occasion, its modernization alliances will have only limited impact. For now, however, the outlook is clouded. Russia is no longer an empire, but it is no nation-state yet, either. Put differently, it is yet to become a republic—in the literal meaning of the word, *res publica*. Russians need to unite in a joint enterprise, but they first have to agree on the rules and agree to stick to them.

While the private is still king in Russia, virtually completely overshadowing the public, there are indications that this universal aloofness from fellow countrymen may be coming to an end. The idea of individual survival and success allowed the more energetic members of society to rise and prosper. However, it is beginning to dawn on some of them already that their private agendas may not be fulfilled in the future due to the constraints imposed by the ossified system. The system is stronger than any individual, and so individuals need to unite and go public in order to achieve their private goals. It is time that Russian people start coming together and structure their society according to interests and basic worldviews, with a sense of belonging to a single nation that can accommodate them all. The 2010s are likely to see this momentous change in attitude.

In an interesting parallel with its residents, Russia as a unit, an international actor, is also living for itself. There is no ideology, no clear set of values, but a very strong sense of pragmatism. The motto is simple: to survive, and to succeed, using whatever means available. This pragmatism allows no room for empire building. Russian leaders have agreed among themselves: no more expensive ideological nonsense; no more material self-sacrifice; and no more subsidies for others. The Soviet Union acted abroad as a big spender. The Russian Federation is constantly on the lookout for opportunities to make money.

Yet even if Russia is post-imperial, the empire is still not fully out of its elites' minds. The positive thing is that the same elites will not commit their limited resources in support of their nostalgia. As to the population at large, it is adjusting to the abrupt changes at the end of the twentieth century and is slowly healing the huge wounds inflicted upon the previous four generations of Russian men and women by their fellow countrymen, whether acting on behalf of an authority or while rejecting any authority. For the time being, Russia is both pre- and, in some ways, postmodern. What is missing there is the modern element. Ironically, as the Russian leaders emphasize modernity, much of the world is already beyond it. This is a catch-up that may never succeed.

True, Russia is moving toward modernity, by fits and starts. Its current modernization drive—powered from above—is largely motivated by the Kremlin's concerns over its world role. Modernization, which requires pervasive liberalization and eventually a genuine democracy, confronts the Russian state and Russian society alike with serious challenges. It is not clear at all that they will meet these challenges. However, Russia's failure to modernize will almost certainly lead to its marginalization, deterioration, and decay. The 2000s model of success built on ever-rising oil prices has revealed itself as unsustainable. In the end phase of the worst-case scenario, the country's physical disintegration is not to be ruled out.

The Russian leadership faces a difficult, seemingly impossible, dilemma: to leave things as they are means steady decline and ultimate fall, even in the leadership's own lifetime; to start changing things in earnest entails the risk of losing control, power, and property. They may want to be Peter but are afraid to end up like Gorbachev. So for the time being, they act like Brezhnev. Putin in 2010 told members of the Russian Academy of Sciences a story about his former colleagues in the KGB who had furnished the West's best-kept industrial secrets to the Soviet economy, only for those Western innovations to be rejected by the very nature of the Soviet economic system. Now Putin is presiding over a system that is likely to reject all the technology transfers he is trying to organize because corruption, the lack of legal protection, and bureaucratic arbitrariness rule the day. As someone quipped, corruption is not a bug, it is a feature of the present system. Crunch time will come sometime during the 2010s when the essential failure of modernization as currently conceived and practiced will be clear to all.

This raises serious challenges also to Moscow's foreign policy.* For now, two decades after the breakup of the Soviet Union, Russia has shed communism and abdicated from its historical empire. These two great

---

* Beginning from here, the text is partially drawn from my article, "Russia Reborn: Reimagining Moscow's Foreign Policy," *Foreign Affairs*, vol. 88, issue 6, November-December 2009.

feats of self-liberation are not to be ignored, and their significance is not to be minimized. The Russian Federation, however, is still looking for a new place and a new role in the world. So far, it sits uncomfortably on the periphery of affluent Europe and dynamic Asia while apprehensively rubbing shoulders with the Muslim world. However, the new freedom from geopolitical involvement in Europe and Asia allows Russia to concentrate on itself and to use the whole world as a resource and a market.

Throughout the 1990s, and the early 2000s, Moscow tried exiting from the empire by means of integrating into, and then with, the West. These efforts failed, both because the West, which then held the initiative, lacked the will to adopt Russia as one of its own, and because Russian elites eventually chose to embrace a corporatist and conservative policy agenda at home and abroad.

As a result, in the second presidential term of Vladimir Putin, Russia abandoned its goal of joining the West and returned to its default option of behaving as an independent great power. It redefined its objectives: soft dominance in its immediate neighborhood; essential equality with the world's principal power centers, China, the European Union, and the United States; and senior membership in a global multipolar order.

Half a decade later, that policy course revealed its failures and flaws. Most were rooted in the Russian government's inability and unwillingness to reform the country's energy-dependent economy, the noncompetitive nature of Russian politics, and a trend toward nationalism and isolationism. In terms of foreign policy, Russia's leaders failed to close the book on the lost Soviet empire. It is as if they exited the twentieth century through two doors at the same time: one leading to the globalized market of the twenty-first century, and the other opening into the Great Game of the nineteenth century.

As the recent global economic crisis has demonstrated, the model that Russia's leaders chose in the 2000s—growth without development, capitalism without democracy, and great-power policies without international appeal—is unsustainable. Not only would Russia fail to achieve its principal foreign policy objectives, it would fall further behind in a world increasingly defined by instant communication and open borders, leading to dangers not merely to its status but also to its existence. Russia's foreign policy needed more than a reset: it required a new strategy and new policy instruments and mechanisms to implement it. In short, Russia needed to focus on overcoming its economic, social, and political backwardness—and use its foreign policy to meet this supreme national interest.

It was the Russian leadership's concern over the loss of Russian power in the world, not only vis-à-vis the West, but also in comparison with the rising powers of the former Third World, that has prompted the policy of modernization, and—within it—a modernization of Moscow's foreign policy. The Kremlin's thinking behind it was probably like this: Whatever we may think of the veracity of international ratings, the country is definitely going south. Without mastering advanced technology and building a capacity for innovation, Russia will cease to be regarded as a great power. If that happens, it will probably start disintegrating. Energy resources will not save it, as nuclear arsenals did nothing to save the Soviet Union. Thus, the dilemma is stark: modernization or marginalization.

Russian leaders also recognized that the country cannot modernize on its own and should not even try it. In the globalized world, it needs to reach out to the modernization resources of the advanced countries. These are the countries of the Organization for Economic Cooperation and Development (OECD). Russia should strike modernization alliances with them, to allow technology transfers, investment, support of innovative ventures, and so on. These modernization allies are members of the European Union, to begin with Germany, France, and Italy; and the United States.[1] The West is back as Russia's ally.

This analysis and conclusion lead to serious foreign policy implications. Instead of passionate defense of a diminished status and focusing on where Russia stands in the international pecking order, foreign policy was ordered to serve as a provider of external modernization resources.[2] For this, it needed a proper environment: a relationship with the West finally free of the war risks which, as the war with Georgia had demonstrated, were not entirely absent two decades after Malta. Hence, Moscow's efforts in the field of European security, which have run beyond seeking assurances of NATO's non-enlargement to the east. Hence, a willingness to resolve the issues pertaining to the Arctic by legal or negotiated means. Hence, the remarkable rapprochement that Moscow has initiated with Warsaw.

In principle, turning Russia into a modern independent power center is feasible—provided that the country manages the task of integration. However, this power center will have a relatively weak pull and a fairly short reach. A Russian empire at the height of its glory can not be restored, even informally. In order to become modern and newly powerful, Russia needs to develop a new vision of the world and an appropriate agenda for dealing with it.

The "vision thing" is fundamentally important. The country and the state the Russian leadership strives to build belong in the early twentieth century. As they go about it, they lay emphasis on tight control; vertical, hierarchical relationships; order and discipline; but in reality, they are mired in corruption. Managing networks, building trust, creating a system of incentives and disincentives, living by the rules and on some system of basic values is still out of reach for them, though they all have heard about these things—and even use them to create surrogates for manipulation. Unless this changes in a fundamental way, what follows is hardly relevant.

If changes are coming, Moscow's first priority should be strengthening Russia's own economic, intellectual, and social potential. It must start overcoming the deficiencies of its institutions, to begin with the rule of law and the legal system, and make them comparable to those of the West. Modernization conceived in terms of technology transfers and innovation oases is too narrow to succeed. Attempts to restore a "soft" equivalent of an empire will not add to Russia, only take away from it. This does not mean that Russia should ignore its immediate neighbors (which would be impossible) or shy away from close cooperation with them (which would be foolish). Russia's current demographic crisis requires that it learn to win over people rather than collect their lands and seek to integrate them as full citizens.

Soft power should be central to Russia's foreign policy. Russia possesses precious and virtually unused elements of this kind of power across the post-Soviet world; the Russian language is used from Riga to Almaty, and Russian culture, from Pushkin to pop music, is still in big demand. If Russia rebuilt its infrastructure, its neighbors would be increasingly attracted to opportunities for higher education—especially in science—and research and development in the country. And if Russia manages to enact fundamental changes in how its political system and economy are run, the benefits could be dramatic: Russian businesspeople would no longer be perceived as agents of the Kremlin and would be more welcome abroad; a Russian-language television channel could become a sort of Al Jazeera for Russophones; and the Russian Orthodox Church, if it were seen as a transnational institution and not an extension of the state, could gain authority outside Russia. But such an outcome would require transcending the view that Russia is defined by its leader—whether Yeltsin, Putin, or Medvedev—and envisaging instead a Russia of multiple actors in which the nation, and not the authority, is sovereign.

In such an approach, Russia's policy toward Ukraine could become a useful standard. Rather than insisting that Ukraine join some integration project that Moscow leads, Russia must reach out to the Ukrainian people directly, to attract new business opportunities, new workers, and new students.

The Caucasus is another important test: Solving the conundrum of Russia's relationship with Georgia and the final status of Abkhazia and South Ossetia is a sine qua non of Russia's goal of assuming the role of a benevolent regional leader. This will take a serious effort. In the meantime, settling the conflicts in Nagorno-Karabakh and Transnistria will require Russia to work alongside the EU, the United States, Turkey, and Ukraine, not to mention the parties to the conflict themselves. Taking a leading role in resolving conflicts in the former Soviet territory will be a testimony to the Russian Federation's capability and willingness to produce international public goods.

Russia has no choice but to build stability in Central Asia, to prevent the region from becoming a generator of regional tension. Working closely with Kazakhstan, it can turn the CSTO into a more effective instrument to prevent, manage, and resolve conflict. Working with China and other members of the Shanghai Cooperation Organization, Moscow needs to assume responsibility for managing security in the center of the Asian continent. This may include moderating among Asia's giants, China and India, and the regional powers, Pakistan and Iran.

Of particular importance in that regard is Afghanistan. Alongside other countries in the area, Russia will need to make sure that, once the U.S./NATO operation in Afghanistan is over, the country does not again become a safe haven for terrorists threatening the world and the seat of a never-ending conflict that permanently destabilizes the region.

Reducing religious extremism and strengthening the forces of moderation needs to be the centerpiece of Russia's foreign policy all along its extended southern flank. With the indigenous Muslim population that has grown by 40 percent since 1989, Russia has the capacity to play a useful role in the Christian-Muslim dialogue.

As a leading energy producer, Russia's obligation is to help assure energy security in the world by harmonizing, to the extent possible, the interests of producers and consumers, as well as the rights and responsibilities of transit countries. These could be embedded in a new charter with the EU. To begin rethinking its role as an energy power, Russia could focus on raising its appallingly low energy efficiency. This can also be a major contribution to the international effort to stem greenhouse gas emissions.

Last, but certainly not least, are big opportunities in the field of environmental protection. Russia's obligation to itself and the global community is keeping in good shape the vast resources of fresh water, forestland, and clean air, most of them situated in Siberia.

Russia needs hard power, too, but the kind that addresses the challenges of the present, not the past. It needs a well-trained and well-equipped army to deal with crises along its long border, as well as a modern air force and a modern navy. In many cases, Russia will not be acting alone. It will need to master the mechanisms of military and security cooperation in Eurasia with its allies in the CSTO, its NATO and EU partners, and its Asian neighbors, such as China, India, Japan, and South Korea.

Moscow's new foreign policy vision prioritizes relations with developed countries. Luckily, the EU, Japan, and the United States are Russia's neighbors, a fact that Russia can use to further development in those areas near these shared borders, from Kaliningrad and the Kola Peninsula to Kamchatka and the Kuril Islands. Because of its proximity and Russia's European roots, the EU is Russia's most important partner for modernization. A 2005 EU-Russian agreement defined four areas for cooperation—economics, justice and internal security, cultural and human contacts, and external relations—precisely the areas in which closer ties with the EU would contribute to Russia's transformation.

Russia's long-term goal should not be to join the EU but to create a common European economic space with it. When Russia finally joins the WTO, a pan-European free-trade area—with Turkey, Ukraine, Kazakhstan, Belarus, the Caucasus, and other countries joining—will become a realistic goal. Energy could form the underlying material basis for this common space, but for that to happen, energy trade between the EU and Russia must be less contentious. Visa-free travel between Russia and the Schengen countries would also be a central human element of this new arrangement. The statement by the European Commission's former president, Romano Prodi, that the EU and Russia "share everything but the institutions" remains sound and valid.

As Europe's own experience shows, such a common economic space can exist only in an atmosphere of trust and confidence. Russia will not be able to modernize without support from the more advanced economies. Of all the OECD members, the EU is Russia's most important modernization resource. There are compelling economic interests; geographical proximity; cultural affinity; close historical ties. For Moscow, Europe no longer starts at the Elbe but at the Narva and the Neman. And, most importantly, Europe itself has profoundly changed. Multilateralism there has taken over from historical multipolarity, and it is time Moscow, too, adjusted its policies.

To fully tap into that resource, two conditions need to be met. The first is mutual exiting from the Cold War mentality. From that, a historic

understanding with the United States is indispensable. The second is reconciliation between Russia and its neighbors in Central and Eastern Europe.
The twin goals of this strategy should be (a) a Euro-Atlantic Security Community as a zone of stable peace embracing North America and the whole
of Europe; and (b) a pan-European Economic Area. Even if these goals are
met, Russia will be able to keep its basic strategic freedom. It can stay away
from military alliances and tight economic unions. Russia's own geography
is the reason for that.

Russia is not so much a Eurasian country—both Turkey and Kazakhstan are better suited for that description—as a Euro-Pacific one. Its territory extends all the way to the Pacific, from Chukotka to Sakhalin. The
United States is a near neighbor to the east, and Canada is the next one
behind it. Combining Russia's European and Pacific roles will not come
easily, and much will depend on how Russia will be able to manage its relations with its biggest land neighbor, China.

China is one of Russia's leading trading partners and is a fast-growing
market that could also become a major source of capital investment in Russia. In addition, Beijing is an indispensable partner in assuring security and
stability along Russia's borders, from Central and Northeast Asia to the
greater Middle East. Thus, Moscow has no alternative but to seek friendly
and cooperative relations with Beijing. A key challenge for Russia's foreign
policy will be to learn to live alongside a China that is strong, dynamic, assertive, and increasingly advanced.

To avoid becoming an adjunct to the Chinese economy and a political
semi-vassal of Beijing, Russia will need to focus on its Far Eastern territories much more than before. It will have to achieve dual integration: Pacific
Russia's integration into the Russian Federation and Russia's integration as
a whole into the Asia-Pacific.

Russia's cutting-edge, twenty-first-century frontier lies to the east,
where it has both a need and a chance to catch up with its immediate Pacific
neighbors: China, Japan, and South Korea. Beijing, Tokyo, and Seoul all
look to the Pacific. The global power shift toward the Pacific necessitates a
new focus in Russian foreign policy. I have written elsewhere[3] that if Peter
the Great were alive today, he would decamp from Moscow again—only
this time to the Sea of Japan, not the Baltic.

As such, Russia would do well to think of Vladivostok as its twenty-first
century capital. It is a seaport, breathing openness. Its location within easy
reach of East Asia's most important cities—Beijing, Hong Kong, Seoul,
Shanghai, and Tokyo—puts Russia in immediate contact with the world's

currently most dynamic peoples. In addition, Vladivostok's location close to the Russo-Chinese border would actually serve as an ultimate guarantee of peace and territorial integrity.

A new emphasis on the Pacific Rim would not only develop the Russian Far East but also the many time zones that lie between Vladivostok and St. Petersburg. Such a focus would help develop all of Siberia. It would also push Russia to pursue economic and geostrategic opportunities in the Arctic Ocean, which is emerging as a resource-rich and potentially productive area. The Arctic—which brings together Europe, North America, and Russia—is a region whose very harshness requires cooperation.

Adopting a new role after 500 years as an empire, seventy years as an ideological warrior, and over forty years during the Cold War as a military superpower will be difficult. Russia's post-Soviet comeback disproved forecasts that it was going to descend into irrelevance. Russia has survived the recent economic crisis. But it does have a long way to go before it becomes a modern state capable of pursuing a foreign policy that fully serves its needs, not its nostalgia. Russia will not, and need not, formally join the West as its former satellites have done and its erstwhile borderlands may do. But as it becomes more modern as a result of its domestic transformation—and adapts its foreign policy accordingly—it can emerge as a serious, desirable, and, yes, indispensable partner, as well as a resourceful player.

NOTES

Introduction

1. Winston S. Churchill, *The World Crisis* (New York: First Free Press, 2005).

2. I do not propose to give a full account and analysis of the end of the Cold War. What I do is a thumbnail sketch. Readers will find exhaustive treatment of that vast topic in other authors' works, including (my selection) Mary Elise Sarotte, *1989: The Struggle to Create Post-Cold War Europe* (Princeton, N.J.: Princeton University Press, 2009); Angela Stent, *Russia and Germany Reborn: Unification, the Soviet Collapse, and the New Europe* (Princeton: Princeton University Press, 1999).

3. International Institute of Strategic Studies, *The Military Balance: 1988–1989* (London: IISS, 1989).

4. In the eyes of the military, Eduard Shevardnadze, who as foreign minister was negotiating the redeployment agreements, was made the main culprit. This had fateful implications not only for Shevardnadze, but for Russian-Georgian relations after the fall of the USSR.

5. For a very good first-hand account of that, see Karen Brutents, *Nesbyvsheesya: Neravnodushnye Zametki o Perestroyke* (Unfulfilled: Partial thoughts on Perestroika) (Moscow: Mezhdunarodnye, 2005).

6. According to historian and well known demographer Sergei Maksudov.

7. Andrei Amalrik, *Will the Soviet Union Survive Till 1984?* (Gloucester, Mass.: Peter Smith Publisher Inc., 1970).

8. Andrei Amalrik, *Dissidents: Memoirs and Commentaries* (Ann Harbor, Mich.: Ardis Publishers, 1982).

9. Henry Kissinger, *Diplomacy* (New York: Simon & Schuster, 1994).

10. This included Yegor Gaidar, the historian Alexander Yanov, and others.

11. Anatoly Chernyaev, *Shest' let s Gorbachevym: Po dnevnikovym zapisyam* (Six years with Gorabachev: Based on diary entries) (Moscow: "Progress"-"Kul'tura," 1993).

12. Anatoly Chernyaev, *1991: Dnevnik Pomoshchnika Prezidenta SSSR* (1991: Diary of the assistant to the president of the USSR) (Moscow: Terra, 1997).

13. Yegor Gaidar, *Gibel imperii: Uroki dlya Sovremennoi Rossii* (Destruction of an empire: Lessons for modern Russia), Second Edition (Moscow: ROSSPEN, 2007).

14. Dmitri Furman, "SNG kak Poslednyaya Forma Rossiyskoy Imperii" (CIS as the last form of the Russian empire), in *Posle Imperii* (After the empire), edited by Igor Klyamkin (Moscow: Fond Liberalnaya Missiya, 2007), 82.

15. Ibid., 79.

16. In the early 2000s, Turkey has raised its international profile dramatically, partially as a result of the dimming hopes of European integration. On the contrary, Germany, firmly embedded within the EU, has been eschewing a more active international role, not to speak of a leading one.

17. Thomas Graham, "The Sources of Russia's Insecurity," *Survival*, vol. 52, no.1 (February–March 2010): 55–74.

18. Vasily Klychevsky, *Kurs Russkoy Istorii* (The course of Russian history) (Moscow: Sochineniya v 9 Tomakh, 1997); Geoffrey Hosking, *Russia: People and Empire, 1552–1917* (Cambridge, Mass.: Harvard University Press, 1998); Richard Pipes, *Russia Under the Old Regime*, Second Edition (London: Penguin, 1997).

19. Nikolay Trubetskoy, *Nasledie Chingiskhana* (The heritage of Genghis Khan) (Moscow: Agraf, 2000).

20. Natalia Tikhonova, "Postimperskiy sindrom ili poisk natsionalnoy identichnosti" (Post-imperial syndrome or the search for a national identity), in *Posle Imperii* (After the empire), edited by Igor Klyamkin (Moscow: Fond Liberal'naya Missiya, 2007), 157–58.

21. Robert Cooper, *The Breaking of Nations: Order and Chaos in the Twenty-First Century* (New York, Atlantic Monthly Press, 2003).

22. Dmitri Trenin, "Russia Leaves the West," *Foreign Affairs* (July–August 2006).

23. Vladimir Putin and Robert Kocharian, Press Conference Following Russian-Armenian Talks, Yerevan, Armenia, March 25, 2005, http://archive.kremlin.ru/eng/speeches/2005/03/25/2234_type82914type82915_85953.shtml.

24. Vladimir Putin, "Rossiya na poroge Tretyego tysyacheletia" (Russia on the doorstep of its third millennium), *Nezavisimaya gazeta*, December 30, 1999, www.ng.ru/politics/1999-12-30/4_millenium.html.

25. Putin's speech at an election rally, Luzhniki Stadium, Moscow, November 21, 2007, http://archive.kremlin.ru/eng/speeches/2007/11/21/1735_type82912type84779_153676.shtml.

26. President Putin's remarks at the Munich Security Conference, February 5, 2007, http://archive.kremlin.ru/eng/speeches/2007/02/10/0138_type82912type82914 type82917type84779_118123.shtml.

27. Dmitri Trenin, "Russia's Coercive Diplomacy," Briefing Paper, vol. 10, issue 1, Carnegie Moscow Center, January 2008.

28. See remarks by German Chancellor Angela Merkel at a joint press conference with Dmitri Medvedev, St. Petersburg, October 2, 2008, www.kremlin.ru/text/appears/2008/10/207176.shtml.

29. For a comprehensive chronology of the war, see Mikhail Barabanov, Anton Lavrov, Vyacheslav Tseluiko, *Tanki Avgusta: Sbornik statey* (Tanks of August: A collection of articles) (Moscow: Tsentr Analiza Strategiy i Tekhnologiy, 2009) www.cast.ru/files/the_tanks_of_august_sm.pdf.

30. Dmitri Medevedev's remarks at a meeting with members of the Valdai Club, September 12, 2008, http://kremlin.ru/appears/2008/09/12/1518_type63374type 63376type63381type8; Medvedev's remarks to NGO representatives, September 19, 2008, www.kremlin.ru/text/appears/2008/09/206639.shtml; The President's Address to the Federal Assembly of the Russian Federation, November 5, 2008, www.kremlin.ru/text/appears/2008/11/208749.shtml; see also "Conversation With Vladimir Putin," a national call-in event held on December 4, 2008, www.vesti.ru/doc.html?id=229865&cid=1.

31. "Official Interim Report on Number of Casualties," *Civil Georgia*, September 8, 2008, www.civil.ge/eng/article.php?id=19384.

32. Cf. WikiLeaks revelations on that score: Scott Shane, "Fearing Russia, Baltics Turned to NATO," *New York Times*, December 7, 2010.

33. Dmitri Rogozin interview with Vladimir Pozner, Channel One (Russia), December 5, 2010.

34. Dmitri Medvedev, interview with Channel One (Russia), August 31, 2008, http://archive.kremlin.ru/eng/speeches/2008/08/31/1850_type82912type82916_206003.shtml.

35. The Declaration of the Moscow Session of the Collective Security Council of the Collective Security Treaty Organization, September 5, 2008, www.kremlin.ru/text/docs/2008/09/206174.shtml; The Dushanbe Declaration of the Member States of the Shanghai Cooperation Organization, August 28, 2008, www.infoshos.eu/?id=39.

36. Cf. Edward Lucas, *The New Cold War: How the Kremlin Menaces Both Russia and the West* (London: Bloomsbury Publishing, 2008).

37. Thomas Graham, "The Sources of Russia's Insecurity," *Survival*, vol. 52, issue 1 (2010): 63.

38. Vadim Tsymbursky, *Ostrov Rossiya* (Russia the island) (Moscow: ROSSPEN, 2007), 7.

Chapter 1

1. Alexander Zinoviev, *Nesostoyavshiysya Proekt: Rasput'e. Russkaya Tragediya* (Missed project: Crossroads of a Russian tragedy) (Moscow: AST Moskva, 2009).

2. Putin is not alone in his assertion. Leonid Kuchma, Ukraine's second president, having called the disintegration of the Soviet Union "a great historic event," which "resurrected Ukraine," adds in the same breath that it was also a "tragedy of the century," in terms of the socioeconomic dislocations it produced. Cf. Leonid Kuchma, *Posle Maydana. Zapiski Prezidenta, 2005–2006* (After Maidan: Notes of a president, 2005–2006) (Moscow: Vremya, 2007), 165.

3. Natalia Tikhonova, "Postimperskiy sindrom ili poisk natsionalnoy identichnosti" (Post-imperial syndrome or the search for a national identity), in *Posle Imperii* (After the empire), edited by Igor Klyamkin (Moscow: Fond Liberal'naya Missiya, 2007), 62.

4. A poll by IKSI RAN, 2001.

5. Table 18.1, *Obshchestvennoe Mnenie – 2009* (Public opinion – 2009) (Moscow: Levada Center, 2009), 146.

6. Tikhonova, "Postimperskiy sindrom," 164.

7. Mikhail Konstantinovich Gorshkov, Natalia Tikhonova, Aleksandr Chepurenko, Frants Sheregi, and P. Shultse, *Rossiya na rubezhe vekov* (Russia at a milestone) (Moscow: ROSSPEN, 2000); Mikhail Gorshkov and Natalia Tikhonova, *Izmenyayushchayasya Rossiya v Zerkale Sotsiologii* (Changing Russia in sociological perspective) (Moscow: Letniy Sad, 2004); Mikhail Gorshkov and Natalia Tikhonova, *Rossiyskaya Identichnost' v Usloviyakh transformatsii: opyt sotsiologichskogo analiza* (Russian identity in the context of transformation: Experience in sociological analysis) (Moscow: Nauka, 2005).

8. Statement made during his TV appearance on a Channel One talk show, November 7, 2007.

9. For example, Vitaly Treyakov and others.

10. Vadim Tsymbursky, *Ostrov Rossiya* (Russia the island) (Moscow: ROSSPEN, 2007), 21.

11. According to a 2005 VTsIOM poll.

12. Cf. Dmitri Trenin and Pavel Baev, *The Arctic: A View From Moscow* (Washington, D.C.: Carnegie Endowment for International Peace, 2010).

13. Putin's statement at the Russian Geographic Society conference, Moscow, September 22, 2010.

14. Yegor Gaidar, *Gibel imperii. Uroki dlya Sovremennoi Rossii* (Destruction of an empire. Lessons for modern Russia), Second Edition (Moscow: ROSSPEN, 2007).

15. Kuchma, *Posle Maydana*, 104–106, 235.

16. E.g., Sergei Karaganov.

17. Putin's reported remarks at the meeting of the Russia-NATO Council, Bucharest (Romania), April 4, 2008, http://archive.kremlin.ru/eng/speeches/2008/04/04/1949_type82915_163150.shtml.

18. Modest Kolerov, *Noviy Rezhim* (New regime) (Moscow: Dom Intellektual'noy Knigi, 2001), 16.

19. Lydia Andrusenko, "Sil'niy Khod ili Oshibka Prezidenta?" (Strong Move or a Mistake for the President), *Politicheskiy Zhurnal*, issue 29, October 15, 2007, 11.

20. These words belong to Vladislav Surkov, the Kremlin first deputy chief of staff, himself a Chechen. Quoted in M. Muradov, "Krasivy My Vse-taki Narod," *Kommersant*, October 25, 2010, www.kommersant.ru/doc.aspx?DocsID=1528383.

21. Cf., e.g., Shaimiev's speech to mark the millennium of the city of Kazan, August 26, 2005, http://shaimiev.tatar.ru/pub/view/973.

22. I. Begimbetova and V. Boyko, "Borisu Gryzlovu Naznachat Den Prinyatiya Islama," (Boris Gryzlov receives request for day for the adoption of Islam) *Kommersant*, June 3, 2010, 4, www.kommersant.ru/doc.aspx?DocsID=1379947.

23. Kolerov, 12–13.

24. Ibid., 13.

25. Cf. Russian Ministry of Foreign Affairs, "The Foreign Policy and Diplomatic Activities of the Russian Federation in 2008," Moscow, March 2009, www.mid.ru/brp_4.nsf/2a660d5e4f620f40c32576b20036eb06/c77fbfe0819669b9c32575e100338b95/$FILE/THE%20FOREIGN%20POLICY%20AND%20DIPLOMATIC%20ACTIVITIES%20OF%20THE%20RUSSIAN%20FEDERATION%20IN%202008.pdf.

26. See Estonian President Toomas Hendrik Ilves's speech at the Fifth World Congress of Finno-Ugric Peoples, June 28, 2008; V. Kuzmin, "Ilves Isportil Prazdnik" (Ilves ruined the holiday), *Rossiyskaya gazeta*, June 30, 2008, www.rg.ru/2008/06/30/ilves.html.

27. Vadim Tsymbursky, *Ostrov Rossiya*, 25.

28. Quoted in Viktor Larin, *Aziatsko-Tikhookeansky Region v Nachale XXI Veka: Vyzovy, Ugrozy, Shansy Tikhookeanskoy Rossii* (Asian-Pacific region in the beginning of the XXI century: Summons, threats, chances in Pacific Russia) (Vladivostok: DVO RAN, 2010), 8.

29. Larin (2010) quotes figures suggesting that 2 out of 3 adult residents of the RFE have been to China, and at least 15–20 percent to Japan and South Korea. See *Aziatsko-Tikhookeansky Region*, 41.

30. Yuri Znovarev and Alexander Popov, "Russkiy Novy Svet" (The new Russian society), *Expert-Dalniy Vostok*, no. 39 (580), October 22–28, 2007, 6–7.

31. Emil Pain, "Imperiya v Sebe. O Vozrozhdenii Imperskogo Sindroma v Rossii" (Empire in itself: Regarding the re-birth of the empire syndrome in Russia), *Posle Imperii*, Igor Klyamkin (ed.) (Moscow: Fond Liberal'naya Missiya), 102.

32. Cf, e.g., Nikolay Petrov, "All Power to the Regions," *Moscow Times*, October 5, 2010, www.themoscowtimes.com/opinion/article/all-power-to-the-regions/418432.html.

33. Larin, *Aziatsko-Tikhookeansky Region*, 44.

34. Irina Zvyagelskaya, *Stanovlenie gosudarstvo Tsentralnoy Azii. Politicheskie processy* (The establishment of governments in Central Asia) (Moscow: Aspect Press, 2009), 156.

35. Alexander Solzhenitsyn, "Kak Obustroit' Rossiyu," (How to develop Russia) *Komsomol'skaya Pravda* (Spetsial'niy Vypusk), September 18, 1990.

36. See Emil Pain, "Imperiya v Sebe."

37. Igor Zevelev, "Buduschee Rossii: natsiya ili civilizatsiya?" (The future of Russia: Nation or civilization?), *RiGA*, September–October 2009.

38. A. B. Zubov, ed., *Istoriya Rossii. XX Vek: 1894–1939* (History of Russia, XX century: 1894–1939) (Moscow: AST, 2009).

39. Tikhonova, "Postimperskiy sindrom," 158.

40. Lev Gudkov, *Negativanaya Identichnost': Stat'i 1997–2002* (Independent identity: Articles 1997–2001) (Moscow: Novoe Literaturnoe Obozrenie–VCIOM-A, 2004) 193.

41. Andrey Kozenko, Ivan Buranov, Pavel Korobov, and Daniil Turovskiy, "Ataka vtorym tempom" (Second wave of attacks), *Kommersant*, December 16, 2010, 1.

42. VTsIOM figures, as reported by the *Kommersant*, February 24, 2009, 3.

43. By 46 percent in 2010.

44. Igor Zevelev, "Russia's Future: Nation or Civilization?" *Russia in Global Affairs*, no. 4 (October–December 2009), http://eng.globalaffairs.ru/print/number/n_14246.

45. Cf. D. E. Furman, ed., *Belorussiya I Rossiya: Obshchestva I Gosudarstva* (Belarus and Russia: Societies and states) (Moscow: Izdatelstvo "Prava Cheloveka," 1998).

46. Zvyagelskaya, *Stanovlenie gosudarstv Tsentralnoy Azii*, 49.

47. *Rossiyskiy statisticheskiy ezhegodnik* – 2008 (Statistical yearbook of Russia – 2008), available at www.gks.ru/bgd/regl/b08_13/Main.htm.

48. This is according to Finance Minister Alexei Kudrin. See "Vyskazyvaniya A.L. Kudrina Informatsionnym Agentstvam na Vstreche Ministrov Finansov G-20"

(Akexei Kudrin's speech to the media at the G-20 summit), September 5, 2009, www.minfin.ru/ru/press/speech/index.php?afrom4=04.09.2009&ato4=07.09.2009& type4=&id4=8064.

49. Medvedev's annual address, November 30, 2010.

50. Kingsmill Bond and Andrey Kuznetsov, *Russia: 20 Years of Change: Collapse, Recovery and Transformation*, Troika Dialog, January 2011, http://www.kremlin-ag.de/_files/ downloads/20%20Jahre%20Wandel%20in%20Russland_en.pdf, 21.

51. *Rossiyskiy statisticheskiy ezhegodnik* – 2003, 2007 (Statistical yearbook of Russia – 2003 and 2007), available at www.gks.ru/bgd/regl/b07_13/Main.htm.

52. Anders Åslund, *How Ukraine Became a Market Economy and Democracy* (Washington, D.C.: Peterson Institute for International Economics, 2009).

53. Yaroslav Romanchuk, *Poiskakh Ekonomicheskogo Chuda* (Searching for an economic miracle) (Minsk: Tsentr Mizesa, 2008), http://liberty-belarus.info/images/stories/ book/V_poiskah_ekonom_chuda.pdf.

54. L. A. Fridman, *Ocherki ekonomicheskogo isotsialnogo razvitiya stran Tsentralnoy Azii posle raspada SSSR* (Outlines of the economic and sociological development of the Central Asian countries following the collapse of the USSR) (Moscow: Gumanitarii, 2001), 15–17.

55. Zvyagelskaya, *Stanovlenie gosudarstv Tsentralnoy Azii*, 41.

56. Kolerov, *Noviy Rezhim*, 20.

57. "Soldat Sovetskogo Soyuza" (Soldier of the Soviet Union), Oleg Odnokolenko's interview with Marshal Dmitri Yazov, *Itogi*, December 4, 2010, www.itogi.ru/ spetzproekt/2010/15/150831.html.

58. V. Litovkin, "Parad Reform Ne Zatormozil" (The reform parade has not ended), *Nezavisimoe Voennoe Obozrenie*, issue 17, May 14–20, 2010, 3, http://nvo.ng.ru/ realty/2010-05-14/1_parad.html.

59. Mikhail Barabanov, Anton Lavrov, and Vyacheslav Tseluiko, *Tanki Avgusta: Sbornik statey* (Tanks of August: A collection of articles) (Moscow: Tsentr Analiza Strategiy i Tekhnologiy, 2009), www.cast.ru/files/the_tanks_of_august_sm.pdf.

60. President Bill Clinton made that point during a "town hall" meeting with the students of Moscow University during his trip to Russia in the 1990s.

Chapter 2

1. For a very good Russian biography of Genghis Khan, see Isay Kalashnikov, *Zhestoky Vek* (Severe age) (Moscow: Sovetsky Pisatel, 1980).

2. Cf. Nikolai Sergeevich Trubetskoy, Petr Nikolaevich Savitsky, Georgii Vasil'evich Frolovsky, and Petr Petrovich Suvchinsky, *Iskhod k Vostoku* (Exodus to the East) (Sofia, 1921).

3. Aleksandr Prokhanov, *Pyataya Imperiya* (Fifth empire) (Moscow: Amfora, 2007); Mikhail Yuriev, *Tret'ya Imperiya. Rossiya, Kotoraya Dolzhna Byt* (Third empire. Russia, which it should be) (Moscow: Limbus Press, Izdatel'stvo K. Tublina, 2007).

4. Dmitri Trenin, *The End of Eurasia: Russia on the Border Between Geopolitics and Globalization* (Washington, D.C.: Carnegie Endowment for International Peace, 2002).

5. Andrei Kozyrev, *Preobrazhenie* (Transformation) (Moscow: Mezhdunarodnye otnoshenia, 1995), 5.

6. For an early assessment of these policies, see Dmitri Trenin, "Realpolitik Moskvy" (Realpolitik Moscow style), *Nezavisimaya gazeta*, February 9, 2004, www.ng.ru/courier/2004-02-09/9_realpolitik.html.

7. Leonid Kuchma, *Posle Maydana: Zapiski Prezidenta, 2005–2006* (After Maidan: Notes of a president, 2005–2006) (Moscow: Vremya, 2007).

8. For a good Russian account of the Orange Revolution, see Andrei Kolesnikov, *Perviy Ukrainskiy. Zapiski s Peredovoy* (First Ukrainian: Memories from the front) (Moscow: Vagrius, 2005).

9. See Pavlovsky's interview in *Expert* magazine, December 2004. T. Gurova, "Revolyuziya, Eyo Vozhdi I Eyo Tekhnologii" (Revolution: Its leaders and its technology) *Ekspert*, no. 46 (446), December 6, 2004, www.expert.ru/expert/2004/46/46ex-ukr-pav_27653.

10. See Dmitri Medvedev's interview with Valeriy Fadeev, "Sokhranit' Effektivnoe Gosudarstvo v Sushchestvuyushchikh Granitsakh" (To keep the effective state within existing borders), *Ekspert*, no. 13 (460), April 4, 2005, www.expert.ru/expert/2005/13/13ex-medved_5168.

11. Kuchma, *Posle Maydana*, 280.

12. Ibid., 97–98.

13. Putin's press conference following talks with President of Ukraine Viktor Yushchenko and the Second Meeting of the Russian-Ukrainian Intergovernmental Commission, The Kremlin (Moscow), February 12, 2008, http://archive.kremlin.ru/eng/speeches/2008/02/12/2018_type82914type82915_160088.shtml.

14. Kuchma, *Posle Maydana*, 176.

15. Sergei Karaganov, "Magia tsifr 2009: Ili Neokonchennaya Voyna" (The magic of 2009 numbers, or an unfinished war), *Rossiyskaya Gazeta*, no. 4867 (Federal'niy Vypusk), March 13, 2009, www.rg.ru/2010/03/13/karaganov.html.

16. Vladimir Soloviev, "Iz Ukrainosti v Krainost'" (From Ukraine to extremes), *Kommersant*, no. 71 (4371), April 22, 2010,www.kommersant.ru/doc.aspx?DocsID=1358173&print=true.

17. Several astute observers, including Stephen Sestanovich, U.S. ambassador-at-large in the former USSR during the Clinton administration, drew parallels between the two men.

18. The author's conversation with Zviad Zhvaniya, then-prime minister of Georgia, November 2004.

19. As related by Igor Ivanov, who was negotiating on Russia's behalf.

20. See Dmitri Trenin, "How To Make Peace With Georgia," *Moscow Times*, August 9, 2010; and Sergei Markedonov, "Mozhno li Segodnya Dobit'sya Mira s Gruziei?" Polit.ru, September 9, 2010, www.polit.ru/analytics/2010/09/09/georgia.html.

21. Cf. Arkady Dubnov's comment in *Vremya Novostei*, "Pridnestrov'em Zaimetsya Kazakhstan" (Kazakhstan takes up Trandsneister), *Vremya Novostei*, no. 45, March 19, 2009, www.vremya.ru/2009/45/4/225315.html.

22. "The Military Doctrine of the Russian Federation 2010," www.scrf.gov.ru/documents/33.html.

23. Statement made during his meeting in Moscow with members of the Core Group of the Munich Security Conference, October 20, 2010, http://eng.kremlin.ru/news/1173.

24. Helmut Kohl, *Erinnerungen 1982–1990* (Memories, 1982–1990) (Munich: Droemer Verlag, 2005), 961.

25. *Obshchestvennoe mnenie – 2009* (Public opinion yearbook – 2009) (Moscow: Levada Center, 2009), 166.

26. Cf. SVOP's (Committee on Foreign and Defense Policy) report, *Politicheskiy Kontekst: Interesy Zapada, Stran Tsentral'noy azii i Vostochnoy Evropy I Rossii. Rekomendazii* (Political context: The interests of the West in the countries of Central Asia and Eastern Europe and Russia. Recommendations), June 21, 1995, http://svop.ru/live/materials.asp?m_id=7009&r_id=7044.

27. As in an interview on *BBC Breakfast With Frost*, March 5, 2000, available at http://archive.kremlin.ru/eng/speeches/2000/03/05/1426_type82916_134555.shtml.

28. In conversations with NATO Secretary General (1999–2004) Lord Robertson.

29. "NATO-Russia Relations: A New Quality," Declaration by Heads of State and Government, Pratica di Mare air force base, Italy, May 28, 2002, http://archive.kremlin.ru/eng/events/articles/2002/05/156782/161245.shtml.

30. George N. Lewis and Theodore A. Postol, "European Missile Defense: The Technological Basis of Russian Concerns," *Arms Control Today*, October 2007, 13–18, www.armscontrol.org/act/2007_10/LewisPostol.

31. Alexandr Batygin, "Po Edinym Pravilam Igry" (Based on the only rules of the game) *Soyuz. Belarus-Rossiya*, no. 476 (40), October 21, 2010, www.rg.ru/2010/10/21/tamozh-soyuz.html.

32. On the safe limits of NATO enlargement, see Dmitri Trenin, "Thinking Strategically About Russia," Policy Brief, Carnegie Endowment for International Peace, December 2008, http://carnegieendowment.org/files/thinking_strategically_russia.pdf.

33. Bruce Jackson, "A Turning Point for Europe's East," *Hoover Digest*, April 1, 2010, www.hoover.org/publications/policy-review/article/5292.

34. James Marson, "Ukraine, Eastern Europe Worries About Losing Clout in Washington," *Kyiv Post*, September 24, 2009, www.kyivpost.com/news/nation/detail/49399.

35. Taras Stets'kiv, "Natsionalniy interes segondnya" (Today's national interest), *Zerkalo nedeli*, issue 32, August 29-September 4, 2009, www.zn.ua/1000/1550/67040.

36. Sergey Tigipko, "Nashe mesto na karte mira" (Our place on the world map), *Zerkalo nedeli*, issue 32, August 29-September 4, 2009, www.zn.ua/1000/1550/67039.

37. Alyaksandr Lebedko, as quoted by Anton Khodesevich, "Lukashenka Stavit na Tamozhnyu" (Lukashenka sets his sight on tariffs), *Nezavisimaya Gazeta*, March 19, 2009, www.ng.ru/cis/2009-03-19/6_Lukashenko.html.

38. For an analysis of the Chechen war, see Dmitri Trenin and Alexey Malashenko, *Russia's Restless Frontier: The Chechnya Factor in Post-Soviet Russia* (Washington, D.C.: Carnegie Endowment for International Peace, 2004).

39. Ivan Sukhov, "Net 'Vostoka,' i 'Zapada' Net" (There is no East and West), *Vremya Novostey*, no. 207, November 10, 2008, www.vremya.ru/2008/207/4/26635.html.

40. Alexey Malashenko, *Ramzan Kadyrov: Rossiyskiy Politik Kavkazskoy Natsionalnosti* (Moscow: ROSSPEN, 2009).

41. See eyewitness reports by Ivan Sukhov, "Khalva s Garantiey" (Peace with a warranty), *Vremya Novostey*, no. 153, August 27, 2007, www.vremya.ru/2007/153/4/185693.html.

42. Dmitri Medvedev, "Vystuplenie na Rasshirennom Operativnom Soveshchanii s Chlenami Soveta Bezopasnosti," Speech at an Expanded Operational Meeting with the Members of the Security Council, Makhachkala, Dagestan, June 9, 2009, http://kremlin.ru/transcripts/4383.

43. As announced by Ingushetia's President Zayavil Yevkurov, "V Ingushetii Za Pyat' Let ot Ruk Terroristov Pogible Bolee 400 Militsionerov, Zayavil Evkurov" (In Ingushetia in five years more than 500 policemen have died at the hands of terrorists), Newsru.com, October 3, 2010, www.newsru.com/russia/03oct2010/evk.html.

44. Cf. an interview with Adil'gerey Magomedtagirov, Daghestan's Interior Minister. (The minister has since been killed.) Ivan Sukhov, "My Budem Bit'sya do Poslednego" (We will fight until the end), *Vremya Novostey*, no. 45, March 19, 2009, www.vremya.ru/2009/45/4/225224.html.

45. Sergei Mashkin, "Oproverzhimye Dokazatel'stva" (Disputable evidence), *Kommersant*, no. 201 (4501), October 28, 2010, 1, www.kommersant.ru/doc.aspx?DocsID=1530053&print=true.

46. Alexey Malashenko, "When the War Ended," *Pro et Contra*, no. 5–6 (43), September–December 2008.

47. Sergei Markedonov, "A Strategy for North Caucasus: don't mention politics or religion!" openDemocracy.net, November 1, 2010, www.opendemocracy.net/od-russia/sergei-markedonov/strategy-for-north-caucasus-don%E2%80%99t-mention-politics-or-religion.

48. "Kak v koloniyakh" (Like in the colonies), *Vedomosti*, no. 198, October 20, 2010, 1.

49. Ibid.

50. Cf, e.g., Alexey Malashenko, "Tsena Voprosa" (The price of a question), *Kommersant*, no. 45, March 16, 2009, www.kommersant.ru/doc.aspx?DocsID=1137091&print=true.

51. For an excellent analysis of post-Soviet Central Asia, see Martha Brill Olcott, *Kazakhstan: Unfulfilled Promise* (Washington, D.C.: Carnegie Endowment for International Peace, 2002), and *Central Asia's Second Chance* (Washington, D.C.: Carnegie Endowment for International Peace, 2005). For a discussion of U.S., Russian, and Chinese policies in the region, see Eugene Rumer, Dmitri Trenin, and Huasheng Zhao, *Central Asia: Views from Washington, Moscow, and Beijing* (Armonk, N.Y.: M. E. Sharpe, 2007), 75–136.

52. Alexander Khramchikhin, "OSK 'Tsentr' Protiv Tsentralnoy Azii" (OSK [Central Command Center] against Central Asia), *Nezavisimoe Voennoe Obozrenie*, issue 40, October 22–28, 2010, 1, 6–7, www.nvo.ng.ru/concepts/2010-10-22/1-osk.html.

53. Kuchma, *Posle Maydana*, 175.

54. Khramchikhin, "OSK 'Tsentr' Protiv Tsentralnoy Azii."

55. For a longhand option, cf. Dmitri Trenin and Alexey Malashenko, *Afghanistan: A View from Moscow* (Washington, D.C.: Carnegie Endowment for International Peace, 2010).

56. "Rossiya i SShA Vpervye Proveli Sovmestnuyu Operatsiyu v Afganistane, Razgromiv Chetyre Narkolaboratorii" (Russia and the U.S. held their first ever joint operation in Afghanistan, destroying four drug labs), Newsru.com, October 29, 2010, www.newsru.com/world/29oct2010/fsknafghan_print.html.

57. Zbigniew Brzezinski, "An Agenda for NATO," *Foreign Affairs*, September–October 2009.

58. Also, the number of Russian-designed S-27 (J-11 in Chinese) aircraft produced beyond the 200 allowed under the license is not known. Cf. "Druz'ya-Soperniki" (Friends-Rivals), *Vedomosti*, no. 43 (2313), March 12, 2009, www.vedomosti.ru/newspaper/article/2009/03/12/185719.

59. Bobo Lo, *Axis of Convenience: Moscow, Beijing, and the New Geopolitics* (Harrisonburg, Va.: R. R. Donnelley, 2008).

60. Cf. the debate between Anatoly Tsygankov and Dmitri Trenin, "Kitay dlya Rossii: Tovarishch ili Gospodin?" (China for Russia: Friend or master?), *Indeks Bezopasnosti*, no. 2 (82), 2007, 147–56.

61. Cf. Wen Liao, "China Crosses the Rubicon," *Moscow Times*, June 19, 2009, 8.

62. For a full version of this argument, see Dmitri Trenin and Vasily Mikheev, *Russia and Japan as a Resource for Mutual Development: A 21st-Century Perspective on a 20th-Century Problem* (Moscow: Carnegie Moscow Center, 2005), http://archive.carnegie.ru/en/pubs/books/9402jap_engl.pdf

63. For a full version of this argument, see Dmitri Trenin and Vasily Mikheev, *Russia and Japan as a Resource for Mutual Development: A 21st-Century Perspective on a 20th-Century Problem* (Moscow: Carnegie Moscow Center, 2005). Cf, e.g., Alexander Khramchikhin, "V perspective – Arkticheskiy Front" (In perspective: The Arctic front), *Nezavisimoe Voennoe Obozrenie*, issue 4, February 6–12, 2009, 4, http://nvo.ng.ru/wars/2009-02-06/4_arktika.html; "Mnogopolyarnyy Mir Stanovitsya vo Mnogom Pripolyarnym Mirom" (Multipolar world is becoming a largely circumpolar world), *Nezavisimaya Gazeta-Nauka*, June 24, 2009, www.ng.ru/science/2009-06-24/12_mnogopoliarnyi.html.

64. Konstantin Gaaze and Mikhail Zygar, "Rossiya Pomenyaet Vneshnyu Politiku" (Russia will change its foreign policy), *Russian Newsweek*, no. 20 (288), www.forbes.ru/ekonomika/vlast/49383-rossiya-pomenyaet-vneshnyuyu-politiku.

65. Dmitri Medvedev's Presidential Address to the Federal Assembly of the Russian Federation, The Kremlin (Moscow), November 30, 2010, http://eng.kremlin.ru/transcripts/1384; Vladimir Putin on CNN "Larry King Live," December 2, 2010, www.premier.gov.ru/eng/events/news/13147.

Chapter 3

1. Sergey Aleksandrovich Kulik, Andrey Nikolaevich Spartak, and Igor Yurievich Yurgens, *Ekonomicheskie Interesy i Zadachi Rossii v SNG* (Economic interests and goals of Russia in the CIS) (Moscow: Institute of Contemporary Development, 2010), 5, www.insor-russia.ru/files/Intrest_Books_02.pdf.

2. Ibid., 6, 8.

3. "Missiya Rossii" (Russia's mission), lecture by Anatoly Chubais, St. Petersburg, September 25, 2003, www.chubais.ru/blog/view/611.

4. Kulik et al., *Ekonomicheskie Interesy*, 9.

5. Ibid., 11.

6. Ibid., 29.

7. Sergei Chernyshev, "Towards a United Eurasia," *Russia in Global Affairs*, no. 3, May–September 2010, http://eng.globalaffairs.ru/print/number/Towards-a-United-Eurasia-14999.

8. Kulik et al., *Ekonomicheskie Interesy*, 12.

9. Ibid., 15.

10. Leonid Kuchma, *Posle Maydana. Zapiski Prezidenta. 2005–2006* (After Maidan: Notes of a president, 2005–2006) (Moscow: Vremya, 2007), 47.

11. Kulik et al., *Ekonomicheskie Interesy*, 17.

12. Ibid., 34.

13. Ibid., 18.

14. Kuchma, *Posle Maydana*, 83.

15. A. Gevorkian, *Tri Strany – Tri Mifa. Sotsialno-ekonomicheskie I Politicheslie Transformatsii Kazakhstana, Gruzii, Ukrainy* (Three countries, three myths: Socioeconomic and political transformations of Kazakhstan, Georgia, Ukraine) (Moscow: Regnum, 2008), 61.

16. Alexandr Gudkov, "Kirgiziyu Ostavili Bez Kerosina" (Kyrgyzstan left without kerosene), *Kommersant*, no. 60 (4360), April 7, 2010, www.kommersant.ru/doc.aspx?DocsID=1349904.

17. Kulik et al., *Ekonomicheskie Interesy*, 38.

18. Ibid., 23.

19. Andrei Suzdaltsev, "Politics Ahead of the Economy," *Russia in Global Affairs*, no. 1 January–March 2010, http://eng.globalaffairs.ru/print/number/n_14783.

20. Ibid.

21. Petr Netreba, "Dobro Uhodit v Tamozhenny Soyuz" (Goods go to the customs union), *Kommersant*, no. 50 (4350), March 24, 2010, www.kommersant.ru/doc.aspx?DocsID=1341995.

22. Kulik et al., *Ekonomicheskie Interesy*, 41.

23. Ibid., 25.

24. Gevorkian, *Tri Strany*, 64.

25.   Igor A. Nikolaev, Tatiana E. Marchenko, and Marina V. Titova, *Strany SNG I mirovoy krizis: obshchie problemy I raznye podkhody* (CIS countries and the world financial crisis: Common problems and different approaches) (Moscow: FBK, June 2009), 27.

26.   Kulik et al., *Ekonomicheskie Interesy*, 26.

27.   Kuchma, *Posle Maydana*, 175.

28.   Valeriy Panyushkin and Mikhail Zygar, *Gazprom. Novoye russkoye oruzhie* (Gazprom: Russian weapon) (Moscow: Zakharov, 2008), 22.

29.   *Rossiyskiy statisticheskiy ezhegodnik* – 2009 (Statistical yearbook of Russia – 2009), available at www.gks.ru/bgd/regl/b08_13/Main.htm.

30.   Panyushkin and Zygar, *Gazprom*, 148.

31.   Vladimir Putin, "Interviyu Ispanskim Sredstvam Massovoy Informazii" (Interview in the Spanish media), Moscow, February 7, 2006, http://archive.kremlin.ru/appears/2006/02/07/1759_type63379_101129.shtml.

32.   Kuchma, *Posle Maydana*, 54.

33.   Kulik et al., *Ekonomicheskie Interesy*, 28.

34.   Leonid Grigoriev and Marsel Salikhov, *GUAM – Pyatnadzat Let Spustya* (GUAM – Fifteen years later) (Moscow: Regnum, 2007), 171–72, http://common.regnum.ru/documents/guam.pdf.

35.   Panyushkin and Zygar, *Gazprom*, 126.

36.   Yaroslav Romanchuk, "Belorussiya i Rossiya Posle Lukashenko," (Belarus and Russia after Lukashenka) *NG-Dipkurier*, October 18, 2010, www.ng.ru/courier/2010-10-18/11_belorussia.html.

37.   Alexey Grivach, "Minsk Ne Otsenil Komforta" (Minsk didn't value comfort), *Vremya Novostey*, no. 127, July 17, 2008, www.vremya.ru/2008/127/8/208554.html.

38.   Alexander Gabuyev, "Rossiya Povyshaet Davlenie Gaza" (Russia increases pressure on gas), *Kommersant*, no. 53 (4108), March 26, 2009, www.kommersant.ru/doc.aspx?DocsID=1144186.

39.   Alexander Gabuyev and Irina Granik, "Iran I Rossiya Sovpali v Kaspiyskom More" (Iran and Russia have common interests regarding Caspian Sea), *Kommersant*, no. 150 (4205), August 18, 2009, www.kommersant.ru/doc.aspx?DocsID=1222581.

40.   Panyushkin and Zygar, *Gazprom*, 172.

41.   Alexandr Gabuyev and Natalia Grib, "Gazovy Neurozhay" (Gas crop failure), *Kommersant*, no. 196 (4496), October 21, 2010, www.kommersant.ru/doc.aspx?DocsID=1525677.

42.   Milana Chelpanova, "Vostochny Prizyv" (The East's appeal), *Kommersant* (Prilozhenie "Neft I Gaz"), no. 60 (4360), April 7, 2010, www.kommersant.ru/doc.aspx?DocsID=1347156.

43.   Viktor Larin, *Aziatsko-Tikhookeansky Region v Nachale XXI Veka: Vyzovy, Ugrozy, Shansy Tikhookeanskoy Rossii* (Asian-Pacific region in the beginning of the XXI century: Summons, threats, chances in Pacific Russia) (Vladivostok: DVO RAN, 2010), 9, www.ng.ru/courier/2010-10-18/11_belorussia.html.

44. Ibid.

45. Kuchma, *Posle Maydana*, 296.

46. Kulik et al., *Ekonomicheskie Interesy*, 31.

47. Ibid., 112.

48. Ibid., 33.

Chapter 4

1. These figures are by Memorial. See http://www.memo.ru.

2. See *Rossiya v Tsifrakh – 2010* (Statistical yearbook of Russia – 2010), http://www.gks.ru/bgd/regl/b10_11/IssWWW.exe/Stg/d1/05-01.htm.

3. National Intelligence Council, *Global Trends 2025: A Transformed World*, www.dni.gov/nic/PDF_2025/2025_Global_Trends_Final_Report.pdf.

4. Population Division of the Department of Economic and Social Affairs of the United Nations Secretariat, *World Population Prospects: The 2008 Revision*, http://esa.un.org/unpp.

5. UN Development Programme, *Russia, National Human Development Report: Russian Federation, 2008* (Moscow: UNDP, 2009), http://hdr.undp.org/en/reports/national/europethecis/russia/NHDR_Russia_2008_Eng.pdf.

6. UN Development Programme, *World Population Prospects*.

7. UN Development Programme, *Russia, National Human Development Report: Russian Federation, 2008*.

8. Ibid.

9. M. Sergeyev, "Gusa Khiddinka Otdelyat ot Tadzhikov" (Gusa Khiddinka is separated from Tajiks), *Nezavisimaya gazeta*, March 19, 2009, www.ng.ru/economics/2009-03-19/4_gastarbaitery.html.

10. Zhanna Zayonchkovskaya, Nikita Mkrtchyan, and Elena Tyuryukanova, "Rossiya Pered Vyzovami Immigratsii" (Russia faces immigration issues), in *Postsovetskie Transformatsii: Otrazheniye v Migratsiyah* (Post-Soviet transformations: Reflections on migration), edited by Zhanna Zayonchkovskaya and Galina Vitkovskaya (Moscow: Adamant, 2009), 17, http://migrocenter.ru/publ/pdf/transform.pdf.

11. L. L. Rybakovskiy, "Migratsionnaya situatsiya v Rossii na styke XX-XXI vekov" (The migration situation in Russia at the junctures of XX-XXI centuries), www.migrocenter.ru/publ/konfer/kavkaz/m_kavkaz049.php.

12. Lyudmila Maksakova, "Uzbekistan v Sisteme Mezhdunarodnykh Migratsiy" (Uzbekistan in the global migration system), in Zayonchkovskaya and Vitkovskaya (ed.), *Postsovetskie Transformatsii*, 328.

13. Irina Pribytkova, "Migratsii i Vremya: Ukrainskiy Variant Razvitiya" (Migration and time: The Ukraine variant of development), in *Postsovetskie Transformatsii*, 78.

14. Lyudmila Shakhotko, "Belorusskoe Migratsionnoe Prityazhenie" (The pull of Belarusian migration), in *Postsovetskie Transformatsii*, 159.

15.   Rybakovskiy, "Migratsionnaya situatsiya v Rossii."

16.   Zayonchkovskaya et al., *Postsovetskie Transformatsii*, 24.

17.   A. Kornya, A. Nikolsky, and D. Malkov, "Pereselyat Nekogo I Ne Na Chto" (No one to resettle and no funds), *Vedomosti*, no. 53 (2323), March 26, 2009, 2.

18.   Viktor Larin, *Aziatsko-Tikhookeansky Region v Nachale XXI Veka: Vyzovy, Ugrozy, Shansy Tikhookeanskoy Rossii* (Asian-Pacific region in the beginning of the XXI century: Summons, threats, chances in Pacific Russia) (Vladivostok: DVO RAN, 2010), 20.

19.   Zayonchkovskaya et al., "Rossiya pered vyzovami migratsii," 11.

20.   Ibid., 56.

21.   Anastasia Bashkatova, "Rossiyskie Gastarbaitery Vyrvalis v Lidery" (Russian guest workers became leaders), *Nezavisimaya Gazeta*, November 10, 2010, www.ng.ru/economics/2010-11-10/4_gastarbaiter.html.

22.   Pavel Zhuravel, "Vy Nuzhny Zdes I Seychas" (We need you here and now), *Expert-Ukraine*, no. 41 (44), October 31, 2005, www.expert.ua/articles/18/0/1097.

23.   Shakhotko, "Belorusskoe Migratsionnoe Prityazhenie," 170–71.

24.   Valeriu Mosneaga, "Migratsii v Respublike Moldova v Transformatsionnom Kontexte" (Migration in the Moldovan Republic in transformational context), in Zayonchkovskaya et al., *Postsovetskie Transformatsii*, 198.

25.   Ibid., 200.

26.   Leonid Grigoriev and Marsel Salikhov, *GUAM – Pyatnadzat Let Spustya* (GUAM – Fifteen years later (Moscow: Regnum, 2007), 37, http://common.regnum.ru/documents/guam.pdf.

27.   Arif Yunusov, "Trudovaya Immigratsiya iz Azerbaidzhana: Strategii I Riski Immigratsii v Rynok Truda" (Labor migrants from Azerbaijan: Strategies and risks of immigration in the labor market), in Zayonchkovskaya et al., *Postsovetskie Transformatsii*, 237.

28.   Elena Sadovskaya, "Kazakhstan v Tsentralnoaziatskoy Migratsionnoy Subsisteme" (Kazakhstan in the Central Asian migration system), in Zayonchkovskaya et al., *Postsovetskie Transformatsii*, 285.

29.   A. Gevorkian, *Tri Strany – Tri Mifa. Sotsialno-ekonomicheskie I Politicheslie Transformatsii Kazakhstana, Gruzii, Ukrainy* (Three countries, three myths: Socioeconomic and political transformations of Kazakhstan, Georgia, Ukraine) (Moscow: Regnum, 2008), 63.

30.   "Luchshie ne nuzhny," *Vedomosti*, November 12, 2010, 1.

31.   Zayonchkovskaya et al., *Postsovetskie Transformatsii*, 33.

32.   "Luchshie ne nuzhny," *Vedomosti*, November 12, 2010, 1.

33.   Table 17.8, "Obshchestvennoe Mnenie – 2009" (Popular opinion – 2009), Levada Center, 2009, 144.

34.   Cf., e.g., Nikolay Orlov, "Velikaya kitayskaya expansiya" (The great Chinese expansion), *Rossiya*, March 11, 2004; Ivan Sas, "Aziatskaya pnevmonia – u rossiyskikh granits" (Asian pneumonia – At the Russian borders), *Nezavisimaya*

Gazeta, March 18, 2003; AiF-Moskva, November 6, 2002; Natalia Timashova et al., "Rossiya kitayskaya" (Russia and China), *Novye Izvestia*, September 5, 2003; Alexander Danilkin, "Kto ni popadya" (Just about anybody), *Trud*, May 28, 2004.

35. Quoted in Vilya Gelbras, *Kitaytsy v Rossii: skolko ikh?* (The Chinese in Russia: How many?), *Demoscope Weekly*, no. 45–46, December 3–16, 2001, www.demoscope.ru/weekly/045/rossia01.php#a01.

36. Eduard Salmanovichi Kulpin-Gubaidullin, "Rossiya i Kitay: Problemy Bezopasnosti i Sotrudnichestva v Kontekste Globalnoy Borby za Resursy" (Russia and China: Problems with security and cooperation in the global context of the war on resources), *Polis*, no. 6, 2008, 150.

37. Zayonchkovskaya et al., *Postsovetskie Transformatsii*, 12.

38. Vilya G. Gelbras, *Rossiya v Usloviyakh Globalnoy Kitayskoy Migratsii* (Perspectives on Chinese migration to Russia), (Moscow: Muravey, 2004); Gelbras, "Perspektivy Kitayskoy Migratsii v Rossiyu" (Perspectives on Chinese migration to Russia), "Status-Kvo" Dialog, April 29, 2005, www.statusquo.ru/689/article_777.html.

39. Vladimir Razuvaev, "Kitayskaya Ekspansiya v Rossiyu: Vozmozhnosti i Riski" (Chinese expansion into Russia: Opportunities and risks), *Rossiyskaya Gazeta*, no. 4190, October 6, 2006, www.rg.ru/2006/10/06/kitay.html.

40. Rybakovskiy, "Migratsionnaya situatsiya v Rossii."

41. Alexander Dzadziev, "Migratsionnye Protsessy v Respulikakh Severnogo Kavkaza" (Migration process in the North Caucasus), *Kavkazsky Ekspert*, no. 4, 2006, http://rcnc.ru/index.php?option=com_content&task=view&id=75&Itemid=1.

42. Ibid.

43. Ibid.

44. Valeri Tishkov, "Russkoe Naselenie Respublik Severnogo Kavkaza" (Russian people in the North Caucus), www.valerytishkov.ru/cntnt/publikacii3/kollektivn/puti_mira_/russkoe_na.html.

45. Roy Medvedev, *Kazakhstanskiy Proryv* (Kazakhstan's breakthrough) (Moscow: Institut Ekonomicheskikh Strategiy, 2007), 98.

46. Arkadi Dubnov, "Sdelka 'Gaz-Lyudi' Proshla Proverku Vremenem" (Gas–People deal withstood the test of time), *Vremya Novostey*, no. 135 June 25, 2008, www.vremya.ru/2008/133/5/209059.html.

47. Tatiana Ivzhenko, "Okhotniki za Pasportami" (Passport hunters), *Nezavisimaya Gazeta*, March 19, 2009, www.ng.ru/cis/2009-03-19/1_hunters.html.

48. Anatoly Vishnevsky, "Konets Severotsntrizma" (End of sovereignty), *Russia in Global Affairs*, no. 5, September–October 2009, www.globalaffairs.ru/print/number/n_14035.

Chapter 5

1. Yevgeny Primakov, "Mezhdunarodnye otnosheniya na poroge 21-go veka: problemy I perspektivy" (International relations on the eve of the twenty-first century: Problems and prospects), *Mezhdunarodnaya Zhizn*, 1996, issue 10, 3–13.

2.   "Rising from the knees" became a refrain with many pro-Kremlin commentators in the second half of the 2000s.

3.   As reported by Dimitri Simes in his book, *After the Collapse* (New York: Simon and Schuster, 1999), 19.

4.   The issue was not, as some authors (notably, Mark Kramer, "The Myth of a No-NATO Enlargement Pledge to Russia," *Washington Quarterly*, April 2009, 39–60) correctly point out, that Mikhail Gorbachev had never been given assurances as to non-expansion of NATO membership beyond its Cold War boundaries. The Russians thought they had unilaterally wound down the confrontation, dissolved their empire, and embraced Western values. They expected, in turn, to be embraced by the West. What they saw instead was the expansion of the Cold War military alliance toward their borders. Their conclusions about why this was happening were often wrong, but their concerns were genuinely felt.

5.   For a reference to Viktor Chernomyrdin's comment, see Konstantin Smirnov and Vladislav Dorofeyev, "Skazano: ES!" (Russia files in Europe said: EU!), *Kommersant-Vlast*, no. 27 (233), July 29, 1997, www.kommersant.ru/doc.aspx?DocsID=13702.

6.   Vyacheslav Nikonov made that argument in the mid-1990s. Cf. *Epokha peremen. Rossiys 90-kh glazami konservatora* (The Nineties through the eyes of a conservative), collected articles (Moscow: Yazyki Russkoy kul'tury, 1999).

7.   To use the phrase coined by Alexander Vershbow, U.S. Ambassador to Russia in the early 2000s. Cf. Andrey Ivanov, "NATO budet delit'sya" (NATO will share), *Kommersant*, November 21, 2001, www.kommersant.ru/doc.aspx?DocsID=295303.

8.   For the author's extensive analysis of this, cf. Dmitri Trenin, "Russia Leaves the West," *Foreign Affairs*, July–August 2006.

9.   Cf., e.g., Vitaly Panyushkin and Mikhail Zygar, *Gazprom. Novoye russkoye oruzhie* (Gazprom: Russian weapon) (Moscow: Zakharov, 2008).

10. Putin's comments reported by *Rossiyskaya Gazeta* on November 22, 2007, www.rg.ru/2007/11/22/putin-forum.html.

11. Molotov, as quoted by Felix Chuev, *Sorok besed s Molotovym. Iz dnevnika Feliksa Chueva* (Forty interviews with Molotov: From the diary of Felix Chuev) (Moscow: Terra, 1991).

12. Foreign Minister Sergei Lavrov, "Russian Foreign Policy and the New Quality of Geopolitical Situation," *Diplomatic Yearbook*, 2008, www.mid.ru\\brp_4.nsf\\ e78a48070f128a7b43256999005bcbb3\\19e7b14202191e4ac3257525003e5de7? OpenDocument.

13. Putin's speech at the Munich Security Conference, February 10, 2007, http://archive. kremlin.ru/eng/speeches/2007/02/10/0138_type82912type82914type82917type 84779_118123.shtml.

14. See Sam Greene (ed.), "Engaging History: The Problems and Politics of Memory in Russia and the Post-Soviet Space," Carnegie Moscow Center Working Paper, issue 2, 2010.

15. Levada Center, *Obshchestvennoe mnenie 2009* (Public opinion 2009), table 21.18, 193.

16. Ibid., table 21.17.

17. See Gennady Khazanov, "Mozhno Li Podedit' Terrorizm?" (Is it possible to defeat terrorism?), *Kommersant–Vlast*, no. 13(867), April 5, 2010, www.kommersant.ru/doc. aspx?docsID=1347413.

18. Levada Center, *Obshchestvennoe mnenie 2009* (Public opinion 2009), table 21.16, 193.

19. Georgiy Kasyanov, "Holodomor I stroitelstvo natsii" (Holodomor and the building of a nation), *Pro et Contra*, no. 3-4 (46), May–August 2009, 24–42.

20. Dmitri Medvedev's remarks at the meeting with Russian ambassadors and permanent representatives to international organizations, Moscow, July 15, 2008, http://archive. kremlin.ru/eng/speeches/2008/07/15/1121_type82912type84779_204155.shtml.

21. Lev Gudkov, *Negativnaya Identichnost': Stat'i 1997–2002* (Negative identity: Articles from 1997-2002) (Moscow: Novoe Literaturnoe Obozrenie – VCIOM-A, 2004) 21, 25.

22. For an eyewitness account, see Andrei Kolesnikov, "Pravda protiv pravoty" (Pravda against the right), *Kommersant*, April 8, 2010, www.kommersant.ru/doc. aspx?DocsID=1350471.

23. Ibid.

24. Andrei Popov, Deputy Foreign Minister of Moldova, on *Razvorot*, Echo Moskvy Radio, March 3, 2010, www.echo.msk.ru/programs/razvorot/662535-echo.phtml.

25. Alexei Miller, "Rossiya: vlast' I istoria" (Russia: Power and history), *Pro et Contra*, no. 3-4 (46), May–August 2009, 14.

26. Mikhail Morozov, "Istoriya v stile 'pop'" (History in the style of "pop"), *Iskusstvo kino*, issue 1, 2009, http://kinoart.ru/2009/n1-article2.html.

27. Gudkov, *Negativanaya Identichnost'*, 647.

28. Anatoly Torkunov, "O paradoxakh I opasnostyakh 'istoricheskoy politiki'" (Paradoxes and risks of "historic policy"), *Nezavisimaya Gazeta*, July 18, 2007. www.ng.ru/ideas/2008-07-18/7_istpolitika.html.

29. Gudkov, *Negativanaya Identichnost'*, 33.

30. Roy Medvedev, *Raskolotaya Ukraina* (Divided Ukraine) (Moscow: Institut Ekonomicheskikh Strategiy, 2007) 136.

31. Georgiy Kasyanov, "Holodomor I stroitelstvo natsii," 24–42.

32. For an analysis of Ukrainian textbooks see L. Moisseenkova and L. Martsinovsky, "Rossiya v Ukrainskikh Uchebnikakh Istorii: Novoe Videnie ili Proyavlenie Konkurentsii na Ideologicheskom Rynke? Vzglyad iz Kryma" (Russia in Ukrainian history textbooks: New views or manifestation of competition in the ideological market? Views from Crimea), *Starye I Novye Obrazy v Sovremennykh Uchebnikakh Istorii*, (Old and new evidence in modern history textbooks) edited by Frank Bomsdorf and G. Bordyugov, Moscow, 2004, http://his.1september.ru/2003/45/2-2.htm, 139.

33. Kuchma, *Posle Maydana. Zapiski Prezidenta. 2005–2006* (After Maidan: Notes of a president, 2005–2006) (Moscow: Vremya, 2007), 94.

34. Nursultan Nazarbayev, *V potoke istorii* (In the flow of history) (Almaty: Atamura, 1999), *Epitsentr mira* (The center of the universe) (Almaty: Elorda, 2001), *Kriticheskoe desyatiletie* (Critical decade) (Almaty: Atamura, 2003).

35.   Roy Medvedev, *Kazakhstsnskiy Proryv* (Moscow: Institut Ekonomicheskikh
        Strategiy, 2007), 41.

36.   For example, by Oleg Rumyantsev, a prominent political activist in the early 1990s.

37.   Levada Center, *Obshchestvennoe Mnenie 2009* (Public opinion 2009), table 16.2, 138.

38.   Igor Yakovenko, "Imperiya I Natsiya" (Empire and nation), in *Posle Imperii* (After the
        empire), edited by Igor Klyamkin (Moscow: Fond Liberal'naya Missiya, 2007), 60.

39.   Boris Tarasov, "Potomki Pravoslavnykh" (Orthodox descendants), *Vremya Novostey*,
        no. 132, July 24, 2008, www.vremya.ru/2008/132/4/208929.html.

40.   Ivan Sukhov, "Krest na Krest" (Cross with a cross), *Vremya Novostey*, no. 132, July 24,
        2008, www.vremya.ru/2008/132/4/208913.html.

41.   Mikhail Zygar, Pavel Korobov, Georgiy Dvali, and Aleksandr Zvorsky, "Prikhod
        Nezalezhnosti" (Parish square), *Kommersant*, no. 129 (3946), July 25, 2008, www.
        kommersant.ru/doc.aspx?DocsID=915678.

42.   Vadim Venediktov, "Parad Tzerkovnykh Suverenitetov" (The parade of church
        sovereigns), *Nezavisimaya Gazeta – Religii*, October 20, 2010, http://religion.ng.ru/
        events/2010-10-20/3_parad.html.

43.   Roy Medvedev, *Raskolotaya Ukraina*, 28.

44.   Irina Zvyagelskya, *Stanovlenie Gosudarstv Tsentralnoy Azii. Politicheskie Protsessy* (The
        formation of Central Asian governments: Political processes) (Moscow: Aspekt
        Press, 2009), 81.

45.   Levada Center, *Obshchestvennoe Mnenie 2009*, table 16.1, 138.

46.   Kuchma, *Posle Maydana*, 285.

47.   Roy Medvedev, *Raskolotaya Ukraina*, 105–106.

48.   Vladimir Soloviev, "SNG Popadet pod Vliyanie Rossii" (CIS is coming under
        Russian influence), *Kommersant*, no. 133 (3950), July 31, 2008, www.kommersant.ru/
        doc.aspx?DocsID=917672.

Conclusion

1.   Dmitri Medvedev's speech at a meeting with Russian ambassadors and permanent
        representatives to international organizations, July 12, 2010, transcript, http://eng.
        kremlin.ru/transcripts/610remarks.

2.   See internal Ministry of Foreign Affairs document, republished in Konstantin Gaaze
        and Mikhail Zygar, "Rossiya Pomenyaet Vneshnyu Politiku" (Russia will change
        its foreign policy), *Russian Newsweek*, no. 20 (288), May 11, 2010, www.forbes.ru/
        ekonomika/vlast/49383-rossiya-pomenyaet-vneshnyuyu-politiku.

3.   Dmitri Trenin, "Russia Reborn: Reimagining Moscow's Foreign Policy," *Foreign
        Affairs* (November–December 2009): 64–78.

INDEX

Abel, Rudolf, xiii
Abkhazia, 30–37, 48–49, 61
  Black Sea Fleet's support of, 77
  dependence on Russia of, 76, 94, 96,
    97–98, 110, 121, 239
  ethnic Russians in, 195
  Gali region of, 99
  geopolitical stalemate in, 98–99
  language use in, 228
  official recognition of, 111, 121, 133, 137
  as Russian Federation
    buffer zone, 53, 142
  Russian passports in, 198–99
Abramovich, Roman, 53, 96
Adenauer, Konrad, 234
Afghanistan, 133, 239
  economic aid to, 145
  opium production in, 129–30
  Pashtuns of, 131
  projected breakup of, 50
  Taliban regime in, 106, 129, 130
  U.S./NATO war in, 16, 28, 35, 106,
    130–31, 132, 239
  in USSR's zone of influence, 23
  USSR war in, xi, 1–2, 6, 7, 9, 131, 203
Ajara, 48, 95
Akayev, Askar, 58, 130–31
Aland Islands, xi
Alaska, 21, 53, 139–40
Albania, 23, 109
  See also Kosovo
alcoholism, 177
Alexander II, Tsar, 10
Alexi II, Patriarch, 225, 226
Alexi Mikhailovich, Tsar, 20
Algeria, xii, 23, 144
Aliyev, Haydar, 49, 99
Alliance for European Integration, 48, 110
al-Qaeda, 120, 129
Amalrik, Andrei, 8
Angola, 5, 9, 23, 144
Anti-Ballistic Missile Treaty of 1972, 107
Arctic, 242
  climate change in, 141

collective decision making for, 141
energy resources in, 168–69
geopolitical interests in, 140–42
militarization of, 141
Russian claims in, 43–44, 94, 140
Arctic Council, 141
Armenia, 5, 36
  demographics of, 178t, 181, 194t
  economic challenges in, 72, 170
  energy supplies in, 164
  ethnic consolidation in, 181
  ethnic Russians in, 181, 194t
  free trade treaty of, 154
  geopolitical interests of, 99–100, 110,
    122–26
  IMF loans to, 152
  international participation of, 80
  labor migration from, 153, 185
  Nagorno-Karabakh conflict in, 6, 49,
    239
  nation building in, 67
  political system of, 75, 82
  referendum of 1991 of, 5
  Russia's relationship with, 76, 122, 149,
    151, 152
  Turkish reconciliation with, 124
Asia-Europe Meeting (ASEM), 79
Asia-Pacific Economic Cooperation (APEC),
  53–54, 55, 211
Astana, 109
Aushev, Ruslan, 118
Autocephalous Ukrainian Orthodox Church,
  224
Azerbaijan, 36, 49
  demographics of, 177, 178t, 181, 194t
  economic challenges of, 72, 170, 172
  energy industry in, 122–23, 158, 166, 171
  ethnic consolidation in, 181
  ethnic Russians in, 181, 194t
  foreign investment in, 150–51
  geopolitical interests of, 99–100, 110,
    122–26
  international participation of, 81

ABOUT THE AUTHOR

Dmitri Trenin is director of the Carnegie Moscow Center and has been with the Center since its inception.

Trenin retired from the Russian Army in 1993. From 1993–1997, he held posts as a senior research fellow at the NATO Defense College in Rome and senior research fellow at the Institute of Europe in Moscow.

He served in the Soviet and Russian armed forces from 1972 to 1993, including experience working as a liaison officer in the External Relations Branch of the Group of Soviet Forces (stationed in Potsdam) and as a staff member of the delegation to the U.S.-Soviet nuclear arms talks in Geneva from 1985 to 1991. He also taught at the war studies department of the Military Institute from 1986 to 1993.

Trenin has published widely on Russian political and security issues and is the author of *Getting Russia Right*, *Russia's Restless Frontier: The Chechnya Factor in Post-Soviet Russia* (with Alexey Malashenko), and *The End of Eurasia: Russia Between Geopolitics and Globalization*.

CARNEGIE ENDOWMENT FOR INTERNATIONAL PEACE

The Carnegie Endowment for International Peace is a private, nonprofit organization dedicated to advancing cooperation between nations and promoting active international engagement by the United States. Founded in 1910, its work is nonpartisan and dedicated to achieving practical results.

As it celebrates its Centennial, the Carnegie Endowment is pioneering the first global think tank, with flourishing offices now in Washington, Moscow, Beijing, Beirut, and Brussels. These five locations include the centers of world governance and the places whose political evolution and international policies will most determine the near-term possibilities for international peace and economic advance.

OFFICERS

Jessica T. Mathews, President
Paul Balaran, Executive Vice President and Secretary
Tom Carver, Vice President for Communications and Strategy
Thomas Carothers, Vice President for Studies
Marwan Muasher, Vice President for Studies
Douglas H. Paal, Vice President for Studies
George Perkovich, Vice President for Studies

BOARD OF TRUSTEES

Richard Giordano, Chairman
Stephen R. Lewis, Jr., Vice Chairman
Kofi A. Annan
Bill Bradley
Gregory Craig
William H. Donaldson
Mohamed A. El-Erian
Harvey V. Fineberg
Donald V. Fites
Chas W. Freeman, Jr.
James C. Gaither
William W. George

Patricia House
Linda Mason
Jessica T. Mathews
Raymond McGuire
Zanny Minton Beddoes
Sunil Bharti Mittal
Catherine James Paglia
J. Stapleton Roy
Vanessa Ruiz
Aso O. Tavitian
Shirley M. Tilghman
Rohan Weerasinghe